Now I Get My Chance

Now I Get My Chance

Journals & Letters on a Bowing Pilgrimage

by

Heng Sure Ph.D.
and
Heng Ch'au Ph.D.

Volume Seven

Buddhist Text Translation Society
Dharma Realm Buddhist University
Dharma Realm Buddhist Association
Burlingame, California U.S.A.

Now I Get My Chance
Journals & Letters on a Bowing Pilgrimage. Volume Seven.

Published and translated by:

Buddhist Text Translation Society
1777 Murchison Drive, Burlingame, CA 94010-4504

© 2007   **Buddhist Text Translation Society**
             Dharma Realm Buddhist University
             Dharma Realm Buddhist Association

First edition 2007

16 15 14 13 12 11 10 09 08 07   12 11 10 9 8 7 6 5 4 3 2

ISBN 978-0-88139-912-7

Printed in Malaysia.

Note: Contents previously published under the title "With One Heart Bowing to the City of Ten Thousand Buddhas"

Addresses of the Dharma Realm Buddhist Association branches are listed at the back of this book.

Library of Congress Cataloging-in-Publication Data

Heng Sure, 1949-
  Now I get my chance / by Heng Sure and Heng Ch'au.
    p. cm. -- (Journals & letters on a bowing pilgrimage ; v. 7)
  ISBN 978-0-88139-912-7 (hard cover : alk. paper)
  1. Spiritual life--Buddhism. 2. Heng Sure, 1949- 3. Heng Ch'au. 4. Buddhist pilgrims and pilgrimages--California. I. Heng Ch'au. II. Title. III. Series.

  BQ5625.H4665 2007
  294.3'43509794--dc22

2007002701

Contents

Preface

Three steps, one bow – three steps along the side of the highway, then a bow to the ground, so that knees, elbows, hands, and forehead touch the earth, then rise, join the palms together, and take three more steps, then begin another bow. Hour after hour, day after day, for two and a half years, this was how they made their pilgrimage. In China, devout Buddhists sometimes undertake the arduous and prayerful practice of three steps, one bow, for the last few hundred yards of a journey to a sacred site. But this was California, and these two pilgrim-monks were young Americans. Dressed in their robes and sashes, carrying no money, armed with nothing but discipline and reverence, they walked and bowed 800 miles along the narrow shoulder of the Pacific Coast Highway. Progressing a mile a day, they bowed from downtown Los Angeles north along the coast, through Santa Barbara and along the Big Sur, through San Francisco and across the Golden Gate, then 100 miles farther north to the City of Ten Thousand Buddhas, a newly founded religious and educational center in Mendocino County. As they bowed, their prayer was that the world would be free of disaster, calamity, and war.

The silent monk in the lead was Heng Sure. Originally from Toledo, Ohio, he had found his way in 1974 to Gold Mountain Buddhist Monastery in San Francisco. There on a side street of the Mission District, an eminent Chinese monk, the Venerable Master

Hsuan Hua, was living in obscurity as he carried out his pioneering work of transplanting the Buddhist monastic tradition to the West. Moved by Master Hua's virtue and wisdom, Heng Sure joined other young Americans in taking a monastic name and the full ordination of a Buddhist monk.

During his subsequent studies, Heng Sure read of a bowing pilgrimage made in the 1880's by the Venerable Hsu Yun ("Empty Cloud"), who was the most distinguished Chinese monastic of his generation. Master Yun had bowed every third step across the breadth of China; it had taken him five years. Heng Sure knew that Master Yun had been patriarch of the Wei Yang Lineage of the Chan School, and he knew that his own abbot and teacher, Master Hua, was the current patriarch, having received the lineage transmission from Master Yun in 1949. Inspired by this close connection, Heng Sure asked Master Hua if he could undertake his own pilgrimage of three steps, one bow. Master Hua approved, but said, "Wait."

Heng Sure had to wait a year. What he needed, Master Hua said, was the right companion and protector. It was to be Heng Chau. Originally from Appleton, Wisconsin, Heng Chau had come to Berkeley to study martial arts, and he had become an adept in several traditions. When his tai-chi teacher finally told him, "Chan is higher than any martial art," Heng Chau crossed the Bay to study at Gold Mountain Monastery. He soon heard about Heng Sure's vow, and he asked if he could bow with him. Within a week Heng Chau took novice precepts and made a formal vow to bow beside Heng Sure, as well as handle the logistics of cooking, cleaning, setting up camp, and talking with strangers.

Thus the pilgrimage began. Master Hua saw them off as they left Gold Wheel Monastery in Los Angeles on 7 May 1977. To Heng Chau, the martial artist, he said, "You can't use your martial arts on the pilgrimage. Heng Sure's vow is to seek an end to calamities, disasters and war; so how can you yourselves be involved in violence? If either of you fights – or even indulges in anger – you will no longer be my disciples." For protection from the dangers of the

road, Master Hua instructed them to practice instead the four uncon-
ditional attitudes of the Bodhisattva: kindness, compassion, joy, and
equanimity. It was by no means the last time that the two bowing
monks would need their teacher's advice.

On the road, the two pilgrims followed their monastic discipline
strictly – eating one vegetarian meal a day; never going indoors,
sleeping sitting up in the old 1956 Plymouth station wagon that
served as their shelter. In the evenings after a day of bowing they
studied the Avatamsaka Sutra (Flower Adornment Sutra) by the light
of an oil lamp. They translated passages into English and attempted
to put into practice the principles of the text in their day-to-day
experiences on the road, as their teacher had encouraged them to do.
The monks guarded their concentration by avoiding newspapers, by
leaving the car radio silent, and by keeping to a strict meditation
schedule. Heng Sure held a vow of silence for the entire journey, and
it became Heng Chau's job to talk with the many people who stopped
along the highway with questions. Occasionally the visitors were
hostile, and some threatened violence, but the greater number were
curious, and often the curious became the monks' protectors,
bringing them food and supplies until the monks had bowed their
way out of range.

Everything important that happened on the highway – the
mistakes and the growth, the trials and remarkable encounters, the
dangers and the insights, the hard work with the body and in the mind
– the pilgrims reported in letters to Master Hua. He would answer in
person by visiting them from time to time, giving them indispensable
spiritual guidance, admonishment, humor, and timely instructions –
both lofty and mundane. These letters are the contents of this volume.
They were not written with the thought that they would be published.
Rather, they were a medium in which the two monks attempted to
speak to their teacher as openly and sincerely as possible about their
experience on the road. As such, the letters preserve an unadorned
account of an authentic spiritual journey.

The Venerable Master Hsuan Hua

A Brief Portrait

"I have had many names," he once said, "and all of them are false." In his youth in Manchuria, he was known as "the Filial Son Bai"; as a young monk he was An Tzu ("Peace and Kindness"); later, in Hong Kong, he was Tu Lun ("Wheel of Rescue"); finally, in America, he was Hsuan Hua, which might be translated as "one who proclaims the principles of transformation." To his thousands of disciples across the world, he was always also "Shr Fu" – "Teacher."

Born in 1918 into a peasant family in a small village on the Manchurian plain, Master Hua was the youngest of ten children. He attended school for only two years, during which he studied the Chinese Classics and committed much of them to memory. As a young teenager, he opened a free school for both children and adults. He also began then one of his lifelong spiritual practices: reverential bowing. Outdoors, in all weathers, he would make over 800 prostrations daily, as a profound gesture of his respect for all that is good and sacred in the universe.

He was nineteen when his mother died, and for three years he honored her memory by sitting in meditation in a hut beside her grave. It was during this time that he made a resolve to go to America to teach the principles of wisdom. As a first step, at the end of the period of mourning, he entered San Yuan Monastery, took as his teacher Master Chang Chih, and subsequently received the full ordination of a Buddhist monk at Pu To Mountain. For ten years he devoted himself to study of the Buddhist scriptural tradition and to mastery of both the Esoteric and the Chan Schools of Chinese Buddhism. He had also read and contemplated the scriptures of Christianity, Taoism, and Islam. Thus, by the age of thirty, he had already established through his own experience the four major imperatives of his later ministry in America: the primacy of the monastic tradition; the essential role of moral education; the need for Buddhists to ground themselves in traditional spiritual practice and authentic scripture; and, just as essential, the importance and the power of ecumenical respect and understanding.

In 1948, Master Hua traveled south to meet the Venerable Hsu Yun, who was then already 108 years old and China's most distinguished spiritual teacher. From him Master Hua received the patriarchal transmission in the Wei Yang Lineage of the Chan School. Master Hua subsequently left China for Hong Kong. He spent a dozen years there, first in seclusion, then later as a teacher at three monasteries which he founded.

Finally, in 1962, he went to the United States, at the invitation of several of his Hong Kong disciples who had settled in San Francisco. By 1968, Master Hua had established the Buddhist Lecture Hall in a loft in San Francisco's Chinatown, and there he began giving nightly lectures, in Chinese, to an audience of young Americans. His texts were the major scriptures of the Mahayana. In 1969, he astonished the monastic community of Taiwan by sending there, for final ordination, two American women and three American men, all five of them fully trained as novices, fluent in Chinese and conversant with Buddhist scripture. During subsequent years, the Master trained and oversaw the ordination of hundreds of monks and nuns who came to California from every part of the world to study with him. These monastic disciples now teach in the 28 temples, monasteries and convents that the Master founded in the United States, Canada, and several Asian countries.

Although he understood English well and spoke it when it was necessary, Master Hua almost always lectured in Chinese. His aim was to encourage Westerners to learn Chinese, so that they could become translators, not merely of his lectures, but of the major scriptural texts of the Buddhist Mahayana. His intent was realized. So far, the Buddhist Text Translation Society, which he founded, has issued over 130 volumes of translation of the major Sutras, together with a similar number of commentaries, instructions, and stories from the Master's teaching.

As an educator, Master Hua was tireless. From 1968 to the mid 1980's he gave as many as a dozen lectures a week, and he traveled extensively on speaking tours. At the City of Ten Thousand Buddhas in Talmage, California, he established formal training programs for monastics and for laity; elementary and secondary schools for boys and for girls; and Dharma Realm Buddhist University, together with the University's branch, the Institute for World Religions, in Berkeley.

Throughout his life the Master taught that the basis of spiritual practice is moral practice. Of his monastic disciples he required strict purity, and he encouraged his lay disciples to adhere to the five precepts of the Buddhist laity. Especially in his later years, Confucian texts were often the subject of his lectures, and he held to the Confucian teaching that the first business of education is moral education. He identified six rules of conduct as the basis of communal life at the City of Ten Thousand Buddhas; the six rules prohibit contention, covetousness, self-seeking, selfishness, profiting at the expense of the community, and false speech. He asked that the children in the schools he had founded recite these prohibitions every morning before class. In general, although he admired the independent-mindedness of Westerners, he believed that they lacked ethical balance and needed that stabilizing sense of public morality which is characteristic of the East.

The Venerable Master insisted on ecumenical respect, and he delighted in inter-faith dialogue. He stressed commonalities in religious traditions – above all their emphasis on proper conduct, on compassion, and on wisdom. He was also a pioneer in building bridges between different Buddhist national traditions. He often brought monks from Theravada countries to California to share the duties of transmitting the precepts of ordination. He invited Catholic priests to celebrate the mass in the Buddha-Hall at the City of Ten Thousand Buddhas, and he developed a late-in-life friendship with Paul Cardinal Yu-Bin, the exiled leader of the Catholic Church in China and Taiwan. He once told the Cardinal: "You can be a Buddhist among the Catholics, and I'll be a Catholic among Buddhists." To the Master, the essential teachings of all religions could be summed up in a single word: wisdom.

* * *

The monks left the bowing route to join the
Master and delegation to a mission in Asia.
They continued their bowing there.

The delegation to Asia lasted two months which inclu

its to Malaysia, Thailand, Singapore and Hong Kong.

The bows were counted and logged. The distance
covered in Asia were then walked-off when the
monks returned to their bowing route at Castroville.

Now I Get My Chance

October 1978

Heng Sure • October 1, 1978
You can't beat the Middle Way

"On the Road Again"

First mistake: impatience. Walked too fast, in a hurry to cover the miles bowed in Asia. Wanted to waste no time but pushed too hard. Seventeen miles in two days brought charley horses and sore toes. Greed for speed actually postponed the bowing. Had I followed the Tao and taken a natural, relaxed pace, concentrating my mind and letting the miles pass as they came, I would have covered the same ground without fatigue, without the jet-plane ups and the sorry, aching down. You can't beat the Middle Way.

> He who acts, harms.
> He who grabs, lets slip.
> Therefore, the Sage does not act and so does not harm;
> does not grab, and so does not let slip.
>
> Lao Tzu

"Artichokes and Skandhas"

Skandas are the parts of people's personalities: forms, feelings, thoughts, actions, and consciousness. The Buddha sees through them and travels freely in the wisdom that goes beyond. We don't see them, so we stumble in the narrow cave-dwelling of the self. The Skandhas are the invisible bars on the cage of personality. The

Buddha opens the cage; cultivation leads us out of the dark, cramped cave.

What do enlightened beings see, once free of the cave? Skandhas and people, says the Sutra, are not different from emptiness; they exist, but only in thoughts. Skandhas have no true substance of their own. Skandhas, like the illusory personalities they support, are empty and false.

Walked through Castroville counting off the miles to our next starting point. Passed Artichoke fields hidden in the morning fog; walked by mile after mile of spiky, silver-green, choke bushes. Castroville claims to be "Artichoke Capital of the World," but what does the title have to do with the town of Castroville? The town has one main street, a boarded-up 5 and 10 cents store, and two coffee shops full of Portuguese artichoke ranchers. If a traveler didn't read the banner across Main Street announcing the October artichoke festival and artichoke queen contest, he'd never know this tiny corner of California supplies most of the artichokes eaten in restaurants and sold in groceries the world over.

Without the sign and the title, Castroville, like the skandhas, is just another town, but it functions all the same. Artichokes come from Castroville, but close your eyes as you pass the sign and the town's fame fades away. The personality comes from thoughts of the skandhas; cultivate an end to false-thoughts and the view of self disappears.

"The Dharmas of the three periods of time and the five skandhas, when named, bring the world into being. When they are extinguished, the world is gone. In this way they are only false names."

Praises in the Suyama Heaven Palace
Avatamsaka Sutra

Heng Chau • October 1, 1978
Feeling more solid then ever

> With repentance and reform as their adornment
> Their cultivation is progressively more solid.
>
> Ten Grounds Chapter
> Avatamsaka Sutra

* * *

First day of road bowing since return from Asia. We are by-passing the freeway on San Andreas Road to Santa Cruz. Narrow shoulders and fast traffic. We decide to bow the railroad tracks next to the highway.

We feel more solid in our resolve than ever and also deeply aware of our faults and the need to become better people. It's said, "Buddhism and the art of becoming a person are the same."

For me that means bringing forth a heart that delights in seeing others succeed and grow strong. Be for people, not jealous and obstructive.

Heng Sure • October 2, 1978
Memories of Asia flood the mind

"Into Santa Cruz County"

Made it! Thirty miles counted on the beads. Stepped the final paces this morning. Will begin the bowing on San Andreas Road in a eucalyptus grove beside the Southern Pacific train tracks. Memories of Asia flood the mind as I walked the quiet, wide-open farm roads. I let concentration slip and found my thoughts transporting me to temple courtyards in Bangkok, Kuala Lumpur, Singapore, Malacca.

Crowds of people crossing grimy, ancient flagstones; some in robes with hands full of smoking incense sticks; some smartly dressed young couples on motorbikes below fierce-eyed temple-guardian statues. Clouds of cigarette smoke drifting through potted bamboos, laundry drying on poles; odors of roasting meat, mountains of exotic fruits on a forest of push carts beyond the twelve-foot, triple-locked, temple gate. Two Western monks and a file of devout lay Buddhists doing three steps, one bow, winding through the throng, hearts concentrated on the pure Dharma-nature.

"They vow that living beings be shaded by wholesome Dharmas and eradicate the hubbub, dirt, and dust of the mundane world."

Ten Transferences Chapter
Avatamsaka Sutra

In a single bow, spanning half the world; in a single thought linking past and present. Clamorous Asian courtyards echo in my memory, deafening in the stillness of this pastoral Pacific country-side; all made from the mind alone.

When the mind is still, one hundred affairs cease.
When the mind moves, ten thousand things appear.

Chan saying

Heng Chau • October 2, 1978
True principle comes forth naturally

Decision and Choices.

How can you tell if something is Proper Dharma and accords with true principle? If it's for everyone, then it's proper and true principle. If it is for self, and self benefits, then deviant and false. True principle comes forth naturally when selfishness doesn't obstruct it.

Heng Sure • October 3, 1978
Bowing, bowing, Who am I?

"San Andreas Road"

Foggy mornings, misty evenings, crystal-clear days. Bowing past horses in rocky pastures, pick-up trucks in rutted frontyards. Bowing pass plump brussel sprouts on the open trench storm drain. Bowing, bowing, Who am I? Bruised feet slowly mend. Mind awhirl.

Heng Chau • October 3, 1978
Giving the City to the world

A local high-school teacher who said he was "spiritually inclined" stopped to check us out. We are going through food and sleep adjustments from Asia. "Culture Shock" is very mild for us, maybe because as left-home people we have no home culture to shock. From our perspective, the whole world is a bit unusual and upside down. And we are the strangest and most weird of all. Trying to get rid of selfishness can look pretty stupid.

The Abbot, for example, has given the City of Ten Thousand Buddhas to the world. He wants *nothing* for himself. Everyone thinks he is nuts, or else they don't believe him. The Dharma Masters in Asia who built Way-places and temples as little nest-eggs for themselves can't handle this kind of "folly". After visiting one such adorned palace in Thailand, the Abbot commented while riding in the car,

"What do you think about my idea of giving the City of Ten Thousand Buddhas to the world?"

Everyone offered an opinion and a little surprise.

"I'm really stupid. You can look the whole world over and never find one as stupid as me."

So it says,

> The Enlightenment Path seems dim,
> To advance seems like retreating,
> The easy way seems rugged,
> High Virtue is like the deep valley,
> Great Pristineness seems dishonored,
> Vast Virtue seems inadequate,
> Mighty Virtue seems lax,
> Real Virtue seems empty.
>
> Tao Te Ching

The Abbot says that the whole world is ripe for this kind of stupidity, or else we won't make it. This is the spirit of the Ten Thousand Buddhas. Self-seeking ruins the world and only selflessness can save it. Then, with a smile, the Abbot says,

"When we open the light at the City of Ten Thousand Buddhas, it's going to be really bright! There will be enough light for everyone. The Buddhas and Bodhisattvas are really going to shine their lights. Everyone will get to bathe in it."

Heng Sure • October 4, 1978
A green polka-dot trail of tasty sprouts

Bonita Drive

Where did all these demons come from? Look inside for the answer. Instead of concentrating on my Dharma, I've been playing sprout-scout and filling my pockets with little emerald-green brussel sprouts as I bow.

> "In making great vows you shouldn't have even one false thought. If you make a big vow and then you have a few false thoughts, they can obscure the great vow... As soon as you have false thoughts, the gods, dragons, and others of the eight-fold division, the good spirits, and the 84,000 vajra-

treasury dharma protectors who follow you must simultaneously retreat. And when the vajra-treasury bodhisattvas retreat, then the retinue of demons attacks."

Master Hua

This morning as I counted bows to bypass a shoulderless section of road, I discovered the local packing plants' driveway, the drop-off point for the trucks full of sprouts that pass us all day long. Greed swallowed good sense and I entered the driveway, following a green polka-dot trail of tasty sprouts.

How can a cultivator of the Way carelessly indulge in thoughts of greed? Still I filled my pockets and lost my purity. Bowing by the Plymouth before lunch, half a dozen cars honked, men in trucks hollered insults, cars swerved off the road to buzz my prostrate body, missing by inches. After the third close call in an hour I recognized my error. Time to repent. The brussel sprouts at lunch tasted like soggy cardboard. Good lesson.

"One thought of greed and you'll lose every time."

Master Hua

Heng Chau • October 4, 1978
The casino in the desert of birth and death

A certain Ch'an Master entered Samadhi for 49 days to check out what happened after death. After the 8th consciousness ("soul") leaves the body it becomes what is called the intermediate skandha body and drifts around in a vast, dark, and cold void. An uncomfortably cold wind and no light surrounds it, while the soul is unaware that it is dead and cannot tell good from evil or perceive things.

Then "doors" or "gates" appear, and if one can recognize and pass through the right ones, rebirth in the heavens or in the Buddha's household lies on the other side. However, the cold wind is fierce and the desire for warmth and light compelling. A dim light will appear in the dark emptiness and if the soul goes for it, it will be reborn as a human or in lower realms. The dim light is the parents (with whom this soul has conditions), engaging the act of sex. The minute the soul goes for the light, it becomes a fertilized embryo in its mother's womb. Human birth is likened to ripping a turtle of its shell while still alive, the experience is this painful.

These discourses can't be proved or verified by science yet. But in our own experiences and states of mind there is a recognition, an intuitive understanding, of things beyond the ordinary realm of our senses.

For example, the Master has said, "If you can bear the pain and can bear being without a partner, then you can pass through the gate." As we bowed the cold, fogged-in highway last night on a long, isolated stretch, I felt very much alone and cold. Suddenly the dim lights of small village appeared. One could hear the voices and laughter of people getting together over dinner. The impulse to "go for it" welled up momentarily. But then I recalled this Ch'an Master's description. And somewhere inside I recognized the truth of these things: birth and death come from sexual desire; amid the cold darkness and gates, we grab for the comfort and the soft lights only to realize too late that we "blew it again."

> The gate of my birth is the door of my death.
> How many wake up to it? How many are still dazed?
> At midnight, the Iron Hero thinks it over:
> The turning wheel of the six paths you yourself stop.
>
> Verse by Tripitaka Master Hua

We bowed past the village without stopping. For the first time I began to see clearly the nature of the man-woman thing, how much of it is motivated by fear of the dark and cold. Basic ignorance of who we are, where we come from, and where we are going keeps us on the turning wheel. "How many wake up!?"

Three Steps One Bow is teaching us that giving into emotions and feelings ends in a lot of suffering, and that bearing what's hard to bear yields an indescribable bliss. Each difficult situation we pass through brings a little more understanding. Each time we are able to do what we thought we couldn't do it, it leaves us lighter on our feet and more tranquil in our minds.

Cultivating the Way is all about patience: don't grab at anything, don't fear anything. Seek nothing outside to lean on; hold on to nothing inside. Withstand the suspense of the not produced, not destroyed. Don't be whipped around by empty emotions and pretty bubbles. Content with what you have, then "Everything's O.K."

> Patience is a priceless jewel,
>> but nobody knows how to use it.
> If you can really use it,
>> then everything will be okay.

Just as fear of the dark vanishes in the light of morning, love and desire fade away in the brightness of self-awakening.

* * *

We drove to Santa Cruz to contact the CHP, County and City Police and to check out routes. The county of Santa Cruz has a "non-dwelling" law: no camping or sleeping overnight in any vehicle within the county limits. Cooperative but skeptical reception. Most people don't know what to make of two monks who "bow once every three steps for a living," as one person put it.

* * *

"The time of your life!" promises a roadside color-burst billboard for a casino in Las Vegas and Reno. A row of dancing girls, sparkling cocktails, swimming pools, keno, blackjack, roulette and slot machines sprinkled with stardust. Heaven on earth, the slick Madison Avenue lie would have you believe. The truth? "Gambling scrambles the mind and distracts one from cultivating the Way," said the Master. And the cocktails?

> "Those who crave intoxicants will descend at death into the Hell of Boiling Excrement and in succeeding lives will be stupid, having lost the seed of wisdom."
>
> Vinaya

And the dancing girls and willing young men?

> "Because of lust, worldly people destroy their bodies and ruin their homes... Sexual desire is the primary root of birth and death. It would be better to die continent then live in licentiousness."
>
> Vinaya

But the number of people who believe in true principle compared to the number of people who believe in the billboards is like a handful of dirt compared with all the dirt on the great earth. We live in a dream, in a make-believe world, and only on the verge of dying do we awaken to our errors and regret a wasted life.

> When a bird is about to die, its cries are sorrowful.
> When a man is about to die, his words are good.
>
> Confucius

* * *

In Nevada, where people live on the edge of civilization and the edge of their own minds, where they face the daily reality of the empty void, gambling and prostitution are legal. Alcohol is consumed in a race against the ever-present, unnamed anxiety that people feel. Facing the emptiness of things, emptiness of a self, they grab at existence (sex), or dive into emptiness (alcohol). All around is desert and the drama of birth and death. Without a method to break out of the conditioned prison of the world, everything seems like a gamble, a question of luck and fate. In the casinos people test their skill and try their luck, hoping to "beat the house." Outside the coyotes sing a cold and lonely song that never leaves our ears.

This world is a casino in the desert of birth and death where the house always wins and every man's a sucker. The big wheel keeps on turning and only Buddhas can show us how to stop it.

> Destroying all existence
>   and the wheel of birth and death,
> Turning the pure and wonderful Dharma wheel,
> Being unattached to all worlds:
> He speaks this way for the Bodhisattvas.
>
> Ten Dwellings Chapter
Avatamsaka Sutra

Heng Sure • October 5, 1978
I don't understand Italian

"Bonita Drive"

"Listen, get this straight. I don't care who you are or what you represent. I want you to scram off my land and right now, you hear me?"

Two long-haired, burly men in tee-shirts glower from their open jeep.

"If you're not down the road by the time I get back I'm going to throw you off myself. Now git!" His commands send puffs of breath into the chilly afternoon air.

I smile, nod, and continue bowing. Still have fifty bows to count in place, the road is too narrow to step and bow. I'm islanded on a narrow shoulder shared by two driveways leading back to shaded, hillside houses. Figure I'll be around the next curve in twenty minutes; best to pretend he speaks Italian and I don't understand Italian. Clearly I'm doing no harm; the man must be my own past angry thoughts returning to me.

"Because of the mind of kindness, they could not harm or vex living beings."

Entering the Dharma Realm, Part II
Avatamsaka Sutra

Why do people sometimes trouble and hassle us without apparent reason? Cause and effect create a complete circle – what we send out returns to us without fail, without error. Because in the past we forgot to be kind, now kindness forgets us.

Heng Chau • October 5, 1978
The same kind of sickness I contracted in Asia

"People are born because of sexual desire, and people die because of sexual desire. If you know how to not become attached to your sexual desire, then you can leave birth and death."

The Venerable Abbot
in Muar, Malaysia, 1978

I went into Santa Cruz with a mind fretting that the food was low and a body fighting the cold and wet fog. I was turned by the women again. Even when I know, the habit persists: grabbing at beautiful forms and the "dim light," and giving away my treasures. Slow, real slow to catch one. Ignorance is really boss.

"The cause of all suffering is ignorance. Ignorance is just sexual desire and young people have it most intensely… They are driven by biological impulses they have no control over, something of the nature they can't understand. This is a function of the human species, particularly when they're young. However, if young people do not get urges tempered, then ignorance will become boss."

The Venerable Abbot
in Muar, Malaysia, 1978

You can finish with birth and cast off death if you can unlock the chain of the vicious cycle of the Twelve Conditioned Links. The first link in the chain is ignorance. Ignorance is just referring to sexual desire, and when it is ended, then all suffering is over.

> When ignorance is the condition,
>   suffering can't be stopped.
> Ending the condition (ignorance),
>   then suffering is all over.
> Ignorance, love, and grasping
>   are affliction's branches.
> Actions create karma
>   and suffering is all that follows.
>
> Ten Grounds Chapter
> Avatamsaka Sutra

The heart can change suddenly and easily, but bad habits leave at their own slow, stubborn speed.

For example, as we drove into Santa Cruz today, I was determined to "subdue myself and return to principle." I firmly resolved to discipline my six sense organs and to not let them run out and unite with the six dusts, specifically: not to be turned by women. Cities are "dusty" places, but I managed to harness my desires and to rein in my sense organs through the busy market plaza. Teeming crowds of gaily-dressed, beautiful people, layer upon layer of fragrance, from perfumes, tobaccos, roast meat, and the music, the emotions, the human comic-tragic drama constantly unfolding on every street corner and in every passing face. Through all of this carnival of red dust I kept my heart down deep inside, still and content, as if alone in a deep forest.

After we finished our errands, we drove to our last stop, the local Police Station, to check city ordinances and map out a route.

"Oh, you'd be wanting to talk to Sergeant Krenshaw in the room across the hall," advised the watch commander, pointing us to an adjacent room. Wouldn't you know it, Sargeant Krenshaw was a young woman! Caught me completely off guard and my mind moved as soon as I heard her voice and caught her warm smile.

I smiled back and spoke with her too long. As a result, I got sick again – the same kind of sickness I contracted in Asia.

Now camped in the quiet night fog on a small hill above the ocean. Outside the eucalyptus trees drop drops of moisture, and their berries 'ting-ping' on the metal roof of the car. As sneezing, fever, chills, and aches set into my body, my thoughts drift inexorably to one of the primary teachings of Buddhism: desire is the cause of suffering. Not only is desire the source of all illness and disease, but it is the root of birth and death itself. I remember the Master coming to see me as I lay sick in my room in Malaysia. He was kind and consoling, but wasted no words in diagnosing my illness.

"It was your old flaw," he said. "False thinking about women brought on your sickness."

Now back in the U.S.A. the old flaw still lingers and so does the old sickness. The Sutra couldn't be more explicit when it says,

> "Living beings are blind and lack the wisdom-eye, so nothing is seen or known (by them). From mother's belly they enter the womb, and are born in this foul, defiled body. Ultimately they end up with white hair and wrinkled faces.
>
> "Those with wisdom contemplate this process and know it all happens from the arisal of sexual desire and impure dharmas...
>
> "I now should never do these things again."
>
> Ten Treasuries Chapter
> Avatamsaka Sutra

* * *

Bowing through Santa Cruz County to the sounds of hanging hammers, power saws, and hard rock 'n roll ringing through the oak woods. The young energy of America tries "living off the land" and commuting to the nearest big city 9-5. Walden, Winterland, and Wall Street all packed together, but not jelling like we hoped it would.

"This is a very desirable place," noted a city cop, "so right away you've got a lot of people and a lot of problems. Then comes a lot of laws and with each law someone suffers and loses something."

> If the people never see such things as excite desire,
> Their hearts will remain placid and undisturbed.
>
> Tao Te Ching

Bowing through a "desirable" area we always find a lot of anger and uptight police. Wanting to get more and wanting what others want surely must be the greatest disaster in the world.

Heng Sure • October 6, 1978
Who among us can claim permanent residence?

"Door Key to the Dharma Realm"

Pack into the Plymouth as mist descends at day's end. No campsite available for miles, only fences and hedgerows. Keep Out! and Private!

Heng Chau drives and drives. We decide to risk a park service road in a eucalyptus grove; hope the neighbors will overlook us in the fog. Like the blowing mist we are migrants.

> "We come with the dust and we go with the wind."
>
> Woody Guthrie

Leave the car to practice standing meditation beneath dripping, pungent, eucalypts. No cars pass, the night is silent, but for the pitter-pat from the leaves. My ears still buzz with the din of Happy Valley, Hong Kong, half a world away: streets packed with humanity, ducks, fishheads, Fiats, double-decker trolleys, beauty parlors, blind and crippled beggars, newsstands and naked children, orange peels and French perfume. Blowing horns, ringing cash registers, open sewers, double-parked Cadillac's, clouds of smoke from restaurant woks, refugees huddled below the grandstand pillars of the race-track clubhouse. Who among us can claim "permanent residency" on this drifting planet? Are we not all transmigrating through space?

As I rejoin Heng Chau for evening ceremony, our beat-up, four-wheeled Way-place with its oil lantern gleaming in the fogbound grove looks a welcome sight. After chanting, we enter the infinite universe of the Avatamsaka Sutra. For a left-home person, the unbound, liberated mind is the door key to the limitless, splendid mansion-home of the Dharma Realm.

> "Able to dwell in all worlds with a heart not at all attached."
>
> Universal Worthy's Practice
> Avatamsaka Sutra

Heng Chau • October 6, 1978
Suddenly, in the space of a few hours

"Santa Cruz Tollgate"

Each new town has its test; each new area its rites of passage. As sure as we have to pass the scrutiny and win the official approval of the visible authorities in every city and change of jurisdiction, so too do we have to pass the inspection of the unofficial and invisible authorities. As we approach the fringe of a town or change in geography, a tollgate of pressure, tension, fast-action encounters crystallizes out of thin air.

For example, for over three days we've bowed undisturbed and unmolested. We didn't see more than a few people from dawn to dusk. Then suddenly, in the space of a few hours, we found ourselves swept into a whirlpool of activity – as tight and rough a tollgate as any we faced.

Three to four cars/trucks full of hostile men took turns driving by, honking, yelling and threatening us.

"Go home. Freaks! Santa Cruz has enough freaks. Go South. Santa Cruz is all freaked-out!"

"We are going to have your car towed to the junkyard if you don't move on."

"Move on!" threatened one man and kicked us off our bowing spot.

A dog hung around us, running in front of passing traffic, causing near-accidents and making a lot of motorists angry at the two monks whom it appeared owned the unruly dog.

Three times people tried to force us off the road with their vehicles. A pick-up cut across both lanes and came charging at us from behind on the shoulder at 50 mph. Just missed.

Ten seconds later a long white-haired Jesus-preacher meandered up and calmly whispered, "What are you doing?" The truck left. "I admire your dedication but I hate what you're caught up in. You're in the grip of the devil. Did ya know that, huh? He's the prince that rules the earth you're bowing to. Only Jesus can save you! Jesus made you! Listen to me! So he ought to know what's best for you," he screamed.

"Yeah, Santa Cruz is a mecca for people who are seeking peace and happiness," he went on. "Have you found it yet!?" he asked threateningly. We kept bowing.

And then the gate seemed to open and the tide slowly turned. Two young men stopped to wish us luck. A man who had seen us in Big Sur drove up: "Good Luck, I know you'll reach your goal!" A sheriff's deputy who apologized for bothering us: "I had to check you out because a neighbor thought you were disguised burglars. It's amazing the things you have to put up with to make a pilgrimage in this day and age, isn't it?" he added. A bright-eyed young couple appeared with fruit and flowers as an offering and a lot of moral support. Both Heng Sure and I felt affinities with them as if we all knew each other already. End of the day. Another "tollgate" squeezed through on our way to the City of Ten Thousand Buddhas.

As suddenly as the tollgate appeared, it disappeared again. Now, the day's over and all is quiet. It was just a test to see if we would move, to see if we really believed in the Dharma and in the power of patience.

> "The power of patience diligently cultivated to the other shore, able to endure the most supreme, still, extinct Dharma, with minds level, equal, and unmoving. Those of boundless wisdom walk this path."
>
> Ten Conducts Chapter
> Avatamsaka Sutra

* * *

We have never been more happy or peaceful in our lives. Bowing always feels like "home." Whatever we get we've got coming to us, and good or bad, "it's all made from the mind alone." Each day is a little brighter inside and a little easier outside as the threads of karma wear thinner and emotions seem to empty themselves.

> "He first eradicates the bonds of views, then all the bonds of desire, the bonds of form, the bonds of existence, and the bonds of ignorance, which decrease to threads... His deviant greed, deviant hatred, and deviant stupidity all become extinguished, and all his good roots become brighter and more pure."
>
> Ten Grounds Chapter
> Avatamsaka Sutra

Heng Sure • October 7, 1978
The Plymouth gets a ticket

Across the freeway and into the Santa Cruz suburbs. No camping sites. We bivouac outside a pet hospital on a narrow paint-striped shoulder. CHP officer tickets the Plymouth for excess smoke! Our first citation in eighteen months of highway travel. I'd better get my false thoughts under control.

Heng Chau • October 7, 1978
The Big Darkness

> "Producing a wholesome joy and desire, they always enjoy cultivating the practice of vast, extensive giving."
>
> Ten Transferences Chapter
> Avatamsaka Sutra

The two people who made an offering at the end of a heavy day left a note: "The givers are grateful." You see few people these days with that kind of deeply happy and honest light. I saw the same glow in the faces of all the people from the City of Ten Thousand Buddhas who greeted our delegation at the San Francisco Airport on our return from Asia.

There is Big Darkness growing in the world. We all sense it and yet it's so huge and so pervasive we can't pin it down or single it out. Unrecognized, it daily festers and grows. When the early Americans came to the New Land their writings talked about escaping from the "foulness, decay and darkness" of the Old World (Europe). In their eyes, America was clean and virginal, full of unstained and purifying energy. Yet even back then a few were able to see that the "seed of pollution" was right within their own minds. Almost prophetically, they predicted that in time, America would become infected with "the foul darkness" because people were bringing the disease with them from the Old Countries, in their minds. The land was new and unspoiled, but the mind was old and as polluted as ever with greed, fighting and ignorance. Buddhism is declining in Asia. An overcast of lightless gloom and faded glory eclipses the temples. The spirit of decay even infects the dwindling Sangha who battle impossible odds just to hold their own. It seems the future of Buddhism is in the West, in America, in the aces and hearts we saw at the airport.

While Heng Sure was bowing yesterday he had the insight, "When I am greedy, selfish, and uptight, I am part of the sickness, part of the darkness." The Big Darkness begins very small. It is the child of our own minds.

There is still hope to destroy the Big Darkness and restore the "wind and light of the original ground." How?

"This means not being selfish and not aiming for self-benefit," the Master emphasized in a speech at Seremban, Malaysia where he offered the City of Ten Thousand Buddhas to the world. "I am one who is willing to be under the feet of all Buddhists, not on top of their heads. I am willing to walk behind every Buddhist and not in front of them. And in this way I maintain the spirit of yielding and of not fighting. From ancient times, all those who had virtue never fought. They never fought for name and for benefit, never got caught up in rights and wrongs."

"We should realize the mistakes that have been made in Buddhism and change them so that its light can shine broadly." So it says,

> Truly recognize your own faults,
> Don't discuss the faults of others;
> Others' faults are just my own.
> Being together with one substance
>   is Great Compassion.

We are back bowing on the highway to the City of Ten Thousand Buddhas with new energy and vigor. The trip to Asia added a sense of urgency and clarity to our cultivation. If we want to change the world and to disperse the Big Darkness then we first must change ourselves by eradicating the poisons from our own minds.

In Bangkok, Thailand, while riding in a car, I listened to the Master say, "I am really stupid." Something really sunk in. "That's it!" I thought, "Everyone else is so smart, seeking this and that for self-benefit, making sure not to take a loss or to give away too much, keeping a little 'nest-egg.' But the Master lives what I've only read about in Sutras and is able to continually renew people's hopes. That is vast, great giving. Totally without a self, he happily transfers all his merit and virtue to others." I now see my work and responsibility as a person: to get rid of all selfishness. Later I told this to the Abbot and he replied, "Yes, the time is ripe now for everyone to bow with a single heart to the City of Ten Thousand Buddhas."

* * *

All day long young men in fast cars and pick-ups were trying to run us off the road. Driving on the shoulders, skidding into us, driving on the wrong side of the road, breaking all manner of laws. Finally at the end of the day the police gave us a citation because too much smoke comes out of the old Plymouth when it first starts up. Life's little ironies keep us from getting too serious.

"Far-Away Returning"

Outside: Cold, damp nights. We are camped in an empty field across the road from an animal hospital and next to a large trailer court by the freeway.

Inside: The joy and mysteries of far-away traveling... wanderings alone with the Tao in the Great Wilderness. They are not external journeys, but explorations of oneself, back to the "beginning of things."

> Now, great also means passing on,
> And passing on means going far away,
> And going far away means returning.
>
> Tao Te Ching

We have left our homes far away, yet each step away is returning.

Heng Sure • October 8, 1978
One more low bow, one less false thought

Bowing in place for three days' worth of impassable freeway "pilgrims prohibited." Counting bows on stones and bottle-caps, contemplating the purity of great Bodhisattvas who,

> "Although they diligently cultivated vigor, they knew that all wisdom ultimately does not come from anywhere… with level wisdom they entered into all countries, with the power of self-mastery they caused all worlds to revolve and mutually enter into one another."
>
> Entering the Dharma Realm
> Avatamsaka Sutra

Perched on a sandy, vacant lot across from the Soquel Village Trailer Park, between a bright yellow Mack dump-truck (for sale), and our road-weary Plymouth, my heart yearns for the self-mastery of the world-transcending heroes. On the Way, one low bow more, and one false thought less.

Homage to the Ocean-wide Assembly of Avatamsaka Buddhas and Bodhisattvas.

Heng Chau • October 8, 1978
Cultivation can look like bitter suffering

> From his first resolution, up to Buddhahood,
> All the Avici (hells) suffering in between,
> In order to hear the Dharma, he can undergo,
> Much more all the sufferings in the human realm.
>
> Ten Grounds Chapter
> Avatamsaka Sutra

All Buddhas were once ordinary people like you and me, who made a wish to become enlightened. But between that first resolution and realizing All-wisdom is a lot of hard work and suffering. Just wishing to be a Buddha, even with utmost sincerity, doesn't make one a Buddha. You have to actually change inside and out, effect a total transformation by cultivating your person. What's it like? It's like jumping into a blazing fire.

> Should a person come and tell the Bodhisattva,
> If you can hurl your body into a huge mass of fire
> I shall bestow upon you the jewel of Buddha-dharma!
> Having heard this, he throws himself in
> without trepidation.
>
> Ten Grounds Chapter
> Avatamsaka Sutra

Between the initial resolve and the fruit is the painstaking labor of smelting a vajra body and mind, a diamond-like vessel that's able to hold the Dharma. The resolve comes easy, attainment is dear. Sticking with your original vision, seeing it through to completion, takes the vigor of a great hero and the patience of the great earth. But to get the Dharma-jewel there is no suffering, no hardship a Bodhisattva can't endure. Cultivation can look like bitter suffering, but when you actually go and do it, you don't notice the aches and anguish. Only the joy is remembered.

* * *

Experiment in "Everything is made from the mind alone." For four days we have been hassled by police and by local cowboys. We've been run off the road and hazed by trucks and cars, cursed by people and bothered by stray dogs; we've been called "weirdoes and baddies." We figure it was because we've been eating too much and sloppy about starting on time, i.e. not keeping our rules of the road.

Today we started everything on time and ate a moderate meal. Results: no hassles, no weirdoes, no problems. Yesterday a pick-up truck backed up to Heng Sure as he bowed and then spun its wheels, covering Heng Sure in a cloud of dirt and stones. Today they returned and backed up to Heng Sure, but after a little heart-to-heart talk, they mellowed and drove away without incident.

A family from San Jose drove out with an offering and found us just as we were about to drive away to camp – perfect timing. And finally the County Sheriff who came out to hassle us about camping and being weird, had a change of heart. We got the okay to stay for the night. He even offered some suggestions on where to camp while bowing through Santa Cruz so as to not arouse suspicion that we are breaking the no-camping law. "I won't hassle you anymore and I'll see what I can do to pass the word on. Have a good night," said the Sheriff.

Lesson: Follow the rules, reduce desires, then every place is peaceful and every day is happy.

> When the nature's in Samadhi demons are subdued,
> Every day is happy.
> False thoughts not arising,
> Then everywhere is peaceful.
>
> The mind stops, thoughts are cut off,
> This is true nobility and riches.
> Selfish greed ended completely
> Is the true field of blessings.
>
> Verse by Master Hua

Heng Sure • October 9, 1978
Buddhists don't flog themselves

Bowed past acres and acres of greenhouses this morning and heard a voice from a passing pick-up on Soquel Drive:

"What do you guys do for fun, flog yourselves?"

Buddhists don't mortify the flesh; we cultivate to discipline the body and to subdue the mind. Cultivation is like gardening. Self-disciplined work on the mind-ground takes strenuous effort. Most people seek comfort. The labor of cultivation can look like punishment to folks who value saving labor, cutting corners, seeking pleasure.

But Buddhists don't flog themselves. We recognize the mind as a weed-choked field. Cultivating to clear the mind of desire, anger, and delusion is a great gift to the self, not a torture. There is no lasting happiness until we resolve the one great matter of birth and death. There is no more having fun once we see through to the heart of things. The body dies and departs without asking permission.

By cultivating the Dharma we make the most of the fleeting years in our fragile bodies. We come to the world to pay off our debts, to purify accounts, to return to the mind's true source. Until the work is done there is no more pleasure source. Until the work is done there is no more pleasure in seeking "fun." Cultivation may look backwards to some, but things are not always what they seem. The temporary discomfort of disciplined cultivation is like tilling soil, clearing weeds, and tending blooms in the mind's greenhouse garden of enlightenment. The fun follows the work.

"...repeat Amitabha's name, see clearly birth and death, then enjoy happiness beyond the reach of others."

Venerable HsuYun
Song of the Skin Bag

Heng Chau • October 9, 1978
They made room to stay together no matter

"The Bodhisattva Mahasattva has entered into the level nature of all dharma. He has not thought of any living being not being family or friends."

Ten Transferences Chapter
Avatamsaka Sutra

I came from a Wisconsin family whose roots were firmly planted in the land. Half of the relatives still live in the country, running farms handed down from father to son for four generations. Something about working the soil, planting and harvesting in natural rhythm with the seasons, instills a healthy blend of common sense, tolerance and reverence for the spiritual. Closeness to nature tends to level things out and to expand the mind's measure.

So even though I did a lot off-the-wall stunts and took some wrong roads while growing up, my family never rejected or disowned me. With patient humor and sometimes with bruised pride they made room to stay together no matter what I did. Conflicts and differences were settled among ourselves and with outsiders in the spirit of regarding everyone as family and friends.

This attitude has stayed with me through the years, only to grow and to mature within Buddhism. On the pilgrimage we look at everyone as our fathers and mothers, sisters and brothers. We have our fallings-out, our thick and thins, and passing thoughts of ill-will, but there's no room for hatred, grudges or anger. We are all of us, "going through a state" and "searching for ourselves." And after all the rope I was given, how can I not respect and value the ultimate rightness of regarding everyone with kind eyes? No matter what happens, there's just no problem when we can look at things in this way. A gentle smile and patient shrug of the shoulders handles almost every situation. There's a lot to laugh at, especially ourselves, but there's nothing in this life worth getting angry about.

> "Even if there is a living being who has a thought of hostility towards the Bodhisattvas, the Bodhisattva looks on him with kind eyes as well: and to the very end he never shows the slightest anger."
>
> Ten Transferences Chapter
> Avatamsaka Sutra

Heng Sure • October 10, 1978
Simple unadorned praises, chants, and mantras

"Big, Pure, and Bright"

Four words describe the Avatamsaka: big, pure, bright, and alive. The Sutra lives because it springs from the heart of the biggest, purest, and brightest being: the Buddha. The Buddha's Dharma-practices can look lifeless: slow, earthly bowing, still, tranquil Ch'an meditation. The sounds of cultivation are heart-beat basic: simple unadorned praises, chants, and mantras. But they are full of life and the methods of liberation transmitted from the Sages of antiquity. These are living Dharma treasures of "The most supreme of persons from time past."

From the outside nothing much seems to be going on. But inside, a single step onto the road of cultivation opens up a world never before imagined, a world above the dust, a world big as the universe, pure as empty space, bright as the harvest moon, endlessly alive as the Buddha's perfect human heart.

> The most supreme of all persons from time past,
> Their merit and virtue beyond measure and unattached.
> Courageous heroes, foremost, incomparable.
> The ones who leave the dust walk this path.
>
> Ten Practices Chapter – Avatamsaka Sutra

Heng Chau • October 10, 1978
The best of all the healing professions

Three cars full of angry, doped-up, young men sped up and squealed to a halt in a cloud of dust. Jumping out of their cars cursing and spitting on the ground, they grabbed rocks and surrounded us. Even though we were in town, a small redwood grove and park on Soquel Avenue concealed us from public view. We were isolated and out of the sight of witnesses, neighbors, and traffic.

We continued bowing and after a few minutes of sharp and tense questions and answers, one by one they relaxed. As we talked on the roadside they slowly dropped the rocks hidden in hands held behind their backs. "Thunk, thunk, thud." The stones fell limply to the ground as the men stepped closer and let down their guard.

"Well man, we just wanted to check you out, ya' know," said one in a husky, half-apologetic voice.

"Yeah!" chimed in another. "You're really stupid. Did you know that?! You're really stupid," still trying to bait us into a fight.

"What do you guys do?" I asked.

"Oh, us? We work and get stoned all the time," they answered.

After a few more questions they quietly drove away. "No harm meant, really. We was just testing you out."

After they left I thought of how I used to see alienated and mixed up people as hapless victims of a competitive and disjointed society whose culture drove nearly everyone to madness and to the end of their ropes.

But people make the society and karma makes the people. The conditions of our lives and our lot are molded by our hands. Not God, not the government, not the "Man" or the system, determine our fate. Not heredity, the stars and planets, or even "lay luck." Everything that happens to us comes from the karma we alone create. So it's said,

> The way of people is harmony
> With merit and error interspersed.
> On virtuous deeds you rise, offenses make you fall.
> It has nothing to do with anyone else at all.
>
> Master Hua – from The Ten Dharma Realms
> Are Not Beyond a Single Thought

Good causes reap good results; bad causes reap bad results. The superior person makes his own destiny superior, just as sure as the petty person makes his destiny petty. And no matter how bad the circumstances of your life, they can be reversed by returning to the good. No matter how thick and rich your blessings, they can be depleted by enjoying them and by turning away from the good. So in this world some of us blow hot while others blow cold, some climb up while others get trodden-down, but when all is said and done, it's the ones who keep the ancient, constant rules of the Tao that live the best of lives. The Master told us once,

> "Wealth and honor are the branches, virtue is the root. Nothing in this world endures unless it's created from virtuous conduct. What opposes the Tao is soon destroyed."

From the point of view of the young men who "work and get stoned all the time" a Buddhist monk's life is really stupid. But from the viewpoint of, say, a Midwestern daily pasture in the old-fashioned small town where I grew up, working and getting stoned all the time would merit the worst epithet a person could receive: "He didn't amount to anything." If you didn't respect and take care of yourself and benefit society, if you disgraced and burdened your parents and piddled your life away on running after selfish pleasures, this was both stupid and pathetic. Folks actually felt embarrassed and ashamed for someone like this.

A Buddhist monk, on the other hand, would be okay. Most people knew this world was temporary and respected those who "had a calling" to lead a spiritual life as priests, nuns, monks, and mystics – as long as they did it right and proper, that is, joined an order, renounced money, sex, name and fame, and dedicated themselves to helping others. "Been better if he'd become a Catholic priest, of course," they might say, "but Buddhists are a good group. At heart we're all the same and everyone's got their own way."

The value of a religious calling was unquestioned. Highly regarded as models and symbols of people's own inner needs and spiritual longings, a priest or monk, sister or nun contributed to the community's health and well-being as much as a doctor, farmer, lawyer or teacher. Although the soul is invisible, few denied its existence or the need for looking after it.

For most of human history, when people got sick in body or mind they turned to the local "doctor" for help. Shaman, witch doctors, healers, sorcerers, medicine men responded with hit-or-miss methods, that however strange they might seem to us, worked as well, perhaps even better, than their modern counterparts. Although the names have changed, the roles remain remarkably the same. Where I came from, sick people went to either MDs, priests, or psychiatrists – sometimes all three, just to be sure.

The problem with MDs was they could only patch up the body and they charged too much money. The Fathers relied mostly on faith, rituals and tradition. When it came to dealing with the mind and all its myriad states, they were stumped and could only shrug and say, "Trust in God." Psychiatrists also over-charged and although they delved beyond the realm of the senses and blind faith, they were far from the Tao and the noumenal truths beyond the path of words and thought. The workings of karma, the Seventh and Eighth Consciousnesses, the trail of ghosts and karmic shadows, bad energy and obstacles following us from past lives – none of this could be detected by psychoanalysis or by an ink blot test, or cured with a bottle of tranquilizers and an electric shock-treatment.

A Buddhist Sanghan combines the best of all the healing professions and avoids the worst short-comings. In an unbroken tradition of tough training and rigorous spiritual cultivation, a left-home person learns the secret of birth and death, the root causes of all suffering and sickness, and the medicine to health them. They ask for neither money nor thanks, and only wish to benefit others and to bring all living beings to Unsurpassed, Proper, Equal and Right Enlightenment.

> "He vows that all living beings become an indestructible medicine tree that can completely cure and save all living beings."
>
> Ten Transferences Chapter
> Avatamsaka Sutra

Heng Sure • October 11, 1978
Cutting through internal afflictions

"In the stillness of Dhyana, meditating by oneself, one forever severs all doubts and delusions. One's mind is not weary, nor is one lax or lazy. Ever increasing in progress and cultivation, one perfects all Buddhadharmas."

Entering the Dharma Realm
Avatamsaka Sutra

"Cutting Through"

Saturday morning in Santa Cruz fogbank I took charge of my mind during Ch'an meditation. Since leaving for Asia over three months ago, my meditation has been turbid and restless. We've bowed in America now for three weeks and passed a rough gauntlet of demon-tests, hostility, and hard times. Why have Aptos, Soquel, and Santa Cruz felt like a long, bad dream? Because I've let my mind flounder in a fuzzy, scattered fog not different from the mist that circles the Plymouth this dawn.

When you're concentrated, it's magical.
When you're scattered, there's nothing.

During the first 48 hours after returning to the Highway, I forced a 30-mile march. Result: bruised arches and unbalanced energy. Constant spinning from black-out sleeps through Sutra lectures to careless chats and useless philosophizing. Left the wisdom-sword hanging on a nail in my mind's closet. False thoughts flourished, desires beckoned, afflictions struck, concentration dribbled away.

With so much internal confusion, other states arose to match: young men buzzed us in high-speed strafing runs, pick-ups spun tires in the gravel, blasting the Plymouth with "dirt-offerings." Police and civil authorities, usually helpful and genial, have not yet connected with the spirit of our trip.

In the morning fog I resolved to cut through and to clear my mind. Sat long, refused to nod, and refused to follow the pain. Found the right spot and grew still, absorbed in concentration once more. What a relief! Felt rusty gears turn, deep inner breath exhaled; a quiet voice said, "Back to work again. Good."

Heng Chau • October 11, 1978
All we saw was ourselves

A local family stopped to offer supplies and support. "We meditate a lot when we go camping, but not as much as I'd like," said the husband. "My life feels like a whirlpool. I keep spinning and spinning and getting closer to the center."

They related this experience of their first meeting with the Venerable Abbot:

"Well, at first we weren't impressed. He looked so young and healthy – too much so to be an Abbot, so I crudely said, 'Who are you?' I thought he was one of the assistants. I've never seen anyone his age look so youthful! Anyhow, we got no reply. In fact, the Master said nothing to us at all that first time. It was like looking into a big mirror; as if he was empty inside. All we saw was ourselves!"

"Good Man, if there are living beings who have not planted good roots, who have not been gathered in by good friends, who are not protected or remembered by all Buddhas – such people will never be able to see me. Good Man, if there are living beings who get to see me, they will obtain irreversibility from annuttarasamyaksambodhi."

"There wasn't any of the usual, 'Hi! How are you… what 'ya been doing, et cetera,'" said the husband.

"It wasn't until later that we came to appreciate what a rare and valuable experience that was," said his wife.

I thought of one of Good Wealth's advisors, the Bhikshuni Lion Sprint. Because of her vast vows and her virtuous conduct,

> "All those who beheld her did not do so in vain. Whoever got to see her obtained an unforgettable experience and gift. She was like a clear, pure pool, in that her mind was without filth or turbidity. She was like a wish-fulfilling gem, in that she everywhere bestowed to all who sought from her... She was like the King of Wondrous Incense, in that she could cause those who saw her to obtain clear coolness in their minds."
>
> Entering the Dharma Realm
> Avatamsaka Sutra

After they left, as we bowed, I remembered one of the vows the Abbot made at age nineteen, on the anniversary of Guan Yin Bodhisattva's enlightenment:

The man's words echoed: "It was like looking into a big mirror... all we saw was ourselves!"

> "I vow that all living beings who see my face or who even hear my voice will fix their thoughts on Bodhi and quickly accomplish the Buddha Way."

* * *

> "He single-mindedly recollected how he should rely upon the Good Knowing Advisor... how towards the Good Knowing Advisor he should never be in opposition or rebellious."
>
> Entering the Dharma Realm
> Avatamsaka Sutra

My cultivation progressed dramatically in Asia because the Abbot held tight reins on this headstrong novice. The Master was exacting and demanding, yet not unreasonable, and always acted in my best interest, not for his own. Whenever I started to scatter and to climb on conditions, the Good Advisor came down swiftly. His firmness helped me gather back my energy and focus my mind. I swallowed my rebellious pride and as a result, grew immeasurably as a person under the wise and kindly care of a skillful teacher. And yet, even though I didn't oppose him, initially I tried to counter-control and manipulate him with fawning and with buttering-up. It didn't work.

"…How towards the Good Knowing Advisor he should
not have any thoughts of flattery and deceit."

Entering the Dharma Realm
Avatamsaka Sutra

I tried to ply the Abbot with special food during meals. He saw right through my deception and said, "No, I don't want any. Eat your own food, end your own birth and death." I tried to give him medicines which he flatly refused. I would praise him and he'd ignore it. My ingratiating smiles earned a scowl. I'd start to climb on a situation by talking *hwo swo* (Chinese for rapping meaningless chatter), and he'd cut me off in mid-sentence. While bowing, my false thoughts would drift to a table of sweet drinks usually set out and stocked full in every temple. I'd turn to sneak off for a drink only to find the Master standing there staring right through me. So it's said,

It is difficult to encounter a Good Knowing Advisor.
It is difficult to get to dwell together with him.
It is difficult to please him.
It is difficult to follow him, but now I have met you
    and obtained good benefits.

Entering the Dharma Realm
Avatamsaka Sutra

Why is it so difficult to please and follow a true teacher? Because he is always pure and lofty: thus, thus unmoving. His mind and will dwell in constant, proper concentration. He has no greed for offerings or benefits, no seeking for name or fame. The only thing that makes a Good Advisor happy is when a disciple brings forth the mind for the Way and lays to rest his greed, anger, and stupidity.

I felt rejected and policed at first, but later came to recognize and to appreciate the compassion and sympathy behind the Master's stern facade. It was exactly what I needed to keep from wandering down a perilous path. His skillful guiding and teaching led me through a door to a place I had never been before. Once through, everything looked different. As if borrowing his eye, for a few moments, I was able to see the actual nature of dharmas – they are false and empty affairs. All the difficulty and harshness was worth that brief, clear seeing; all the scoldings forgotten in that quiet moment of joy.

> "A good teacher is a lamp that tends towards All wisdom, for he enables me to recognize safe and perilous paths. A good teacher is an eye that tends towards All-wisdom, for he enables me to obtain the door of seeing the nature of dharmas."
>
> Entering the Dharma Realm
> Avatamsaka Sutra

Heng Sure • October 12, 1978
We just do our thing

"Expanding the Fishbowl"

It's been this way in each new town we enter. At first, two monks in an antique car arouse suspicions. Our every move is on display. Nervous homeowners reach for the phone to report to the authorities when we blow our noses, when we brush our teeth, when we sit to meditate. Heng Chau and I have learned to relax inside the fishbowl. Our protection is cautious, proper deportment in walking, standing, sitting, in every moment of the day. We have no private space so we can't be casual or sloppy in the least.

Gradually people lose their fear of the unusual pedestrians. We present no edges, seeking nothing, our clothes are modest, we just "do our thing," keep bowing, don't sell or buy. Slowly the message of peaceful contemplation and non-contention emerges from the bowing. Hard stares soften. The fishbowl expands. Looking at us as we look within, the viewer's vision returns, the fishbowl becomes the self-nature, the questions return to the asker.

First day in any town: "What do you creeps think you're doin'?"

Third day: "Pardon me. I've seen you every day on my way to work and I had to find out what you hope to accomplish. I don't know whom you represent, but I see you believe in your work. I admire your dedication. Could you tell me about your purpose?"

> "These Bodhisattvas know kindness done for them, and know to repay that kindness. Their minds are well-disposed for the good, and they are pleasant to associate with. They are upright and gentle, not acting like a dense thicket."
>
> Ten Grounds Chapter
> Avatamsaka Sutra

Heng Chau • October 12, 1978
They shine on each others' thrones

"The Ultimate Goal"

> "You should now believe that the knowledge and vision of the Buddha is simply your own mind, for there is no other Buddha."
>
> Sixth Patriarch Sutra

The police are in a hurry for us to hurry. They know where we shave and where we relieve ourselves. They know when we rise in the morning and what kind of tea we drink at night. But they don't know our "sound" and police like to know everything. So they keep coming back, watching and trying to figure us out.

"I mean, really, what's the ultimate goal?" asked the officer on duty last night.

The ultimate goal is the knowledge and vision of the Buddha, and the Buddha is just our own mind.

* * *

There is no problem so big that a day of bowing can't solve.

* * *

"Good Friend"

> "His mind neither relies or dwells on any external dharmas, and yet he does not forget the Bodhisattva's practices, nor does he leave good advisors. Upholding all the vast, great practices and vows of a Bodhisattva, he constantly takes delight in being of service to all his good friends."
>
> Ten Transferences Chapter
> Avatamsaka Sutra

The Bodhisattva has no self. In his "friendships," he seeks and expects nothing, yet he gives with a heart that never runs dry. He wants only for all beings to become Buddhas, a model, a catalyst, and even a crutch to this end. But he never is confused by emotional love and by selfish desire. At all times the Good Knowing Advisor[1] acts only to encourage people to use their own wisdom, to stop false thinking and to break attachments, to go towards the good and to stand on their own two feet. Everything is impermanent and even the best of friendships must end. The Good Knowing Advisor, therefore, is the ultimate friend. Drawing near to him is temporary; the friendship ends in Buddhahood. And so he vows,

---

[1.] "Good Knowing Advisor" is the English translation taken from the Chinese *shan zhi shi* (善知識). The term originally comes from the Sanskrit *kalyana-mitra*, meaning "a wholesome friend, a virtuous friend." And in Chinese, the phrase interchangeably appears as *shan yo*, literally "good friend."

"I vow as long as there is a single living being who has not accomplished Buddhahood, I too will not attain the Right Enlightenment."

The Bodhisattva acts in a way that brings out the Buddha-nature in others without looking for thanks or fearing betrayal. Have no attachments, and produce the mind that dwells nowhere, then one can happily be of service to all one's good friends.

> Neither great nor small,
> Neither come nor gone,
> In world systems like motes of dust
> They shine on each others' thrones.

* * *

"Just as lights do not conflict with one another, so too, people, should not clash; they should allow their lights to shine on one another like the lights interpenetrating at the interstices of the circular net canopy of the Great Brahma King."

Ten Dharma Realms

Heng Sure • October 13, 1978
Go for it!

"Soquel"
Cultivation is the first real thing I've ever done. Cultivation's goodness goes beyond our knowing, beyond words. The True and the Real are hard to hold close, but just having the chance to seek the unsurpassed Dharma makes all the difficulty worthwhile. The time used in bowing to the Buddha feels especially valuable, like nothing else in the world.

Voice from a passing car: "Hey man, you better do something about your life."

Voice heard from shoe-tip level as footsteps approach, pass, pause, and return, indrawn breath and a tone of admiration: "Go for it!"

> The unsurpassed, deep, profound, subtle,
>   and wonderful Dharma
> In hundreds of millions of kalpas
>   is difficult to encounter.
> I now see and hear it, receive and maintain it,
> And I vow to understand the Thus Come One's
>   true and actual meaning.

Verse on Opening a Sutra

Heng Chau • October 13, 1978
Kindness, compassion, joy and giving

Monk: "Master, how should we handle people who want to fight with us, or intend to harm us?"

Master: "You must be patient with every single state. Patience will win. You must not be angry with anything. No matter what comes, don't get angry."

Monk: "Some people are really mean and tough. It could get violent."

Master: "Don't ever use force to oppress people. Use virtuous conduct to move people… No matter what situation you must use the four unlimited minds of compassion, kindness, joy and giving to deal with it."

There is no higher gung fu than the four unlimited minds of kindness, compassion, joy, and giving. Every potentially violent situation we've met has been turned with this attitude; with the unlimited hearts, not the force of hands.

Yesterday, for example, a gang of young street toughs started taunting us and tossing rocks while we bowed in a bike lane. We didn't move and didn't get angry or afraid. They sensed this I think, and mellowed. After awhile, they came over to watch us bow and to ask some sincere questions. The leader of the gang in particular, was moved and read our hand-out aloud in his broken, skip-school, street-English.

We parted friends, respecting each others' right to "weirdness." The hardness in their eyes and faces had given way to softness, to acceptance and a bit of warmth.

People ask, "What do you hope to accomplish?" The answer is: nothing. When we bow sincerely things seem to accomplish themselves. But when we try to accomplish something then nothing gets done. We are learning to have deep faith in our instructions. Why? They work! Non-contending is the greatest of power. Kindness is yielding, compassion is softness and together they can overcome any obstacle and disarm the fiercest foe.

> "That the yielding overcomes the resistant and the soft conquers the hard is a fact known by all men, yet utilized by none."
>
> Lao Tzu

* * *

"Passing Sounds…"

Angry: "Hey we told you to get out of Santa Cruz, goddammit! Next time we see you we're going to run you over. I mean it!"

Welcome: "Ah, a divine pilgrimage!"

Shock: "I can't believe it. You're putting me on!"

Strange Threat: "Why don't you do that in your place of worship. You lost your brain? Where did you… how about if I kick you in the ass, how about that!?" says an older lady, who then takes our picture and leaves.

Advice: "You'd be more effective in a closet!"

Optimistic: "Ahh, you'll find Santa Cruz to your liking. Yes sir, there's some real mellow, holy vibes here."

Question: "But where did they come from?"

Directions: "Go home!"

Requests: "Please come and be our guests. Take a bath, have a hot meal, relax…"

Jesus: "Jesus loves you, Heng Chau," on a 6-lane street from a stranger.

?: "But where did they come from?"

Cool: "How weird! Get down baby! Get down!"

Sales: "Buy some downs? Wanna buy some downers? Uppers?"

?: "But where did they come from?"

Thanks: "Does my heart good to see you bowing. Just watching, I feel peaceful. Thanks."

> Proper mindfulness and reflection
>   are apart from discriminations.
> All the gods and men cannot disturb it.
> Although they hear praise or slander of the Buddha
>   or of the Buddhadharma, or of the Bodhisattvas
>   and the conduct they practice,
> They do not retreat.
>
> Ten Dwellings Chapter
> Avatamsaka Sutra

* * *

"In cultivation, what you can see is not real. The truth of what is going on is invisible. Anything that is visible is false… Yet right within the false you want to cultivate the true."

the Abbot in Singapore, 1978

"Urban Camping"

This is the second county in which we have run into a "no-overnight-camping" law. There are ways around it.

That night we parked in the middle of abandoned junk cars and old school buses. Our '56 Plymouth fit right in and even though we were in the middle of town, no one saw us. We spent the night in the "graveyard of the rusted automobiles," invisible.

Sometimes after bowing we drive to a park or an open field area to meditate and do evening ceremonies. About 11 P.M. or so when the police "sweep the streets" we cruise and quietly coast to a resting niche in a residential area or anywhere in the "invisible zone" (where you are so invisible you pass unnoticed). One night it was the parking lot of the busy Avalon Restaurant and another night, next to the police station. No one noticed.

The trick is to not get uptight or have any plan. Just patiently wait and watch for everything to tell you what to do. Everything speaks the Dharma. Within the visible we make ourselves invisible; within the false we cultivate the true.

Heng Sure • October 14, 1978
Just an ancient riddle

"Verse for Reversing Adversity"

> Guard your treasures.
> Forsake pleasures.
> Patiently endure; renounce.
> Thoughtless, kind, compassionate.
> Happy, calm, and pure.
> There's no self and there's no other.
> Just an ancient riddle:
> Not produced and not destroyed.
> Empty, false, and Middle.

Heng Chau • October 14, 1978
If you can see all marks as no marks

"Apart from Marks"

We bow the sidewalks in silence, yet we aren't deaf. Scores of people stop to advise, threaten, praise, ridicule, question, convert and "just say my piece," as one man put it today. Sometimes I contemplate a specific idea from the Sutra and let my mind wander where it will, like a jazz musician – improvising rhythms and contrapuntal melodies that always weave back and keep to the same theme, or simple songs. Today's theme was "marklessness," and the Light Enlightenment Chapter of the Avatamsaka provided the melody when I read this A.M.:

> The Buddhadharma is subtle, wonderful,
>   and hard to measure,
> All words and phrases cannot come up to it.
> It is not harmonious or in disharmony,
> Its substance and nature
>   are still and quiet apart from marks.

It's said that the whole world and all the myriad things are constantly proclaiming the subtle and wonderful principles of the Flower Adornment Sutra. It surely seemed that way today. In an uncanny, almost playful and delightful way, encounters and incidents that normally would have broken up our concentration and intruded on our quiet space, blended in as effortlessly and creatively as a jam session of professional jazz musicians. Everything and every person spoke to the main melody, "marklessness," yet each was as unique and as different from the other as a piano from a saxophone, as a flute from a bass fiddle.

For example, an excited man roared up on a motorcycle and breathlessly said, "Do you speak English? Listen, I got something to say to you!" He gulped a breath of air and forced it down. "At the exact moment you bowed across that street, a huge limb fell out of a tree on the very same street. Everybody came outside and they are all excited. It's really neat!" he smiled, eyes all lit up. The people saw it as an omen, a sign from nature announcing our presence maybe, or as a display of power, or I don't know what. It was probably a coincidence and we certainly do not intend or even think about such things. Still, it spoke the Dharma we heard from the Abbot that all marks are set up by the mind.

"Everything is made from the mind alone," means however you see things, that's how they are. Basically there's nothing going on at all, but we go out and look for things to do, adding a head on top of a head. So we say, "it's all made from the mind alone."

"Marklessness" means anything that has shape and form is empty and false. The real thing is apart from appearances and found only by awakening to the self-nature, not by looking outside and attaching to marks and to what can be perceived by the senses. So it's said,

> "The Thus Come One does not compose his substance by manes of marks. But only with unmarked, still, extinct Dharmas."

Light Enlightenment Chapter
Avatamsaka Sutra

A commuter from Santa Cruz stopped to say,

"I had to stop and tell you you're putting out really good vibes. I watched you for three days now and each time I see you my mind trips out."

Another person comes to offer encouragement:

"No matter what anyone says or does you keep at it. I know you will anyhow, but I wanted to say that. I know you will make it all the way."

Kind words, sweet praise, coming from sincere people with good hearts. But if we attach to the good marks we are only setting ourselves up to be blown over by the bad ones. And so the Sutra says to return the light and seek the true and actual Dharma within. It is apart from praise or slander, good and bad, color, caste and all appearances and words.

> If one uses the qualities
>> of awesome virtue, color and caste
> To look for the guiding
>> and regulating master among men,
> This is a sick vision,
>> a perverted view,
> Which will not bring knowledge
>> of the most supreme Dharma.
>
>> Light Enlightenment Chapter
>> Avatamsaka Sutra

"What you are worshipping doesn't exist," shouts an irate preacher as we bow down Soquel Avenue. "I'll pray for you so you find what's truly true – god!"

In a way the preacher is right. The Buddha does not exist, at least in the way we think of things existing or not existing. A Patriarch upon enlightening once said, "All Buddhas are not," meaning the Buddha's state is completely without marks and attachments, something we ordinary people can't image. So our teacher says to us, "If you can name it and talk about it, you are still only on the surface." The unobstructed, unbound, nowhere-dwelling mind of great, perfect wisdom is the Buddha. All beings potentially have this Buddha-nature, and all can equally become Buddhas – even god, and yet until we are enlightened, we can't even imagine such a state.

> The Thus Come One's form and shape,
>> and all is characteristics,
> Are beyond the reckoning

of anyone in the mundane world.
For hundreds of thousands of nayutas of aeons
  these thoughts have been together.
His form, appearance, and awesome virtue
  have turned without limit.

Light Enlightenment Chapter
Avatamsaka Sutra

"I admire your dedication, but this (bowing) is getting you nowhere in the hereafter. Not all roads lead to heaven," warned a worried Christian in Aptos.

But we aren't going to heaven and aren't seeking the hereafter. We don't bow to the East, or to the sun, or kiss the earth, or anything else that can be named and labeled. Ultimately, all roads lead nowhere, and that nowhere is said to be wonderful past words. Everything with marks and names is false and impermanent, including the heavens.

All with marks is empty and false.
If you can see all marks as no marks,
Just this is seeing the Thus Come One.

Vajra Sutra

The prize-winning piece comes at the end of the day from a neighbor who strolls over to talk as I make tea on the tailgate. We are camped under a branching Cypress Tree at the edge of a lonely street that dead-ends into the sand dunes of Soquel Cove in the Monterey Bay. He walks right up and joins me, rubbing his hands above the flames of the Coleman stove and rounding his shoulders against the chilly, salt-sea night air.

"People think Jesus is coming again. But they're wrong," he says, matter-of-factly.

"Jesus isn't coming; the UFOs are coming. They're out there watching us like a farmer watches a corn crop grow. When they come, they're going to take some of us with them – alive, right out into outer space!" he exclaims.

"The rest they will leave here on earth to blow themselves up with nuclear weapons and pollution. It says so in the Bible!" he says with confidence and authority.

"Oh?" I say.

"Yeah! Do you read the Bible?" he asks.

"Once upon a time..." I answer.

"Well, I've read it!" he states irrefutably.

"Oh!" I say.

"Yessir, you bet. What are you going to do?" he demands urgently, almost worried.

"About what?" I ask.

"Whey they come. When the UFOs come. Are you going with them into outer space or are you staying here?"

"We will just keep bowing," I answer.

"They're coming real soon, I know it..." he says, voice trailing off as he looks up at the stars and scans the skies.

I pour the tea in our thermos, pack away the camp stove, and crawl inside the car to meditate before sleep. As I nod in that half-awake, half-asleep twilight state, the melody returns to tie together the whole day's separate pieces. The first verse I read that morning came back, at first faintly, then louder and clearer, rounding out the circle and finishing the concert called "apart from marks":

> The Buddhadharma is subtle, wonderful
>   and hard to measure.
> All words and phrases cannot come up to it.
> Neither harmonious nor in disharmony,
> Its substance and nature are still and quiet,
>   apart from all marks.

Light Enlightenment Chapter
Avatamsaka Sutra

Heng Sure • October 15, 1978
The more we relax the deeper we sink

"Unwinding"

Tired this evening and tight as a coiled spring. Finished bowing along a street of shops. Families passed in station wagons, full of brown-paper packages, noodles, and popcorn-munching kids; smells of BarBQed chicken and clouds of muzak tantalized the senses like dancers' veils. Even though I'm tired and tense, this is the time to increase vigor or my mind will run out to play, to seek a party, and to mix with the dust. If I'm not careful my hard-earned concentration will scatter before I settle into meditation.

> When you concentrate, it's magical;
> When you scatter, there's nothing.

Made it into the Plymouth and put body in the disciplined posture of Ch'an. Put mind to work reciting the Great Compassion Mantra. Before long the beckoning feelings of the marketplace seemed transparent and ordinary. No happiness compares with the fullness of self-reliance. We have all the need inside. Seeking the good life outside the mind depletes our original share; instead of relieving suffering, running out after sense-gratification increases suffering.

Seated in full-lotus, a flood of images came to mind: New York City business people sipping martinis on commute trains, auto-plant workers in Michigan chugging cans of malt liquor at the bowling alley, Irish factory men lining tavern railings, noses deep in pints of stout; Taiwanese farmers, cheeks bulging with bright-red betel nut, squatting in a circle around the village's coke machine; Japanese moms and dads leading kimono-clad youngster to the neighborhood ofuro bathhouse after dinner; countless millions of faces across the globe staring mesmerized into the blinking television screen.

People seek to escape tension. There are many ways to wind-down and to relax pressure. But worldly unwinding is like a whirlpool: the more we relax the deeper we sink. In Buddhism, this is called,

"Born drunk, we die in a dream." Cultivators reverse the flow, "Return to the root and go back to the origin."

Just at the point of "I can't take it any longer," cultivators return states of tension, fatigue, anger, frustration, to the mind that produces them. Using Dharma methods like Ch'an meditation, in one thought of concentration and bearing what is hard to bear, afflictions vanish and wisdom appears. Tension melts into ease, desire transforms into delight.

"Returning the light to illumine within" is the only way to truly unwind. Sitting in meditation is relaxing beneath the cool shade of wisdom-canopy.

> "They vow that all beings be covered by wholesome dharmas and eradicate the hubbub, dirt, and dust of the mundane world."
>
> Ten Transferences Chapter
> Avatamsaka Sutra

Heng Chau • October 15, 1978
Accord with conditions, nothing is fixed

> "And now life in its turn evolves into death. For not only nature, but man's being has its seasons, its sequence of spring and autumn, summer and winter."
>
> Chuang Tze

Bowing through Cabrillo College, south of Santa Cruz. Passing under a maple tree with its falling bright orange and yellow leaves, I wondered why when leaves die everyone thinks it's beautiful, but when people die we cry.

In the Avatamsaka it says the Bodhisattva is "constantly without worries or regrets." Why? Because the Bodhisattva's nature is always in Samadhi. Always in Samadhi is just always non-attached. Non-attachment is the basic nature of people. The natural mind doesn't know how to worry because it never stops long enough to pick up any burdens.

> When one attends to the here and now,
>   the false returns to the true.

Master Hua

All my worries come from thinking about the future; all my regrets come from thinking about the past. To "attend to the here and now" is just to take it as it comes and to leave it when it goes. A worried mind is just a thought, it isn't real. When we die we have to leave all our worries and troubles behind. Why not leave them behind before we die?

> Disgusted with the three existences,
>   not greedy or attached,
> He intently seeks the Buddha's wisdom,
>   with no other thought.
> Hard to fathom, hard to think of
>   and beyond compare,
> Limitless and boundless,
>   by troubles unoppressed.

Ten Grounds Chapter
Avatamsaka Sutra

"No Fixed Dharmas"

Traveling with the Abbot in Asia was a classroom in non-attachment. "When you step out the front door you need to be a little expedient," said the Abbot as we left Gold Mountain Monastery at the outset. "There are no fixed dharmas, do you understand?" I nodded yes, but as it turned out, I did not understand at all. We

crossed and re-crossed a dozen different datelines and countries, all
with different times, customs, diets, laws, and languages. The Master,
quite at ease, juggled eating times and deportment to the point I
didn't know whether I was coming or going. Not knowing whether
you're coming or going, and not minding in the least, is non-attachment. Non-attachment is just like the wind.

> The Bodhisattvas dwell in the world, yet,
> They are not attached to any dharmas,
>   either inside or outside.
> Like the wind which travels
>   through the skies without hindrance,
> The Great Knight's concentration is also like this.
>
> Light Enlightenment Chapter
> Avatamsaka Sutra

For example, in one temple, the Abbot threatened to fast
because the hosts repeatedly ignore our delegation's request for
simple food. During lunch the Master openly supported us in
turning down a rich gourmet fare of mock meat, candied vegetables,
and fine-flavored delicacies. Cultivators cannot do the Buddha's
work if they eat good food and indulge their appetites, so we
boycotted the goodies and ate plain rice and fruit.

But, less than a week later, at a donor-sponsored meal-offering,
the very same rich food was served. The Master ate it without a word
or the slightest misgiving. One of the left-homes respectfully said,
"But Master, this is that exact same good food!" The Abbot,
straight-faced, calmly replied, "No. This isn't that kind of food. Eat
up! This is different."

> "Levelly and impartially he teaches and transforms them
> without labels, without any conditions or calculating, without
> any falseness, and far apart from all distinctions, seeking, and
> attachments."
>
> Ten Transferences Chapter
> Avatamsaka Sutra

The meaning, I suspect, was that although the food was identical, the conditions under which it was served were different. The Master was simply according in both cases and concentrating on teaching and transforming both the donors and his young, inflexible disciples. I doubt if the Master himself knew the taste of the food at all, or even cared. So the Gold Mountain manifesto in part says:

> We accord with conditions and do not change.
> We do not change, yet we accord with conditions...

Malaysia and most of Asia travel about uninhibited by traffic laws, stop lights, rules or right-of-way, speed zones, divider-stripes, lanes, or even traffic cops. My linear and square Western mind thinks in black and white, in iron-cast moulds of do's and don't's. Consequently, the Asia highways and city streets looked like keystone cops mayhem to me. People pass any time they get a notion, drive as fast or as slow as they feel, turn without signaling and often just take the shortest distance between two points, every-man-for-himself course. Yet for nearly two months and thousands of miles, we never saw a single mishap while traveling. Whereas in the U.S., with its clear-cut rules and glow-in-the dark, follow-the-dotted-line safety precautions, we witnessed two accidents before we left the airport parking lot and saw a multiple, rear-ending collision on the freeway an hour after landing.

What's the difference? In Asia, no one has any expectations about what the other guy is going to do. So Asians drive in the here and now and are prepared for anything – they expect the unexpected. Americans, on the other hand, drive by the book and expect the other guy to obey the rules. And of course, people being people, they do not follow the rules or behave predictably and smash into each other constantly.

As with cars and clocks, so too with cultivation and with things spiritual. I am learning how to bend and to yield, learning to move sideways and in circles instead of in stiff boxes and headstrong "one-track-onlys." The attached mind prefers logic and reason, but nature prefers spontaneity and follows its own rhymes and reasons that reason cannot understand. So an ancient said,

> "Truly, what is stiff and hard is a 'companion of death;'
> what is soft and weak is a 'companion of life.'"
>
> Lao Tzu

To be soft and weak means to be unselfish and according. It also means there are "no fixed dharmas." But no fixed dharmas does not mean "anything goes," and "let it all hang loose," or "do as you please."

While riding to a Dharma Assembly outside of Kuala Lumpur, I asked the Abbot,

"Master, what does it mean 'nothing is fixed?'"

"It doesn't mean you can go out and steal, kill, take drugs, engage in sexual promiscuity, or lie, and then casually say, 'Oh, it's O.K., I'm not attached, no fixed dharmas!' This is totally incorrect," replied the Master.

"'Nothing is fixed' simply means there's no hard and fast way to go towards the good. There's no fixed way to do what is proper and correct," he explained.

These simple words struck deep and caused me to reflect on a bustle, but dangerous attitude I grew up with. As a child I idolized the Wild-West cowboys and frontiersmen. I grew up in a culture that cherishes freedom but despises the rules; a country born of revolution that boomed to prosperity on the principle that might is right. "Who cares about the law; I got the power, ain't I!?" boasted a famous American "robber baron" tycoon. Thus I and many others came to equate freedom with no rules, and independence with license.

But there is a power and a law that no man can overturn or disregard: the immutable law of causes and effect. The law of karma governs all things under heaven. The only true freedom is that which comes from submitting to its rules. Pure karma is liberation. Independence is the fruit of mastering the rules of cause and effect. The liberated being isn't immune to cause and effect, rather, he is no longer confused by cause and effect. And what are the rules? What is the unchanging and timeless natural law? The precepts. So the Buddha said just before entering Nirvana:

> "All of you Bhikshus, after my extinction, should honor and revere the precepts (Pratimoksha). They are like finding a light in the darkness, or like a poor person obtaining a treasure. They are your great teacher and not different from my actual presence in the world...

> "The precepts are the root of proper freedom; therefore, they are called the Pratimoksha (lit. 'the root of freedom')."

Shakyamuni Buddha

Heng Sure • October 16, 1978
This is the wrong door. Do not enter!

"Out of the Marketplace"

Bowed next to a car dealer's showroom. In the window-glass a reflection caught my eyes. A young woman crossed the sidewalk behind me. An old response stirred briefly; a trace of past habit-energy rose: "Who is she? How do I look?" I recognized instantly as the door to the marketplace of romance creaked open: "This is the wrong door. Do not enter!"

> The gate of my birth is the door of my death.
> How many wake up to it? How many are still dazed?
> At midnight, the Iron Hero thinks it over:
> The turning wheel of the six paths you yourself stop.

Master Hua

A cultivator's heart no longer dwells in the market-place of romance and courtship. I don't dance anymore. Vowed on the spot to never again tie my life to another being in the role of lover, boyfriend, husband, father, or mate. Vowed instead to seek the highest liberation for all beings to benefit the world by realizing All-wisdom and working for the spiritual welfare of others. Bowing by the Santa Cruz auto lot; no price sticker, no discount or rebate on these happy thoughts. Desire has a price but true happiness is priceless.

> "He vows that all beings liberate themselves from the bonds of the home-life and enter into the Buddhadharma, which is not a family-dharma, and that they cultivate pure practices."
>
> Ten Transferences Chapter
> Avatamsaka Sutra

Heng Chau • October 16, 1978
He was a regular old guy

Full moon brings lots of people, lots of action. A lay disciple of the Abbot's was surprised, slightly stunned to discover us bowing in front of his house. "I've been on and off with my practice and had been thinking a lot about it lately and there you show up in my front yard!" he said. He looked a little like a plant too long removed from the sun, fresh wind and rain that suddenly found itself back on the front yard on the first day of spring. Slightly pale and timid, but greatly relieved and ready to come back to the green world, ready to come back to life. "This is just the boost I needed to get back in shape."

He told us he recited the name of Amitabha Buddha and, "Whenever I get lazy and stop reciting, things start going wrong. Then I start reciting again and my problems vanish. Really a mind blower, huh?"

As we bowed down a busy thoroughfare, someone tapped me on the shoulder while I was down in prostration and yelled, "Hey, what are you doing!? What are you doing anyhow!?" It was a "Christian" zealot and friends, out to convert us. With bibles in hand they proceeded to shout verses at us as we bowed on a narrow boulevard of dirt. On our right were rush hour traffic and the "bible blast." On our left two hungry donkeys grazing and sniffing in our ears. Inside it was quite.

Heng Sure's redeemer preached pure Gospel. "Well, all I can say is, if you don't accept what I'm telling you today then you are already condemned!" So she said it over and over again, perhaps six times. It was all she could say.

Mine was less sure of where the correct quotes were and tried a different tack: "I am madly in love with Jesus. Did you know that? Jesus wouldn't have me go out and roll around in the dirt in front of all these people. Buddha is dead. He was a regular ol' guy. But Jesus is alive, right now!" On the other side of pasture fence the donkey pawed the dirt with his hoof, demanding the green grass I was bowing in.

"Now you may not have guessed it but I'm really a spiritual person and I'm free, I'm free! Jesus sent me out to talk to you. So listen to me or else you'll regret it." The donkey pawed and grunted, the cars honked and the preacher continued: "Did you know the Buddha was a liar and a deceiver? When he died he said, 'I'm not who I said I was.' But then it was too late. Too many people were already fooled. But it's not too late for your brother…" and so forth.

After an hour the preachers left. The traffic subsided. I fed the donkeys some green grass and we bowed until sunset.

> "All false views they completely cast away without a trace. They leave behind all heat and vexation. Constantly pure and cool, they dwell on the unobstructed ground of liberation."
>
> Ten Transferences Chapter
> Avatamsaka Sutra

A man came out and offered us his field and a pine tree to camp under the night. "I knew right off you were Buddhists. Welcome!"

We drove back to wash the car at a small run-down row of cabins where the layman who recites Amitabha Buddha lives. We pulled in at dusk and found a small altar in the dirt driveway, adorned with fresh flowers, candles, images, offerings and burning incense. Two other local disciples stopped by and before we knew it, they were all washing and waxing our car after providing mats and a quiet place for us to meditate under some tall pine trees. Later, as the full moon rose and the stillness of evening settled the day's dust, they respectfully approached with folded hands and requested Dharma.

We did the evening ceremony together, bowing and chanting the "Eighty-Eight Buddhas Repentance" in front of the make-shift drive-way altar, reading by flashlight, candles, and the glow of the moon. There we huddled together on mats and blankets and listened to a taped lecture the Master delivered in Hong Kong, translated by Dharma Master Kuo Jing.

"This is America. Buddhism is new here. We are all breaking new ground, inside and out. There are only a few temples and Way-places so we make do in cars and driveways; in abandoned state hospitals and in converted factories. But in our pioneer hearts, these are adornments as fine as any temple in the world."

It's as the Abbot says, "The straight mind is the Way-place."

We drove to camp for the night under the tall evergreen in the secluded field offered by the neighbor. Flowers and thick dew reflect on each other in the quiet meadow by moonlight. Tomorrow morning we will be gone before the dew dries and the flowers fall.

> With no going, no coming, like a mirage or reflection,
> Conditions arise and dissipate and time passes by.
> The door of adornments is opened. Who has come?
> Secluded pathway, falling flowers, deep flowing waters.

[Verses from "Pictures and Praises of Good Wealth's Journey to the South as pointed out to him by Manjushri Bodhisattva" by Ch'an Master Fo Kuo (C.1101 AD.) Entering the Dharma Realm, Vol. II]

Heng Sure • October 17, 1978
Oh never mind, I already know the answer

True principles live in simple words, surrounded by silence. Ordinary words, the same sounds we speak every day, when they carry Buddhadharma from heart to heart, change into pearls of light that please and benefit the ear.

Selfish words carry no light and benefit nobody. The words, "I, me, and mine," illustrate the Self, and defend the phantom Ego. Selfish words never transcend the level of talk. Listened closely today while Heng Chau responded to a Highway Patrolman, a news reporter, a Santa Cruz university student, and a Buddhist layman. He spoke true principles without frills, answered questions with Dharma phrases, then "let the silence be." Refusing to step into the spotlight he tried to reduce words and to remove the mark of Self. His Ego took a loss but he spoke solid Dharma that illuminated the questions, sparked the listeners' ears and lit up our hearts.

> True principle sounds good to everybody:
> In the sea is a spirit named Wholesome Sound
> Whose voice universally accords
>   with the creatures of the sea.
> Completely distinguishing all words and speech,
> He makes them all joyous and happy.
>
> Worthy Leader Chapter
> Avatamsaka Sutra

Layman: "What do you need?"

Heng Chau: "Whatever makes you happy to offer is what we need."

Layman: "How are you fixed for socks? Can we get you some gasoline?"

Heng Chau: "We always feel we have enough of everything. Whatever you would like to offer makes us happiest."

Layman: "You always say that."

Heng Chau: "Because it's true. It was true in the past and it will be true in the future for all left-home people."

Layman: (with a bright smile) "Hard to beat the truth, huh? Let's find the nearest gas station and we'll fill the tank. By the way, how about motor oil? Have you got... Oh never mind, I already know the answer. Ha Ha Ha!"

Heng Chau: (nods, smiles, silently.)

Choosing not to speak for oneself is the cultivation of renunciation (*she* 捨). We pass up the old impulse to seek and climb and to establish personal ties.

True principle sounds clean and bright. Light reflects on all who hear it. Selfish words leave a dull and dusty feeling in the heart.

> As for the place of language of all living beings,
> Within it ultimately there is nothing to obtain.
> If you understand that the names and appearances
>   are all discriminations (made in the mind),
> You will clearly understand that all dharmas
>   are totally without a self.
>
> Ten Transferences Chapter
> Avatamsaka Sutra

Heng Chau • October 17, 1978
You don't need "good" food

Big and small, me and others differ in degree, not kind. All is one. Two is false thought. (So is "one." Still not there, keep bowing).

"With not even one thought arising, the entire substance manifests."

Dream: Shih Fu was steadily climbing a long flight of stairs. I would run and bound in a burst of energy, then stop on a landing to play. When I tried to catch up, the Master was way ahead. Constancy. I woke up with a cold because I fell asleep exhausted and didn't take care to cover up. I had this realization: I use up my blessings, and live off my inner savings. Without renewing blessings or cultivating higher virtue, both are soon exhausted like the prodigal son. I stand and play on the stairs of life thinking it's an escalator. But if I don't keep climbing, the stairs turn into a slide. Life is over and even the richest blessings soon dry up. Wake up from the dream.

> "It is just like a person who in a dream sees himself sliding into a big river. Because he wants to save himself he puts forth heroic courage and comes up with a great expedient and wakes himself up. And because he is awake, all the actions in the dream stop."
>
> Ten Grounds Chapter
> Avatamsaka Sutra

> "If you don't lose your *ch'i* (energy) and essence, then you don't need 'good' food – food that is rich in vitamins, minerals and protein. Your body will maintain a high state of health, balance, and purity naturally."
>
> Shih Fu in L.A.
> November 1977

After two weeks of rice gruel and simple vegetables, Heng Sure and I ate an American, vegetarian, natural-food, balanced meal. It felt like human rocket fuel. After, we were overcharged, full of fire and false thoughts. When we went out to bow, young women came up.

"Hi, what ya' doin'" – more than we've seen in months.

The name of the game is "end desire, preserve wisdom." Food is sex is fame is wealth is sleep. When we indulge in any of these, even in thoughts, we attract trouble and bad energies. Problems come in the form of hecklers, pick-up trucks running us off the road, the weather, each other, and sometimes bad dreams and demons.

When we don't false think it's another world of peace, light, and good fortunes. Bright-eyed, sincere friends and protectors gather around, and Dharma harmony everywhere pervades.

When desire turns us, suffering is boss. If we turn desire, the Pure Land is not far away. One of the biggest lessons of this pilgrimage so far is: what we once took for joy is really suffering; and what we took for suffering, is really joy. Things aren't always what they seem.

All disasters come from desire. Desire is the root of birth and death. Ending desire and purifying the mind is the unalterable, true teaching of the ancient worthies and the single path on which all enlightened beings walk to Bodhi.

> Manjushri, the Dharma is eternally so.
> The Dharma King's only single Dharma
> Does not obstruct people at all,
> But leaves samsara (birth and death) on a single road.
>
> The Bodhisattvas Ask for Clarification Chapter
> Avatamsaka Sutra

Heng Sure • October 18, 1978
A beer offering, without the cup

"Medicine"

> "At all times, in every method I practice, whether I walk, sit, enter or leave, when on the toilet or in the bath, in each movement, looking up or down, with each sight and sound I perceive, I should, with single-minded concentration, recollect the Triple Jewel and contemplate the nature of the mind as empty."
>
> Medicine Master Repentance

Foggy morning, groggy mind. Overturned a steaming cup of hot tea onto my lap, while bare ankles were locked in full lotus.

"That's good tea, really wakes us up, eh?" quipped Heng Chau. A good laugh is good medicine.

"The Great King of Physicians dispenses medicine according to the illness. Specifically: kindness, compassion, joy, and giving are medicine; patience under insult and compliant harmony are medicine."

Medicine Master Repentance

Hobbling along Soquel Drive, feeling foolish and doing a clumsy three limps, one bow, on my lobstered legs. Saw a figure march briskly through the morning mist. It was Heng Chau carrying a tablespoon thrust straight before him like a drum major's baton, leading the band at half-time. He'd brought a spoonful of honey, a vitamin pill, and a mug of tea.

"You're still in shock. I know you'd prefer to avoid sweets, but there's lots of bowing ahead today and you've got to keep the show on the road. Take this," he said.

"…drinking one's fill of sweet dew is medicine, greedily seeking the flavor of Dharma is medicine…"

Medicine Master Repentance

Bowing past Aptos Shopping Plaza at three P.M., a thought occurred to leave the bowing and take a break. At that instant, a pint of beer was tossed from a Chevy pick-up, and soaked me from head to toe.

"We call this an offering of a cup of kindness, without benefit of cup," added Heng Chau as we stuffed the smelly robe and sash into a plastic bag.

Returned to the sidewalk, resolved to wake up and to halt my false-thinking. There are no accidents; cause and effect is not off by the slightest. Time now to return the light and find the source of today's baptisms in scalding tea and stinking beer.

The Medicine Master Repentance provided a solid diagnosis of my state: lack of single-mindedness.

"I will not allow an instant's thought of the Five Desires or worldly affairs, nor will I think of deviant thoughts nor debate and talk with people who are off the Way (externalists). I will allow no laxness or frivolous laughter. I will not gaze at forms or listen to sounds nor will I attach to any dusty states. I will not create bad karma or give rise to afflictions or scattered thoughts. These types of thoughts make me unable to cultivate according to the Dharma. But when I can, in thought after thought, without cease, not leaving the real appearance and without concern for body and life, cultivate this Dharma of repentance on behalf of all living beings, this is called true, actual, single-minded vigor."

Medicine Master Repentance

Heng Chau • October 18, 1978
In plain view but no one seems to notice

One of our Dharma-protectors informed the Master of our tight situation on the road. The Master said it was "a small problem" and it would be okay. Since then, we have not seen the police or had any difficulty finding camping sites. It's like we become invisible at night – we are in plain view but no one seems to notice. Strange.

* * *

Conversation with a little boy on a bicycle:

"I'm a Christian. Hi! I got a church down the street so I can understand what yer doing," he says.

"You can? That's neat."

"Sure. Heck, yes! Hey, did those construction workers kick you off that spot of sidewalk back there?" he asks, slightly worried.

"No. They waited to start work because they knew we were praying and meditating, and we moved when they were ready to start work. So it was good for everyone," I answered.

"That's good," he said, with a big, relieved smile. "I hoped it was somethin' like that. Well, see ya' later."

A small happening, yet even this little boy was speaking Dharma, expressing the natural preference for peace and for mutual kindness all living beings possess.

> "He wishes that all living beings forever pluck out the host of sufferings and that they be mutually kind and loving, without any thoughts of harming."
>
> Ten Transferences Chapter
> Avatamsaka Sutra

Heng Sure • October 19, 1978
But we have no choice

Long night perched in secret beside the Santa Cruz Police Station. A "No-dwelling ordinance" is strictly enforced, but we have no choice. Heads below the window frames, we whisper our chants and wait for dawn. Doing *tai ji* in a trash-littered, vacant lot, stretching on warehouse driveways while the frost crystals on windshields melt and run beneath the rising sun. With no credit ratings, we are rich in invisible means of support.

> In one Buddhaland they rely on nothing.
> In all Buddhalands it is the same.
> Nor are they attached to conditioned dharmas,
> Because they know that in the nature of these dharmas
>   there is nowhere to rely.
>
> Ten Transferences Chapter
> Avatamsaka Sutra

Heng Chau • October 19, 1978
Please regard me with compassion

We hear "freaks" a lot these days from passing cars. Funny, when I was trying to be normal, I felt like a freak inside; now that I am a "freak," I feel more like a real person. I might be getting stupid. But for sure I'm a lot happier.

In Asia when one of the delegates was sick, Shih Fu would suggest eating a piece of fruit in the morning, temporarily relaxing the one-meal-a-day vow as an expedient. The Dharma is fluid and alive, not stiff and unbending.

So this A.M., to help cure a lingering cold, I ate an orange. When I went out to bow, immediately I was accosted by an emotionally "sticky" woman who wanted to take me to her church. Shortly after, two firecrackers exploded next to my head in front of a car garage.

Suddenly the Master's words came to me, "I can't just casually eat anything or at anytime I want, like you. I don't have that kind of Way-virtue." I thought, "Right! Who do I think I am that I can just casually grab a food offering and break vows with it? That's really arrogant. My Dharma protectors probably went on strike and I lost my protection."

There's a right way to do things. So I said, "Before the Buddhas and Bodhisattvas of the ten directions, the Venerable Master and the Assembly, I wish to make known that for health reasons I ate at 'improper times.' This is in no way intended as a retreat from my vows. Regard me with compassion." There were no more problems the rest of the morning.

"With a straight mind, I disciple _____, repent and return my life to the ten directions inexhaustible Triple Jewel. I wish that the Triple Jewell will take pity on me and acts as a clear certifier."

from Avatamsaka Repentance Ceremony

The orange was a small thing and the "disasters" it brought were small too. But the underlying principle was big:

> "Do not consider minor offenses as devoid of disastrous efforts, for although drops of water are very tiny, after a time they can fill even the largest vessel. An offense committed in a single instant may bring the retribution of the uninterrupted hells, and having once lost the human body, one may be unable to get it back for myriads of kalpas."
>
> from Bodhisattva Precepts
> in the Brahma Net Sutra

The small grows into the great, the one into the many. Little thoughts and minor offenses soon fill the largest world-system, and once the vessel starts to splinter and topple, it's too late to make amends and too unwieldy to take in hand. And so, our teacher continually reminds us, "Don't consider the slightest good too small to do; don't consider the slightest evil too minor to avoid."

Heng Sure • October 20, 1978
No giver and no receiver

"Getting and Giving"

Santa Cruz gave us today:

Vegetables from a plump matron in white rabbit fur slippers; rocks from the high school boys; praise and admiration from the KRON newsman; water balloons from the neighborhood toughs; spleen and damnation from the Christian missionary; silent smile and a sack of oranges from a tall, young man.

If we truly had our practice together, we wouldn't have seen anything at all – nobody who gave, and nobody who received.

> "When they cultivate (the practice of giving) in this way, these Bodhisattvas do not see their own bodies, they do not see the objects given, nor the receiver, nor a field of

blessings, nor karma, nor retribution, nor fruition, neither big
nor small…"

Ten Practices Chapter
Avatamsaka Sutra

Heng Chau • October 20, 1978
Sticky glue everywhere, all around us

"He brings forth the mind for Bodhi… because he
desires to exhaustively know the afflictions of the share of
greed… and to cut off the root of all afflictions."

from First Bringing Forth the Mind
Avatamsaka Sutra

The root of all affliction and hassles is greed. A lot of greed and
desire means a lot of affliction. However, if greed and desire are
small, the afflictions are few.

A T.V. newsman said to us today:

"Food, fame, wealth, sex, and sleep are on our minds all the time.
Greed for them is built into our work and our very lives. Desire is
the name of the game and ours is really high pressure!"

Dick and his cameraman are part of a news-action team from
San Francisco who came out to cover the bowing monks. They
arrived hyped-up and harried, but after a half-hour of walking and
talking at bowing speed, they both visibly relaxed and talked about
their work and lives. Something about the bowing mellows anxious
minds and favors introspection.

Newsman: "Our work is cut-throat competition. We live under
constant strain and tension to out-do the other stations and get the
hottest stories first and fastest. We are under heat from within and
from without. Hassles everywhere and all the time!"

Some Jesus people taunt and badger the newsmen as they work.

"Hey, talk to us. Put us on camera," they shout angrily.

"How come you won't put Christ on T.V., huh?! Boy, those monks will talk to reporters, but they won't listen to Jesus."

They continue:

Newsman: "See what I mean!? I wouldn't think of going into a doctor's office or a car garage and start bugging them while they work, but we get that kind of thing all the time – some dodo walks up and starts hassling us, or a weirdo messes up our filming. Does that happen to you two monks, too?"

Monk: "Sometimes, but we find that all the weirdness and hassles come from desire – desire for food, fame, wealth, sex, and sleep are the cause of all the disasters and suffering in the world, said the Buddha. That's one of our biggest lessons on this pilgrimage."

Newsman: "What's that?"

Monk: "That whatever we receive we have coming to us."

Newsman: "You mean you can control it!? Can you actually control it?"

Monk: "Yes, it's all created by our minds alone."

Newsman: "Boy, but how do you begin to turn around thirty-five years of indoctrination? How do you begin to straighten it all out?"

> "It is all because he desires to completely know the
> afflictions of coverings and the afflictions of obstructions...
> It is because he desires to cut asunder the net of all afflictions
> and to purify the nature of All-wisdom, that he first brings
> forth the mind for Bodhi."
>
> First Bringing Forth the Mind
> Avatamsaka Sutra

The wish to "straighten it all out," and the desire to "turn around," are part of bringing forth the Bodhi mind. The cloud-coverings over the pure wisdom-light of our self-nature are our desires. They cause us endless afflictions. Just as the sun gets covered over by clouds, so too does our true, bright nature get obscured by our longings and by our endless cravings.

"How do you begin to turn around thirty-five years of indoctrination?" asked the newsman. As I bowed I pondered his question. How to turn around and go back to our original home is the question of all living beings, not just one man's. Bits and pieces from a Dharma talk the Abbot gave in L.A. came to mind spontaneously as if to answer the newsman. We only see this present life and feel we've been indoctrinated into messed-up and turning in the flow of the suffering paths from beginningless kalpas, in life after life. And so the Venerable Abbot said,

"Because of limitless kalpas of past greed for food, fame, sex, sleep, and wealth, I haven't accomplished Buddhahood. I've been upside down all this time. To not be upside down is to have wisdom. To have wisdom is to be without a self. If you can't be without a self, then you will go on being upside down."

We bowed next to an abandoned lot, overgrown with tall grass, swaying and shimmering in the wind's waves. Rush-hour traffic choked and jerked along on the other side in stark poetic contrast – one side spoke of the natural and of unattached ease, the other spoke of the unnatural and the oppressive burden of attachments. More of the Abbot's talk came to mind:

"My home, my country, my friends and relatives – everything I come in touch with I attach to. We are as if held by an invisible, sticky glue, as if rolling through the paste of the six paths of rebirth. Sticky glue everywhere, all around us. We can't enter Samadhi because we are pulled back by the glue. Glue is visible, but our attachments are invisible."

The Abbot finished with an example of silkworms.

"A silkworm wraps himself up and doesn't know it. He dies without knowing he's cut off his own road, just like people who are born and die and never know why. They are confused when born, confused while alive, and confused when they die. Isn't this too pitiful!?

"So we want to have wisdom. We want to be unattached to self and to dharmas, to break through our attachments to 'me,' and to things. When there is no inside or outside, no subject and no object, no dharmas and nothing to which dharmas can attach, then we can realize true liberation."

A caterpillar slowly inched its way across the sidewalk. Unlike the silkworm who unknowingly wraps himself up and then dies, the caterpillar knowingly crawls inside his cocoon to be reborn as a butterfly. And cultivating the Way is the same.

Heng Sure • October 21, 1978
The thought of benefiting others

Kuo Jya Lee and her son Winston met us in busy downtown Santa Cruz. Mr. and Mrs. Ha had arrived from Hayward moments earlier. At mealtime, Kuo Jya told her story:

"I heard one of the bowing monks was ill and I wanted to bring some medicine and food. I had to take time off from work anyway, because I had the flu. It's no good to live outside when you're sick and I figured it was my job to deliver some good medicine since I live in Pacifica, just a little ways North of here."

She continued, "Only I've never driven alone before. Whenever we go out my husband drives. So I didn't know what to do. I talked Winston, my boy, into coming along to navigate and to give me moral support but he's too young to drive. That coast freeway is really narrow on Devil's Slide, a lot of tricky curves. Little nagging voices told me I was crazy, that I was wasting my time, and would never find you. I called Gold Mountain in San Francisco and got a rough idea of where to start looking. My head was pounding and all but I paid to attention."

"You have faith in the Buddhadharma. So do I," said Kuo Ren Ha.

"You know, when I turned the corner and there you were, my headache and flu were gone, just like that. I'm really happy I didn't listen to those doubts. I've never dared do anything like this before.

The trip went smoothly, no problem. I didn't know I had the strength inside to act alone. But I kept thinking about your being sick and I didn't know who else would take care of you. I'm really happy it all worked out."

> Bodhisattvas should bring forth such thoughts as these:
> Thoughts of benefit, of great compassion, of happiness,
> Thoughts of peaceful dwelling, of pity, of gathering in,
> Thoughts of protecting living beings,
>   of them being the same as oneself...

Ten Dwellings Chapter
Avatamsaka Sutra

* * *

"The thought of benefit is to benefit all living beings, not just oneself. The thought of identity to oneself means Bodhisattvas resolve that if one person has no food it is the same as if they themselves have not eaten; if one person has no clothing it is as if they themselves have no clothes to wear. Seeing living beings in pain it is as if they, too, were in pain."

Master Hua

Heng Chau • October 21, 1978
The best place is sincerely

Newsman, cameras, lots of people and questions... and lots of tests.

Question: "What are people's reactions to you?"

Answer: "Whatever we get we have coming to us. If people are good to us, it's because we've been good to people. If we get hassled, it's because we have hassled others. As we once acted towards people, people now react to us."

Question: "You get a lot of hassles and harassment?"

Answer: "As much as we put out. If we fight in our minds then people fight with us. If our thoughts are peaceful, people make peace with us."

> He is quite free from contention.
> From harming, troubling, and from hatred;
> He knows shame, respect and rectitude,
> And well protects and guards his faculties.

Ten Grounds Chapter
Avatamsaka Sutra

* * *

Day's summary:

— Two news-media interviews.

— Six conversion attempts by other religions.

— One water-hosing while we sat by the road to write in our journals.

— Three rock assaults by gangs of youth. They all missed.

— Two water balloon pepperings.

— Four offerings and positive support.

— A lot of false-thoughts.

— A weary body and a peaceful mind.

This verse carried me through the day:

> He has much happiness and liking,
> And much pure faith as well;
> He has courageous vigor to the utmost.
> Along with much elation and rejoicing.

Ten Grounds Chapter
Avatamsaka Sutra

More newsmen questions…

Question: "Don't you, sometimes, at the end of a long day, wish you could lay back and take in some of life's simpler pleasures?"

Answer: "Something has become very clear to us on this pilgrimage: what we thought was suffering is really joy; and, what we took for joy is really suffering. Cultivating the Way is life's greatest pleasure."

* * *

Dream: An old childhood friend had become a monk and was crying for a parent who had just died. I could see this parent in another world, and told the friend not to feel sad. "This world is just a dream we pass through. Our families are temporary and not real. On a deeper level there are no differences or attachments. Your parents know this and are happy. There is no reason to cry."

After the dream, while meditating, I saw a face in empty space. It kept on changing into the faces of all possible people. All of the people in the world, past, present, and future, were all just slight differences in a single face.

> "He understands that all the mundane world is like a transformation. He clearly understands that living beings are just a single dharma – they do not have two natures."
>
> Ten Transferences Chapter
> Avatamsaka Sutra

* * *

News-reporter: "Is there one place to do it (bowing) that's better than others?"

Answer: "The best place is sincerely."

* * *

In one block of bowing we heard,
"God bless both of you. This is a good thing you're doing!"

"Boy, you are putting out a lot of energy. I drove by and felt it in my car. It's really humbling. Thank you."

"Hey Jack, look at 'em. They're either menials or they're on drugs." Jack: "What's a menial?"

"Thank you for bowing for us. Good journey!"

"I think what you're doing is wonderful – really helping the world out. Too few people do anything like this anymore. Keep it up!"

"Goddamn faggot, queer, weirdo, creeps, mother-…"

* * *

"It's not easy to reduce desire. Even table salt and toothpaste have sugar added to them," noted a local dentist who meditates every day.

> "There is nothing more visible than what is secret, and nothing more manifest than what is minute. Therefore the superior person is watchful over himself when he is alone."
>
> Confucius

When the mind is pure there is natural virtue; its radiance no words can enhance. When thoughts are turbid there is an evil shadow; it's a stain no amount of finespun talk can conceal. We are seen very clearly by people because every stirring of thought shows and every inner feeling leaves its trace. And so what is secret to us is most visible to others, and what is minute within is most manifest without. Truly there are no boundaries or barriers between all that exists. The mind pervades everywhere: each living being is as transparent as clear glass, and every realm interpenetrates without obstruction. We watch over ourselves even when alone, because in truth we are never alone. And in the end, we only cheat ourselves by not being straight and constantly sincere. In this light how could I continue!?

"All the shameful dharmas I personally have done as well
as of those committed by living beings in the past, present,
and future, are completely known and seen by all Buddhas...
In this light, how could I continue!?"

Ten Inexhaustible Treasuries
Avatamsaka Sutra

* * *

"Why don't you go some place exciting when you're done?
Ukiah is kind of dead, isn't it?" observed an antique dealer in Santa
Cruz as we bowed past his shop.

We are camped behind a fire station. Found some time to
exercise by starlight behind a nearby grammar school. Tired, happy,
and determined.

He cultivates the good without fatigue,
His quest intensifying for the Way Supreme;
Such, then is his liking for the Dharma,
That merit and virtue interact with meanings.

Ten Grounds Chapter
Avatamsaka Sutra

Heng Sure • October 22, 1978
This is truly Great Compassion

"Tollgate"

"We must give up our bodies and our minds and our lives
for others. This is truly Great Compassion. Have no self.
Have no thoughts of what is good for me."

Master Hua

Feeling today like a river-boat with a broken tiller in a white-
water current. Can't find the groove and am moving fast in the flow.
Police eye us with hostile glances, cars honk, Italian restaurant owner

makes special trip to scold us while his Sunday-brunch diners stare from red-checkered tables.

Across the river into the civic center, feeling tension in the air as thick as smoke. Today is just that kind of day. Heng Chau talks to campus reporters, the tension builds. We reach the intersection of two main streets, the traffic din peaks; I cross, counting bows, like treading on thin ice. Pick up trucks and motorcycles gun their engines to jump the light.

Just then, with a hearty handshake and a big smile, Bill Ireland from San Luis appears. "Say, there you are! We didn't think we'd find you. Remember me? I'm Gary's grandfather. We've just come down from the City of Ten Thousand Buddhas; went to visit our grandson. He told us where you might be and this is the first street we tried. Good guessing huh? Say, it sure is nippy today. I know you don't talk but Pat and I wanted to stop and see how you two are getting along. Where's your buddy?"

The gunpowder tension melts briefly as the Irelands chat with Heng Chau. They left for San Luis and the pressure returned. We bow on past the county courthouse and jail, feeling shaken, certain we've just crossed a tollgate.

To the left, conga drums reverberate from a throng of dancers; to the right, beer cans shatter store windows, missing our heads by inches. A silent woman appears, holding a baby. The pair sits on the grass before us, unmoving, as if sculpted from stone.

"You two had better be out of town by sunset or it will be the last sunset you'll ever see," snarled a voice from a passing sedan.

Finished the day's bowing on strength from the Venerable Abbot's instructions:

"What we want to do in cultivating the Way is to accept the heroic, selfless energy of Shakyamuni Buddha as he went everywhere to benefit beings. Imitate his vital spirit and have no self."

Heng Chau • October 22, 1978
Very nice, very nice

"300 Yards and a Can of Beer…"

> "With a single mind he properly recollected the Dharma door of wisdom of likeness to illusions… With respect to the various different illusion-like transformations that arise from the illusion-like three periods of time – he universally pondered them all."
>
> Entering the Dharma Realm
> Avatamsaka Sutra

Our daily experiences increasingly take on an "illusion-like" flavor. Even time itself seems like the passing shadow of a cloud's reflection. Slowly we learn to not take things as so real and not attach so much importance to the various different illusion-like transformations. But the illusory wisdom born from impartial, even-mindedness is itself as evasive as the illusory events it tries to ponder. For what is real often seems illusory and what seems illusory often is real. It takes genuine, unattached wisdom to know the difference. Today unfolded with a will-o'-the-wisp quality that on one hand felt so real as to make one's hair stand on end, and on the other hand, so unreal as to pass like a dimly-remembered dream.

* * *

– An old friend walks past without saying a word, staring at us. Her face cracks with emotion. Later while we meditate, she watches from a parked car across the street.

– Two newspaper women ask pointed and loaded questions for ½ hour about Buddhism and politics.

– The Irelands from San Luis Obispo stop on a tense intersection to say hello. Local toughs in pick-up trucks and on motorcycles gathered for a showdown and to "run us out of town." The Irelands had just come from the City of Ten Thousand Buddhas. There is a bright light within them and it disperses the tension and bad vibes at the intersection.

— As we approach the Santa Cruz bridge, a band of conga drummers and gypsy-dancers yell and make merry across the street.

— A young woman and child kneel by our sides and watch as if in a trance, mumbling with half-closed eyes.

— A full can of beer flies past my head and smashes into a storefront. It was thrown hard from a passing truck, and close enough to smell the beer as it passed my face. "Get out of town!" they yelled.

No time to think. The day was like passing through a perilous and difficult wilderness. We squeeze through tight crevices, straddle precipitous ridges, and perch on narrow cliffs, both outside and inside. The Avatamsaka means so much to us because it describes the inner mental terrain and spiritual wandering as well as capturing the outer, real-life encounters. From the nitty-gritty main-drag of a big city to a secluded, wooded valley, from an unexpected whirlwind Ch'an state to a profound, wordless, bowing experience – the Avatamsaka contains and explains them all.

At some point the inner and outer worlds merge indistinguishably, and whether alone or in a crowd, whether in a town or at a forsaken desert mesa, suddenly it's one reality, one time, one place, and one practice: single-mindedness. Then you know there is no stopping, no resting, and no retreating. To obtain the Dharma you will face any difficulty to reach the City of All-wisdom, there is no hardship you can't endure.

> "He progressively traveled. Whether he came to inhabited cities, towns, or hamlets; or passed through perilous and difficult wilderness, cliffs, and valleys, he was without weariness or laxness, and never paused to rest. Then he arrived at the City of Wondrous Light."
>
> From Entering the Dharma Realm
> Avatamsaka Sutra

A little man, resembling a munchkin-type, fairytale character, with black teeth and no shoestrings, walks up and blocks my way. He starts muttering nonsense and then feels my robes saying, "Very nice, very nice." I step around him and keep bowing.

Heng Sure • October 23, 1978
And you'll get there right on time

The winter rains filter into freshets in Cowell Redwood's State Park. The creeks feed together to form the broad San Lorenzo River. The lazy flow bears the myriad raindrops back home to the ocean at Santa Cruz Harbor.

Bodhisattva practices are like drops of rain. Working to benefit other people is the wellspring of Bodhisattva conduct. Practices merge with great vows to save living beings from suffering – the resolve for Bodhi comes forth in our hearts and one day the cultivator enlightens to the Way. Which single drop of rain helped the river reach the sea? Which single practice opened the gate to liberation?

The Avatamsaka says,

> Their wisdom-light is like the pure sun.
> Their many practices are perfect, like the full moon.
> Their merit and virtue is always over-flowing
>   like the great ocean.
> They are undefiled and unobstructed
>   just like empty space.

Frosty morning beneath the clock tower in the heart of downtown Santa Cruz. Bowed up the hill near Old Mission, discussed plans with Heng Chau. Decided to transfer merit an hour before sunset each day. Need last hour of daylight to secure campsite in "non-dwelling" Santa Cruz, where car-living is prohibited. Circled downtown streets last night for forty minutes. Finally shoe-horned into a tight niche beside a gas station. Cutting an hour from bowing will slow pace outside but keeps us "right on time" inside.

Since Asia we've been rushing and forcing. Realized that when pilgrims are in a hurry, greed for progress obstructs the inner journey.

> Too fast and you'll trip.
> Too slow and you'll fall behind
> Not too fast and not too slow
> And you'll get there right on time.

Reorganized schedule to accord with shorter daylight hours of winter: stress practices and vigorous "homework."

```
A.M.
 5:00 Morning Recitation
    Cup of tea, 42 Hands and Eyes
    Ch'an meditation
    Tai ji quan
    Wash-up, break camp
 7:30 Three steps, One bow
10:30 Ch'an meditation
    Lunch
P.M.
12:30 Bow
    Journal writing
 4:00 Wash-up, find camp
    Memorize Sutra
    Ch'an
    Evening ceremony
    Sutra lecture
 9:00 Late Ch'an
    42 Hands and Eyes
    Sleep
```

Heng Chau • October 23, 1978
To be always talking is against nature

Another T.V. news crew comes to film the bowing and to interview us. It takes too much time if we stop so we conduct the interview as we bow – Heng Sure bows and I answer questions as we walk along. The news-people don't seem to mind and it helps maintain the mindfulness of an unbroken bowing rhythm.

A carpenter stopped hammering and sawing on a nearby house to make an offering and to wish us well.

"You're performing a valuable service. It's appreciated," he said.

"They're nuts!" shouts someone from a passing car.

"They're saving our souls," bravely retorts an elderly grandmother standing nearby.

Winter shortens daytime hours, reducing the bowing day. The "no camping overnight" ordinance lengthens the night. We move or are asked to move three or four times, making a single evening seem like three or four separate nights. The space we are limited to shrinks the countryside to the size of a crowded parking lot and we travel in circles sometimes for hours before finding a niche to hide away in.

I am going to limit conversation to bare essentials, talking only to the genuinely interested. It's said,

"To be always talking is against nature."

Tao Te Ching

* * *

"He was able to cause us not to be greedy for states and with few desires, to know contentment."

Entering the Dharma Realm
Avatamsaka Sutra

The big surprise of this pilgrimage is that we need so little to happily get by on. The more things we have the more trouble we invite. Whenever we run out seeking after anything, we take a loss. When we just attend to the here and now, like magic, all our needs seems to naturally meet themselves. There's no reason to be greedy for states of enjoyment – our original state is enough.

Our original natural state is non-attachment. Each tie we establish and bond we make has to be broken sooner or later. Every attachment is a "death spot," a flaw and an outflow in our whole and perfect Buddha-nature. It's said, "The one who knows how to live unattached and naturally content, leaves no room for death to enter and undergoes no more becoming."

> "He who aims at life achieves death… He who has a true hold on life when he walks the land does not meet tigers or wild buffaloes; in battle he is not touched by weapons of war. Indeed a buffalo that attacked him would find nothing for its horns to butt, a tiger would find nothing for its claws to tear, a weapon would find no place for its point to enter in. And why? Because such men have no 'death spot' in them."
>
> Tao Te Ching

* * *

Today the light and happiness and unobstructed freedom I feel can't find words. Everything I ever wanted or needed has been in the pocket of my heart all along!

"Pssst whrrrp," comes a loud whistle from a little old, white-haired lady who strides up and says, "Hey, I saw you on T.V. You're doin' a good thing! God bless you both."

Heng Sure • October 24, 1978
No drink or drug on earth can satisfy

"Drugstore"

Bowed past the Walnut Avenue-Rexall Drugstore. Recalled the dizzy high of the modern pharmacy: pills, potions, powders, lotions; mousetraps and balloons, nuts and novels, comic and coca-cola, safety pins, soap, and Sunday paper; the numbing array of nostrums for every ill. Behind a tall barricade, the white-robed, sanitary druggist deciphers cryptic scribbles from local doctors, then measures and labels potent physics beneath his red-ribboned diplomas and licenses. Pensioners hobble by the forest of drug-racks, discussing oil enemas in quavering voices; high-school boys swarm the after-shave-cologne counter, squirting and sniffing atomizer bottles of Jade East, Bay Rum, Hai Karate, Brut.

Near the exit, a porcelain popcorn machine sizzles beside the nickel-a-ride bucking bronco; lurid magazines inflame desire; the "lucky fortune" scale begs the last pennies from pocketbooks. I used to lose my energy after five minutes in the pharmacy, exhausted by so much stimulation. The labels and ads shouting: New! Bigger! Bargain! Value! Quality! Save! Special! More! Set my thoughts on fire. Once excited, the mind of greed is hard to satisfy.

And it's the mind of greed, not the drugstore, that robs our peace of mind, and leaves behind the feeling of "dust" fatigue: an unscratchable itch, grainy, hot eyes hunger for a new taste sensation, yet full of longing no drink on earth can satisfy; weary of the search, but led and pushed by nameless craving for more and for better.

For example, I used to feel incomplete without English Leather splashed beneath my ears and the New York Times tucked beneath my arm every Sunday. But I felt equally incomplete with these weekend identity totems, purchased at the local Rexall. The mind of greed created the need, and no drugstore could satisfy it.

* * *

"Oh, I don't believe it! Weird! Ha, ha ha, ha! It's a troll. Bobbie, do you believe it?"

"A troll! Kick him, Sally – he's a troll. Ha, ha ha. Hey, weirdo, you're the ugliest piece of shit I've ever seen. What zoo did you escape from? You must be a faggot. Faggot troll! Get your ass out of here!"

The girls were fifteen years old. Their profane curses echoed from the sycamores on Mission Street. Golf ball sized rocks slapped my robe, stinging and sharp. High School girls didn't swear at strangers when I was fifteen. Customs haven't changed so much, have they? After the second round of stones, I came out of shock and saw that I faced a test. At first I tried to laugh off the sudden attack by two innocent looking co-eds. "It's not real. They're warped kids. This generation of young people has lost all moral principle," I thought. "Pay no attention to the abuse. It has nothing to do with you," I console myself.

"Freak. Go home freak. You're a loser, you XXX. XXX." Then foul curses bounced off the pavement like bullets. The sharp rocks spattered on my head and hands like hail. The hazing went on and on. These girls had it in for me! I had to return the light and look within.

They may have been past enmity karma. Maybe they were false thoughts of desire manifesting. Maybe they were demons testing my sincerity. I don't know, but I must have had it coming 'cause I sure got it! Sometimes Bodhisattvas appear as hateful enemies to temper a cultivator's heart of patience and compliance.

> From his first resolution up to Buddhahood,
> All sufferings of the uninterrupted hells in that interval,
> In order to hear the Dharma, he can undergo;
> Much the less all sufferings in the human realm.
>
> The Third Ground
> Avatamsaka Sutra

I used the #1 Dharma-tool for enduring tests of all kinds: patience, and bowed on as if nothing was happening. Reached a gas station lot and there was a friendly Plymouth – it was lunch time and the storm was over.

* * *

"Everybody a Lucky Winner" (When you are content)

Cars full of teenagers cruise by challenging, testing: "Wow, what a drag. You guys are real losers. What do you expect to get out of that?"

We've heard the question in every town from young people anxious to be lucky winners in life. They are brimming with restless energy, seeking the right way to express it. I know that urge and remember how my friends suffered from the "Everybody a Lucky Winner" idea. As teenagers we drove the streets for hours, punching the radio buttons, changing stations in mid-song, seeking to hold that high. The advertisements teased with,

"You deserve a break today, so get out and get away…" "You've got a lot to live…" "Grab for all the gusto you can get…" And then when the gusto gave out we always sang the refrain, "Let's split. This is a drag."

On holidays and on weekends, the highway grows tense; people rev their engines in a desperate search for fun: escape routine, run from boredom, make free time pay, take an upper, get angry, turn the channel, order another round, roll a joint, honk the horn. And when Sunday evening rolls around the road returns to stillness; life is a day shorter, we're left with nothing but the offenses we created and the hollowness from the energy we wasted.

Returning the light, looking within, transforms the ordinary experiences. Bowing looks like a drag, but being "real losers" brings a rare contentment. Cultivation mirrors life: we get back exactly as much as we put into it. And seeking nothing gives back the greatest meaning. It is in expecting to get nothing out of life that we get the most; and in expecting the most that we end up with nothing.

There are no formed or unformed dharmas.
There are no thoughts and no non-thoughts.
Both the existence and non-existence
   of dharmas do not exist,
And one understands
   there is absolutely nothing to obtain.

> Ten Transferences Chapter
> Avatamsaka Sutra

Heng Chau • October 24, 1978
The quiet, peaceful life of a monk

While sitting on the grass outside a pottery shop on Mission Street, two men with folded hands sit next to me and stare. They want me to "rap." I explain we let our bowing talk and try to curb our tongues. A strange man with a backpack walks up and stops, waiting. One of the men with folded palms says to him sternly, "I get a strong reading, a feeling, ya' know, that you are interrupting the natural flow of energy on the sidewalk by standing there."

"Huh, what!?" says the backpackers looking over his shoulders, stunned and thwarted.

They all leave: two folded-handed smilers and a confused backpackers who's mumbling to himself,

"Well, s'cuse my English!"

Minutes later a truck squeal to a halt and two angry clenched-fisted men jump out.

"What the f___ you doin' here man? You're crazy, huh!"

I smile and say nothing. But he is really serious and intends to beat me.

"Don't you smile at me!" he screams, getting red in the face. "I'm gonna kick your …" He starts to reach for me.

"We're Buddhist monks and we are on a pilgrimage," I say.

He stops, fists relax.

"Oh…" His face softens and the red leaves. "Yeah, sure. Okay. We thought you were Krishnas or somethin'." They turn and walk away.

Buddhism stands for peace and compassion, for non-contention and harmony, and people know it. Just the word Buddha or Buddhist can often cause even the most angry and violent natures to become soft and subdued.

> "Universally causing all living beings to destroy their thoughts of anger and harming; to smash their mountains of afflictions, to put to rest all their evil dharmas, so that they would always be without contention and debate, and forever be harmonious and good to each other."
>
> Entering the Dharma Realm
> Avatamsaka Sutra

As the two men walk away, a news reporter strolls up and, seeing the now quiet and mellow visitors and me sitting in the softly blowing grass, says,

"Ah, the quiet, peaceful life of a monk!" Little did he suspect that just seconds earlier, had it not been for the power of a single word Buddha, he would have happened upon two pilgrims receiving a violent beating from local roughnecks. What makes life quiet, peaceful and happy is the Buddha.

> If Buddhas and Bodhisattvas
> Did not appear in the world,
> Not one living being
> Would ever attain peace and happiness.
>
> Verses in Praise on the Summit of Mt. Sumeru
> Avatamsaka Sutra

We camped behind an all-night truck-stop café. Tomorrow we will bow past the city limits of Santa Cruz. Ahead is our second winter and about 75 miles of empty coastline before San Francisco… and whatever our minds create.

"Going and coming, wherever they turn they earnestly cultivate the Proper Dharma… Their steps are peaceful, they travel about: heroic, courageous without fear. The power of pure faith completes the practice of vigor. The paths of evil are eradicated and Bodhi is accomplished.

"The actions of all demons cannot disturb them. They rely on a good and wise advisor to stabilize their hearts. Together with all Bodhisattvas they cultivate the paramita of giving."

Ten Transferences Chapter
Avatamsaka Sutra

Heng Sure • October 25, 1978
The vow for Bodhi never closes

"We Never Close"

Found a camping site beside the Southern Pacific tracks. Nestled the Plymouth between two semi-trailers and didn't light the lamp. Headlights knife through the darkness, as cars and trucks roll into a bustling "we never close" coffee shop.

All night truckers, long-haul salesmen, night-owls, and drifters find comfort in another cup of coffee in the wee hours. Reflected how the dark hours of the soul we all cling to the lie of permanence and pretend at immortality, hoping that the body, like the coffee shop, will "never close."

Stretching stiff limbs in the rail yard lot at dawn beside heaps of salvage: rusting buses, ghostly autos, corpses of truck and a hulking, abandoned tug boat. Contemplating my body as an ownerless vehicle, soon to return to nothingness, abandoned at death by my spirit, four elements scattered, name, family, possessions, wishes, gone and forgotten. Life after life the same. "We always close."

Contemplate the body well and see it all clearly.
Be aware that its dharmas are all empty and false.
Do not use mental effort to discriminate among them.
Who gives rise to your life?
Who takes it away? It's just like a burning ring of fires:
Nobody knows its beginning or its end.

The Bodhisattvas Ask for Clarification Chapter
Avatamsaka Sutra

Swallowed a cup of tea, scraped the grime-frost from the windshield and hustled off to bow. Can't hold on to anything but vows for vigorous cultivation. While this body lasts, working for a better world gives life meaning. Bowed first bow of the day in front of the friendly 24-hour coffee shop mindful that in an impermanent world, the vow for Bodhi "never closes."

Their measureless great vows are difficult to conceive.
They vow to cause living beings to be completely pure.
Their vows are empty,
     without appearances or a place of reliance.
Because of the strength of their vows,
Everything clearly manifests.

First Bringing Forth the Mind
Avatamsaka Sutra

Heng Chau • October 25, 1978
A long dream

While the clothes are in the washer and dryer of an all-night Laundromat, we do our evening ceremonies in the parking lot. The neon street lights give enough to read the Avatamsaka by. A few people nose up to the car windows, smile and check us out. I have these thoughts:

– The best of Buddhism is in the West now. In all of Asia there was nothing that even came close to the real meaning and the living tradition. We are all so lucky!

– Leaving home to cultivate the Way is the wonderful within the wonderful. A cultivator's life is too rich and real to fully understand or appreciate. Every false thought and moment of taking it for granted is like throwing a treasure into the sea. Worldly treasures have a price, but the Dharma is a priceless treasure.

> Like one who gets a treasury store of jewels,
> And is ever after free of poverty's suffering,
> When the Bodhisattva gets the Buddhadharma,
> He leaves the dirt and his mind is purified.
>
> Praises in the Tushita Heaven Palace
> Avatamsaka Sutra

– The light we need to become Buddhas gets scattered and wasted every day. It's given away to T.V., books, food, rapping, shopping, anger, pets, drugs, drinks, flirting, worrying, and waiting for the weekend. Just as tiny drops of water soon fill the largest vessel, so too, do tiny leaks soon empty it.

* * *

"Show Me the Bodhi Road"

Had a long dream last night that seemed to capture recurring themes we both experience on the pilgrimage. The dream felt like a synopsis of the inner journey: the long returning home of the soul.

> "I do not dwell in mundane dharmas, my joy is in leaving the world... He only wants to leave the home life to cultivate the Bodhisattva path and adorn himself with all Buddhas' dharmas."
>
> Ten Transferences Chapter
> Avatamsaka Sutra

Dream: I leave my family and friends, renounce all worldly ties, roles, and positions to cultivate the Way. The journey takes me across the Himalayas, huge snowy peaks. I cross on foot, alone in the winter. But the real journey still lies beyond a remote hinterland. With no maps or plans for food, clothes, or shelter, without guide or provisions, everything is up in the air and "here and now." Since I can't speak the native dialects, even words and language are cut off – truly a stranger in a strange land.

Yet, there is little apprehension and much excitement and exhilaration for the promise of freedom and rare discovery that awaits in the unknown wilderness. I leaf through an Atlas map but there are no charts for this region, only faith and legend. I pass by a large banquet of plump, yellow-robes monks with flushed faces and go to bow in the mountains.

But en route I am burned by beautiful forms and reach for one. Suddenly I'm sliding down an embankment of mud and slime into a tarry and decaying marsh. Too fast, too strong to clamber out. I know I'm dying and that I made a mistake. A voice inside takes note: "Don't repeat this mistake. Love and emotion are false." I am pulled into the pits as if by a rope.

> Greed and love are a strong rope,
> Flattery and deception the reins and bit.
> Doubt and delusion veil one's eyes,
> And one enters the deviant paths.
>
> Stinginess, jealousy, and arrogance abound,
> One enters the three evil places,
> Or falls into the various destinies
> Amid the sufferings of
>   birth, old age, sickness and death.
>
> Entering the Dharma Realm
> Avatamsaka Sutra

I emerge in another world where I can see my own body and countless other form-bodies drifting aimlessly about as if in a silent play or sleep-walking. We are all here, acting out pre-rehearsed scenes of retribution. We are paying off dues from misdeeds and even though I can see that the nature of the suffering (blessings) in this world is illusory and basically unreal; still I can't get out of it and must undergo exact repayment. I recognize the causes of my suffering and the mistakes that brought me here, but am bound to endure what I created.

> "Enduring the grief of the nine kinds of untimely deaths and sinking deeper in the three evil destinies, they suffer all sorts of effects. What one creates, one must endure and the numerous bad retributions are never off even by a hair's breadth. Sooner or later, retribution is certain."
>
> from The Medicine Master Repentance Ceremony

We are countless numbers of men and women, children, and other living beings all brought together to settle old debts in a world of suffering created only from our mixed up karma. The world floats as if on vapors or clouds of gas in empty space, a temporary and ethereal congealing, as uncertain as the morning mist. It is held up only by the power of the thoughts of the being who dwell here – a mirage projected from a state of mind and entangling karma.

> "All worlds in the ten directions are just distinctions made from thoughts of living beings. As for thought or non-thought – there is nothing which can be obtained... And he clearly understands that all the mundane world is like a trans-formation. That all living beings are just a single dharma."
>
> Ten Transferences Chapter
> Avatamsaka Sutra

Everyone's body is semi-transparent and surrounded by a haze, so insubstantial and loosely formed like jelly fish made of fog and the illusory play of light and shadow. Some are vaguely aware it is all a dream, but karmic obstacles numb our senses and drug our true minds. We walk around half-anesthetized, half-awake, and serving our time, painfully serving out our time.

"As for the individual karma of each being, there are worlds in measureless variety. Within them we grasp and cling to existence, and we each receive a different measure of suffering or bliss."

Flower Store World Chapter
Avatamsaka Sutra

Some enjoy a fleeting experience of pleasure and bliss only to lose it moments later; others suffer unbearably and then gain a brief reprieve. Back and forth, bliss and suffering: bliss giving rise to suffering, suffering giving rise to bliss. We grasp and cling, grieve and cry, and it's all unreal, just a play. In the end, there is nothing at all to obtain – the bliss is illusory, the suffering empty. It's all a bad dream we can't wake up from and can't end. Not our true home, just a place to pay off debts.

"Moreover, I will reconsider: the body is empty is still. There is no self and nothing which belongs to a self. There is nothing true or real. Its nature is empty and non-dual. Neither suffering nor bliss exists at all because all dharmas are empty."

Ten Transferences Chapter
Avatamsaka Sutra

I wander through another realm – a dark, unwholesome world ruled over by a powerful demon king. Commanding a malevolent retinue, he oppresses and manipulates scores of good men and women. Deceived by his slick enticements and overwhelmed by his dark power, they follow his bidding like naïve children. No one dares oppose this demon-lord who commits all manner of violent and deviant acts of lust. People go blindly along as if covered by a film of ignorance or in a trance.

Covered by stupidity's darkness,
The fires of greed and anger blaze.
The Demon King becomes the ruler;
Like unknowing children, we follow along.

Entering the Dharma Realm
Avatamsaka Sutra

I speak up and confront him. I plead for rightness and the good, but his followers (slaves) are deaf and dull. A few cock their ears and hear but the demon reigns supreme here. Solid evil, not a corner of softness in his heart. He is pure selfishness, a pro at harming and deceiving – a mirror-opposite of the Bodhisattvas in the Sutra who embody kindness, compassion, joy, and selfless giving. I am somehow protected from his malice and cruelty by the Dharma. He towers over me, but the words coming through me are Sutra words. They are safeguarded and not allowed to be silenced.

I leave this world and find myself bowing with Heng Sure in a strange city of stately Victorian houses and seemingly friendly people. It's all a trap. Nothing is real. The joys, comforts, smiles and open doors are all lures set by demons. We head for the open road to bow in the fresh air and sunlight against on our way to the City of Ten Thousand Buddhas.

I wake up full of gratitude and joy for having met the Dharma and the chance to come back home, a chance to walk the Bodhi-road. We bowed through Santa Cruz as the sunlight broke through the gray morning fog. I recalled the verses the Youth Good Wealth speaks to Manjushri Bodhisattva when Good Wealth first encounters the Dharma and the Virtues of the Buddha. He says,

The Three existences are the home of stupid mortals.
Who create causes that form delusive karma
    and earthly destinies.
The Humane One subdues them all.
Like a lamp, he shows the Way.

One who renounces all evil destinies
And pursues all good paths,
Who transcends the mundane world –
Show me the door to liberation!

In a world that's inverted and full of attachments
May the one with thoughts of
    permanence, bliss, true self and purity,
And the wisdom-eye who can leave all this
Disclose for me the door to liberation!

Well-recognizing deviant and proper paths,
One of fearless discriminating mind,
Who has decisive understanding in all,
Show me the Bodhi road.

from Entering the Dharma Realm
Avatamsaka Sutra

* * *

"People"

The louder they yell, the more they hurt.
The harder they laugh, the deeper they wonder.
Ten thousand faces all sharing one heart,
One heart bowing to Ten Thousand Buddha's City

The people who yell the loudest at the bowing are the ones closest to the pain of existence. Those who mock and laugh outside, inside are full of doubts and wondering if there isn't another way than just to eat, sleep, wear clothes, and grow old to die. But behind all the different faces we meet, there is a single heart, the enlightened nature we all share. And with that single heart we bow to the City of Ten Thousand Buddhas.

Heng Sure • October 26, 1978
The chewing gum religion

"Wrigley's Spearmint Sutra"

Boxcars roll off the main track at the Wrigley plant to deliver drums of chicle and sugar, spools of green paper, cellophane tinfoil, and vats of ink. Farm trucks turn in from the highway to unload crates of mint, strawberries, lemons, limes, oranges and grapes from all corners of California. Pickup campers, VW vans, low-rider Chevies and executive limousines fill the lots at sunrise; the wheels of industry spin and spin. Big wigs write checks to pay hands that push buttons on machine that mix tree sap, syrup, and flavors. Machines print labels, wrap packages, fill boxcars and carry the candied product down the tracks to a gum-chewing world.

More people on the globe recognize the lime-green Wrigley's spearmint label than have ever heard the name Flower Adornment Sutra. Yet, the Sutra has been in the world since Bodhisattva Nagarjuna brought it up from the Dragon's Sea Palace in A.D., the 2nd Century. Lifesavers and chewing gum have been popular for a few short decades. Many folks chew gum religiously every day, but how many religiously consider resolving the matter of birth and death? Death chews up people the way people chew gum. Still most of us pass the fleeting years like we treat a stick of spearmint: sucking the flavor, enjoying life's blessings until they're gone.

The candy-plant speaks the Dharma of impermanence: life's pleasures don't last. They pass as quietly as the fading flavor in chewing gum. Cultivating our way off the endless wheel of suffering is our basic responsibility as people. Faithful cultivation of the methods in the Flower Adornment Sutra opens the way to lasting sweetness and the end of measureless bitter pain.

When he sees people attached to pleasure,
He vows that living beings
Take the Dharma for their enjoyment
Happily delight in it, and never put it down.

Pure Conduct Chapter
Avatamsaka Sutra

Heng Chau • October 26, 1978
Out in the country again

Bowing, meditating at night by kerosene lamp, sewing sashes torn on thorns and brambles. Quiet, clear, crisp autumn weather, long silences and deep looking within. We are out in the country again. Felt the first licks of the northwest winter wind coming to meet us.

It's very still. Then a truck or car roars by. After, very still again. Everything is like that… especially the thoughts and stirrings of my own mind.

It's like a dream, untrue, unreal.
Thought after though is over and gone.
As with the former, the latter is the same.

The Bodhisattvas Ask for Clarification Chapter
Avatamsaka Sutra

Heng Sure • October 27, 1978
Earthy and solid apples

"Blessings"

A vintage pickup slid down a dusty road and rolled to a stop in front of me. A clean-shaven man just my age, popped out and stood on the jalopy's running board. Silent while the truck idled, he looked directly at me. His face showed both bravado and shyness. He had to work up the courage to draw near.

He pushed back his sweatshirt hood. Rough-cut as the sea-coast bluffs, he was not a talker. But the man had something on his mind.

"You fellows use some apples? We grow 'em here and figured you might accept some. You don't talk, huh?"

I nodded and pointed to the Plymouth on the road shoulder beyond the farm drive.

"Put 'em by the car? Right."

More silence, more steady staring, letting his eyes discover what a bowing Buddhist monk was about. He swallowed, nodded, and spoke.

"You two are doing a good thing. We wish you luck."

A bright smile lit up his face. He had said his piece and it had connected. His truck rattled up the hill to the white farmhouse.

We ate the offering of apples for two weeks. They were earthy and solid, like the man who grew them. His roots strike deep in the ocean-side soil of Santa Cruz County. He planted the seeds of future enlightenment in the field of his Buddha-nature with his act of generosity.

> It's like the resourceful, wise monarch
> Who can make his people happy.
> The Buddha's field of blessings is like this:
> Making everybody peaceful and at ease.
>
> The Bodhisattvas Ask For Clarification Chapter
> Avatamsaka Sutra

Heng Chau • October 27, 1978
Looking for one second too long, I was jinxed

T.V. reporter: "You know, after we left you yesterday, we felt really good."

Monk: "Oh?"

Reporter: "Yeah. We got to talking about 'non-attachment' and both of us realized that the few times in our lives that we were really happy was when we were the least attached. Non-attachment is real high for us."

"The ultimate state of Buddhism is non-attachment."
                                                    Master Hua

Reporter: "Have you found ultimate peace and happiness since you've taken up Buddhism?"

Monk: "The ultimate joy for a Buddhist is when others find peace and happiness."

All the wonderful happiness
    that the Bodhisattva obtains,
He dedicates to all living beings...
Not for himself does he seek benefit;
He only wants to make everyone else
    peaceful and happy.

                                        Ten Transferences Chapter
                                        Avatamsaka Sutra

* * *

"It's Only Fair"

A woman rancher in pickup:

"I'm really impressed with your philosophy (Buddhism), especially the part about repaying the kindness of your parents...

I've got a 21 year old son and he gives me a lot of problems. I'm glad someone in the world still believes in filiality."

"Father and mother conceived me, bore me, carried me, and led me by the hand. They protected and guided me – this is called 'kindness.'

"They gave me food and drink, they gave me clothing and shelter, and provided me with medicine, education, and wedding – this is called 'being in their debt.'

"When a son or daughter receives such a great, heavy debt of kindness as this from mother and father, he or she should repay it and return it. It is only fair."

from The New Classic of Filial Piety

Yesterday we bowed into new territory – open, rolling hills and the ocean shore. A station wagon full of strange people pulled up and started pestering Heng Sure to break his vow of silence. He held firm. We picked up such strong "off" vibes that we didn't even look at them.

Later, while we meditated at dusk, they returned and parked inches away from our open car window. I made the mistake of looking at them. As soon as I did I felt my insides twinge. It was a woman. Her face was grotesque and hypnotic. Her eyes and expressions weren't human – her face was as if from another time and world. She caught my glance and rolled back with a deep, eerie cackle. Then they drove away. I didn't look for more than a second before jerking my head around, but she hexed me. (Hexes are viewed as superstitious folly and poppycock by most "modern people" especially in the West. But our experiences from traveling in Southeast Asia made it undeniably clear that hexes are quite real and effectively used as much today as ever. The *gu* poison for example, an extremely pernicious hex, is particularly prevalent in Malaysia and Thailand.)

That night in a dream, I was kidnapped and taken down a road into a dark, damp woods. In a little shed with a water-well, a woman came in and cornered me. She was going to eat me up and drain my life. I yelled, "Wake up, wake up, you gotta wake up, man!" And just as she grabbed me for the final blow, I woke up, reciting the Buddha's name. It was the same woman that came to the car window that night and put the jinx on me. I believe the Buddhas and Bodhisattvas helped me. Went back to sleep and spent an untroubled and peaceful night.

"Poisons are unable to attack. Illness is unable to harm. Untroubled by disasters they are caused to be forever peaceful and happy."

Ten Transferences Chapter
Avatamsaka Sutra

At 11:00 P.M., while we were reciting mantras, a car pulled up and some drunken men passed a ½ gallon of fresh milk through the window. "Peace, brothers," they said, in near unison. We don't drink milk, but accepted to accord.

Heng Sure • October 28, 1978
Oh shit! I lost my temper!

"Noble People Never Show Temper"

Windy morning, no shelter, sand blowing between high-banked road-shoulders. Forcing "progress." I lost my temper and lost ground. Laypeople came with food and medicine. I should have meditated and put my emotional state on ice, but I didn't. I wandered around the car interfering with meal preparations and growing progressively more uptight. My job: attend to inner matters. Transform, temper, straighten the mind, let external affairs go.

When the mind is straight and true, states outside align and balance naturally, as they come. The concentrated mind receives and responds in harmony. When the mind is turbid and emotional, nothing works out. When the violin is tuned flat, the result is cacophony no matter what melody the orchestra plays. So it's said,

> Off by an inch in the beginning,
>   you'll be off a thousand miles in the end.

Instead of following instructions and doing my job, I let the state turn me and scouted a lunch spot on a windblown bluff above the road. Feeling more off-center with each step, I then grabbed a pot holder and scooped up a kettle of vegetables. The metal hook slipped, the steaming pot upended, the vegetables cascaded into the sand.

"Oh, shit!" I said, blowing my top and losing all deportment.

I scrambled to rinse off the squash and beans, picked out the twigs and pebbles, and reheated the pot before the laypeople noticed anything was amiss. I covered the error but couldn't fool myself. Crunching down on a rock hidden in a mouthful of beans as I ate, my face flamed and I knew shame. Forcing cultivation is greed. Greed sparks anger; anger destroys the world.

> Sages never blame others,
>   only evil people blame others.
> Worthies never get angry,
>   only ignorant people get angry.
> Rich people never seek bargains,
>   only poor people seek bargains.
> Noble people never show temper,
>   only lowly people show temper.

Heng Sure • October 28, 1978
Karmic retributions of past sexual misconduct?

Dear Shr Fu,

> Truly recognize your own mistakes,
> And don't discuss the faults of others.
> Others' faults are just my own;
> Being of one substance with everyone
>   is great compassion.
>
> Venerable Master Hua

An old friend of Heng Chau's saw us outside a housing project in Santa Cruz. "His face 'cracked' and after a brief talk, he left rather in a hurry," said Heng Chau. The next morning, just before *zao ke*, I was not yet on guard over my mind and I broke the rules by writing a casual, chatty note to Heng Chau. As I reached for the pen and paper, I knocked the lit stick of incense out of the censer and burned a hole in my jacket. This was a clue that I should be careful and check myself – what is out of harmony here? (But, I ignored the signal and went ahead to take another false step.)

I wrote, "Your friend must think you have not only fallen but have also burned out your circuits – crawling in the gutter in rags, with a friend who looks equally wasted," and gave it to Heng Chau to read.

Even before I saw the look on his face, I knew I had made a mistake. Heng Chau read the note and his expression showed disappointment. He said nothing. I had all of *zao ke* and the following hour of meditation to reflect on and repent of my stupidity. Since I had broken the rules once, now I had to do it again to announce my error and apologize. I wrote,

"Writing that note was a real mistake.

"1) It slanders the Triple Jewel, by calling our appearance 'wasted' and 'in rags.' That breaks Bodhisattva Precept #10, 'Do not slander the Triple Jewel.'

"2) It plants doubt-seeds in your mind ('Does Heng Sure really feel that way about what we're doing?')

"3) It maintains my old bad habit of holding a superior and critical attitude towards others. In fact, I don't feel burned out or fallen – of course I don't feel that way about you. The note was a sarcastic, uncompassionate slap at your friend. In fact, Bhikshu robes are the finest clothes I could wish for. Moreover, I wouldn't trade our work for any king's realm. Now I have to start being worthy of my robes and my vows. I can start by not writing such ignorant, bad-karma notes.

"All I can say is that it was too early in the morning. I didn't have my thought-chopping sword drawn yet. An idle, nasty thought manifested as the note. Sorry for the hassle. 'Others' faults are just my own.'"

Cultivating the Way to Genuine Good Health.

Cultivation is the road back to genuine health. Sutras are the medicine. The Venerable Abbot works like a good doctor, prescribing the most efficacious remedy for whichever of the eighty-four thousand types of afflictions obstruct an individual's way back to peace and happiness.

Originally, all the medicine we need for a complete cure of the big disease – birth and death – we already possess inside ourselves, but we don't see it, don't know how to use it, because of attachments to bad habits and upside-down false thoughts. The teacher-doctor comes in to tell us, 1) that we are sick; 2) that the cause of our sickness is looking outside of our own nature for happiness; 3) that there is a cure available; and, 4) that that cure is cultivation of the Buddhadharma.

Then, because the doctor is kind and compassionate, he gives us the medicine perfectly suited to our needs. But, it is up to us to be brave and take the medicine prescribed. At this point, practice of the Dharma becomes self-therapy, self-healing.

I have to remember that I am sick, must keep my faith in the efficacy of the cure, and must keep taking the medicine. The resolve for health follows faith in the doctor and the cure, and then steady practice allows the cure to happen. Faith, vows, and practice are the prescription for total well-being.

Our passage through Santa Cruz this month has been a mirror of the first stages of the Buddhadharma's cure. I reflected long on my past conduct in terms of the Master's teachings and the Sutra's model of Bodhisattva conduct. Bowing through Santa Cruz, it takes no effort at all to recognize that I am really sick. My past conduct reads like a checklist of the ten evil acts. I have done what demons do: killing, stealing, lust, lying, and taking intoxicants. It's not to say that I have changed since I began to practice good health. But, now I *recognize* how far wrong I've gone and how strong my habits are that still lead me away from health towards my old sicknesses. These habits are strong and not easy to change. But, I want to become a true disciple of the Buddha. No matter how much discomfort I have to endure, no matter how long I have to take the medicine, I am determined to get well again. The Master's state of happiness and health, and the radiant goodness of the Bodhisattvas that live in the Avatamsaka Sutra are simply wonderful – to realize their state of well-being is what I want most of all.

> "They vow that living beings forever escape their sick bodies and obtain the Tathagata's body."
>
> Avatamsaka Sutra
> Ten Transferences Chapter

"Kuo Chen, your worst fault is being sticky with people, especially with women," said the Master, very clearly. This is called "recognizing the sickness." Step #2 is seeing how the disease appears in my behavior; and Step #3 is finding a way to turn it around. The Master's statement is, of course, right on. He pointed out the cycle of cause and effect that brought on my troubles. In this life I have harmed myself and caused a lot of suffering to others by my selfish misconduct. In the past I tied myself into bad relationships with women, which came to fruition in this lifetime as promiscuous, mutually harmful sexual behavior. Before I met the Proper Dharma in this life, I planted more bad seeds which are certain to flower in the future.

"If you can't transcend sexual desire, you will not leave the dust," says the Shurangama Sutra. If I don't end sexual desire completely, just cut it off for good, I won't be able to realize my goal of cultivation as a Bodhisattva and becoming a Buddha. I won't succeed. I believe in cause and effect. I see what I've done in this life, seen the bad I've done, because of past bad karma. I saw the blueprint for the future that I was drawing up for myself, and it wasn't a good one.

I want to change, and in the Dharma I've found a medicine to cure my illness. The medicine is called "Three Steps, One Bow and repentance and reform." Every day I repeat vows to end sexual desire, and I recite a wish that together with all beings I can return to the root and go back to the source of original purity. The vow has a part that says, "I vow that all negative affinities already established will come to fruition in a way other than sexual. I will never again have to endure sexual embrace in order to repay my debts. Any debts owed to me in this regard I now cancel." Does it work? Can I really uproot the bad seeds I've planted in this life so that I don't have to go through the same dance in the future that I endured in this life? I have faith that it will work.

Bowing past a shopping center parking lot in Aptos Village last week, I got an "offering of orange juice without the benefit of a cup," as Heng Chau calls it. Showered with sticky juice from a passing pick-up truck, I thought immediately of my vow.

Later that same afternoon I took a bath in a cup of beer that flew from a blue truck. I repeated the vow with a wish to transfer all merit and virtue of my work so that all beings might return to purity. The next morning I poured a cup of scalding hot tea into my Sierra cup, and reaching for the thermos lid, I tipped the whole cup onto my bare foot. The boiling tea covered my lap as I sat in lotus posture before doing *zao ke*. Scalding burns! And in my head, the memory of how much hot suffering I'd given to others through my lustful, casual, selfish behavior in the past. (Heng Chau's comments: "That's good tea, really wakes you up, eh?") Are these incidents actually my sexual karma resolving itself in another form, as I wished in my vow? I think so; I believe so.

Three Steps, One Bow is making my cure possible. Who throws the orange juice and beer? My Good Advisors. They may be people whom I've hurt in the past. Who are the teenaged Santa Cruz High School girls who shower me with rocks and curses that would make a truck-driver blush? I see them as my own behavior returning to me. They are my friends, my fields of blessings. As the Bodhisattva in the Ten Practices Chapter of the Avatamsaka Sutra says,

> "...as he sees a host of starving beggars coming to request his body's flesh to eat, 'These are my good friends. I am really getting benefit. Without being asked, they are coming to help me enter into the Buddhadharma.'"

I've just begun to see the extent of my illness. But this is a start, and with the good medicine I've got, bit by bit I will get well.

The Master explained the basic source of confused karma:

> "All the problems of the world come from the presence of the self. Without the self, who is there to be unhappy? Who is there to feel pain? The self is an illusion. You should have no self."

That is the voice of the Good Doctor, ripping band-aids off the old wounds, not gingerly pulling at them, one scab at a time, the way most of us do. Shr Fu wants us to get better now! Until we all make it to Buddhahood, he's got to keep returning to doctor his unwell disciples. One of these great aeons, however, we'll all make it. The great hero's work will be done, and we will all be able to gather at the City of Ten Thousand Buddhas and "mutually shine upon each other's lotus thrones, in world systems like motes of dust."

Disciple Guo Chen (Heng Sure)
bows in respect

Heng Chau • October 28, 1978
An old friend, or a brother

> The Bodhisattva knows kindness done for him
> and knows to repay that kindness.
>
> Ten Grounds Chapter
> Avatamsaka Sutra

A crippled man, named Joseph, stopped in a pickup truck. "People have been kind to me, always, so I said to myself, 'If I ever chance to see those boys that are bowing, I'm going to help out.'" He struggled and limped out of his truck, face full of smiles, arms full of offerings, saying, "Now I get my chance."

* * *

CHP officer stopped to see if everything was okay and to check out the Dharma. It was an interesting exchange. When we first came into the county, the same officer thought we were just a lark and not for real. He's watched us bow for nearly three weeks and now in his mind, we are legitimate. He was probing, and a doubting Thomas from the word go. But when he asked what "personal gain we sought," I answered, "Nothing for ourselves. We are doing this for everyone." It stopped him speechless. He saw that we meant it. Somewhere inside, his computer jammed for a minute. "Well, good luck, and I wish you God's protection," he said, right from his heart as he left. We both recognized him as if he were an old friend or a brother.

Heng Chau • October 28, 1978
Are you going with them or staying?

Dear Shr Fu,

We just bowed past the city limits of Santa Cruz. Ahead is about 80 miles of empty coastline before San Francisco, and whatever our minds create. I am happiest when I bow a lot, sit long, and keep my mouth closed. I've noticed that those around me are a lot more natural and peaceful when I cultivate. Minding my own business and tending to my own faults seems to allow others room to grow and move without feeling hassled and obstructed. I've put my mind to not getting worried or angry, no matter what. I've eaten my fill of afflictions for too long. They just pollute the air and give me gray hair and wrinkles. This verse from the Avatamsaka really struck me as the right way to be:

> He is quite free from contention,
> From troubling, harming, and from hatred.
> He knows shame, respect, and rectitude
> And well protects and guards his faculties.

I recite this verse on and off during the day. Without fail it clears the shadows from my mind and leaves me feeling pounds lighter. I have never encountered anything more wonderful or true than the Buddhadharma.

In Santa Cruz we met Don Penners and his family. He is a local dentist who is selling his practice and moving to the City of Ten Thousand Buddhas to live and work. "We are all looking forward to the move. It's the best thing going in the world today. The Master's a great guy!" they said. When they first met the Master they were a little non-plussed. "Well, at first we weren't impressed. He looked so young and healthy – too much so to be a Venerable Abbot – so I crudely said, 'Who are *you?*' I thought he was one of the assistants.

I've never seen anyone his age look so youthful and happy! We got no reply."

"In fact," the Penners went on, "The Master said *nothing* to us at all the first time. It was like looking into a big mirror. All we saw was *ourselves*. It was like the Master was empty inside. There wasn't any of the usual 'Hi, how are you… what you been doing?' It wasn't until later that we came to appreciate what a rare and valuable experience that was. We really got a clear picture of ourselves. It was quite something, frankly!"

We have met some strange people, too. One night while I was making tea on the back of the station wagon, two men pulled up to ask about the pilgrimage. One of them related during a perfectly straight conversation, "People think Jesus is coming again. But they're wrong. The UFOs are coming. They are out there watching us like a farmer watches over a corn crop. When they come, they are going to take some of us with them – alive, right out into outer space. The rest they will leave here on earth to blow themselves up with nuclear weapons and pollution. It says so in the Bible!" he insisted.

"Oh?" I said.

"Yeah, do you read the Bible?" he asked.

"Once upon a time…" I began.

"Well, *I've read it*! So what are you going to do?" he asked urgently.

"About?" I asked.

"When they come – the UFOs. Are you going with them or staying?" he pressed.

"We'll just keep bowing to the City of Ten Thousand Buddhas," I replied.

"You will? Well, I guess, but… well they are coming real soon. I know it…" his voice trailed off as he looked up at the stars.

There are a lot of different ways of looking at things. Heng Sure and I are slowly discovering that, with a proper mind, what is seen is proper; with a deviant mind, what is seen is deviant. Proper knowledge and views are essential, because however we look at things, that's what they become. As the Master wrote in a verse:

> As one plants causes, one reaps the fruit –
> > look within yourself.
> With reverence coming and going,
> > impartial is the Way.

All is well. There's no problem so big that a day of bowing won't solve.

Peace in the Dharma,
Disciple Guo Ting (Heng Chau)
bows in respect

Heng Sure • October 29, 1978
We prefer not to talk about ourselves

"What's News?"

Five T.S. news-teams and two daily papers from the Bay Area have interviewed Heng Chau in the past four days. We seem to have stepped onto the face of San Francisco's mass-media radar screen.

The interviews were all alike. At first the cameras and micro-phones peek and jab, the questions challenge and shock.

"We prefer not to talk about ourselves," says Heng Chau. "Frankly, our personal lives are not very interesting. We bow, meditate, recite, study, and little else. We work to get rid of our greed, hatred, and stupidity; to prevent wars and disasters and suffering of all kinds. We wish only that all beings everywhere will obtain peace and happiness."

The bowing continues while cameras whir. Occasionally Heng Chau pauses to respond to questions, but the message of the bowing penetrates and disarms the high-voltage "action-news probes." The interviews mellow into thoughtful inquiry. Genuine people emerge from behind the shiny lenses and bristling boom-mikes.

In our heart of hearts everybody shares a wish for liberation. We're all looking for the original news-story: "Where did I come from? Who am I? What is life about? Where am I going?" The Buddhadharma responds in that deep place where our basic questions turn. Sooner or later we all get the news.

Newspeople gather answers to the basic questions. They record, photograph, and pass on the bizarre, fanciful ways people behave while traveling from cradle to grave. We meet the Buddhadharma and something registers inside. The Dharma rings true, when we recognize the real, the ancient, and the high road back home. Before long, the questions fall silent. There is only the sound of wind, traffic, and voices reciting.

> Namo Da Fang Gwang Fwo Hua Yen Jing,
> Hwa Yen Hai Huei Fwo Pu Sa.

The newspeople all seem to understand the original story: cultivate the Way, find the news within – no self, no others. Who is there to fight with? What is there to lose?

> All beings in all worlds,
> In every direction without exception –
> None are not brought to enlightenment,
> And to constantly practice like Universal Worthy.
>
> Ten Transferences Chapter
> Avatamsaka Sutra

Heng Chau • October 29, 1978
You have to be very, very patient

Mother and little girl, all smiles: "The flowers aren't fresh and we don't have much food... but we wanted to bring something. We have thought about you a lot!" They were poor and on their way home with meager purchase of groceries. Yet, as little as they had, they still wanted to share and show their support. The sincerity and selflessness of people we meet touches us deeply.

* * *

"True or False: 'Prove It'"

A lot of people cannot "see" anything at all in our bowing. They are people who want us to put into words and "prove" how bowing accomplishes something. They doubt and perhaps fear their own spiritual inclinations. Yet they are touched somewhere, somehow, by the bowing and so they come to see what is inherent in us all.

Some people "see" right away, ask no questions, and require no explanations. They say, "thanks," or smile, and quietly leave offerings. Some bow along. Others bow inside. ("On my way to work, I bow in my mind," said a salesman.)

In all cases, the practices of Buddhism work below the skin and beyond the head. It's not the words that move people, it's the worship; it's not what the intellect can see, it's what the heart alone can fathom.

> Their subtleties are difficult to see;
> They leave thought and transcend the ground
>   of the mind.

> Ten Grounds Chapter
> Avatamsaka Sutra

Life is a real dilemma: what's true and real cannot be grasped; what can be seen and touched is false and empty. The Master put it this way in a lecture in Malaysia:

"If you try to find the True in this world you will not be able to find it. Yes, cultivation is true but you cannot really see it. Whatever you see in cultivation is only a symbol of what is going on. You see only the external appearances in the realm of form. However, what is real, you cannot find. Therefore, don't look for the real apart from the false. It's right within the false that you have to be very, very patient."

* * *

They are not beginning, nor middle, nor end.
They are not expressible in words.
They transcend the three periods of time.
Their characteristics are like empty space.

Ten Grounds Chapter
Avatamsaka Sutra

We are only beginners taking our first wobbly steps down this ancient path. It goes against the grain of most of our notions. But then going with the grain isn't all that great. Going with the flow always ends in suffering and leaves a bitter aftertaste of having "missed my chance in life." Besides, the Great Reversal is a lot of fun and never boring.

If I can be a good person then the world is better by a bit. "Is that all that's going on, just self-improvement?" asks a motorist. If I say "yes" I'd be lying: if I say "no" he wouldn't believe me because I couldn't prove it. So it goes.

"They cannot be described in words... difficult to express, difficult to accept."

Ten Grounds Chapter
Avatamsaka Sutra

As I finish writing this in the car, I feel I am being watched. I look up and there is a man kneeling in the car seat where Heng Sure was sitting just seconds ago. He lays down some apples and walnuts and bows with folded hands. He is very sincere. Then without a word, he shakes my hands, nods appreciation, and disappears as quietly as he came. He knew.

> They are not thought and leave the path of the mind...
> The wise know intellect does not reach them.
>
> Ten Grounds Chapter
Avatamsaka Sutra

Begin daylight savings time. Getting cold at night.

Heng Sure • October 30, 1978
Curing the illusory sickness of birth and death

"Healing the Doctor"

Heng Chau was under the weather as we passed through Santa Cruz. I could not subdue false thoughts of doctoring him. I schemed to get medicines and offered diagnoses. Instead of bowing with single-minded concentration I indulged in false thinking. Result: two sick people!

A Bhikshu has a chance to cure himself of the basic disease of birth and death. Medical doctors save bodies but eventually the best prescriptions fail, the skinbag's time expires. I can spend hours in my mind concocting good medicines for Heng Chau yet find it hard to concentrate for five minutes on my own illnesses. Healing myself is the first step towards truly benefitting the world.

"By cultivating the Way to transform your own greed, hatred and stupidity, you are doing genuine good in the world," says the Venerable Abbot.

The ultimate diagnosis:

Contemplate the mind and the world as one sick being. Repent of faults and change towards the good. When the heart is pure, free of thoughts and selfish desires, we have begun to heal a share of the world's illnesses in the best way.

"It's like a man who dreams his body is troubled by illness and who seeks a physician to concoct medicine and to effect a cure. Once healed, he awakes from the dream to understand that basically no illness existed, nor did the absence of illness exist, how much the less the medicine. Therefore, the illnesses of living beings are one illusory illness, and the medicines of the Tathagata are one illusory medicine."

Medicine Master Repentance

Heng Chau • October 30, 1978
They were greeded, not needed

"Bread and Roses"

"You should use the Buddha's level equality to extend and enlarge your own mind."

Entering the Dharma Realm
Avatamsaka Sutra

In ourselves we recognize others; in others we can find ourselves. On the gut level, we know all is one, yet our small, narrow minds work so hard at creating differences. Buddhism seeks to expand the measure of one's mind until everything and everyone is level and equal.

Who are we, really? What is our "true self?" Listen in stillness to the sound of your own mind and you can find the "real you." Sitting quietly in meditation opens wisdom.

A backpacking disciple of the Master's stopped by with an offering of bread and roses. As he sat drinking tea, looking out over the ocean next to the open door of our car he asked, "I mean, what

do you listen to? What do you follow inside? Where is the mind?"
The story of Shen Kuang came to mind:

Dharma Master Shen Kuang said to Patriarch Bodhidharma
once, "My mind is in pain. Please, Patriarch, quiet my mind."

"Find your mind," said Bodhidharma. "Show it to me and I will
quiet it for you."

Venerable Shen Kuang looked everywhere, and at last said, "I
can't find my mind, Great Master. It is nowhere to be found."

"This is how well I have quieted your mind," said the Patriarch.

At these words, Venerable Shen Kuang understood the meaning
of the Dharma transmission and was greatly enlightened.

We are all "spiritually inclined." No one lives on bread alone. It's
in our basic nature to find our mind. We live on bread and roses.

"No Greed."

> He has no greed for benefits or offerings,
> And he only delights in Buddhas' Bodhi;
> With one mind he seeks the Buddhas' wisdom,
> Concentration undivided with no other thought.
>
> Ten Grounds Chapter
> Avatamsaka Sutra

We have added the "no seeking" rule to our code of the road. No
matter what, our attitude is, "we have enough." We don't ask for
things or look for favors. We no longer suggest or make lists of
"needed items." Our job is to benefit people by becoming "One of
the Way with no mind." Our job isn't to cause people to worry and
fret and look after us.

Whatever people want to offer, that's what we need. If we don't
get something, it wasn't needed. Simple and clean.

In the beginning we worried and false thought up a storm about
our "needs." We were "greedy for benefits and offerings" and all we
got was trouble. Seeking benefits is the surest way to incur a loss.

Somewhere past Santa Barbara we had a change of heart. We resolved to "seek the Buddhas' wisdom" with "undivided concentration" and to let things happen naturally. What happened?

When we needed clothes, clothes arrived. When it turned cold, blankets appeared. The less we thought about food and supplies, the more they took care of themselves. If we were sick, medicine suddenly appeared. Campsites, car repairs, maps, and water, even toilet paper, all came without seeking. However if we hoarded or accumulated too many goods and possessions, then thieves appeared to steal them.

Magic? Faith? Coincidence? It happened too many times to doubt and it had a lot to do with our thoughts. Sincere, focused bowing brought responses; scattered, false-thinking brought nothing but troubles.

Today I noticed our water supply was scraping bottom. There are no towns or gas stations around, nor any streams or wells. I was singing "Namo Guan Shi Yin Pu Sa" to myself while doing dishes. A rancher pulled up in his pickup. He clocked Heng Sure's bowing speed on his watch as he sat with his dog on the back of his truck. He started to leave, then shouted, "Hey, the name's Al. If you need water, take whatever you like from my ranch back there, O.K.?"

"Okay. My name is Heng Chau."

"Good to know ya Heng. Help yourself and good luck."

Were there things we "needed" that did not show up? Yes. And we got by the better without them, proving they were greeded, not needed. Slowly we are coming to trust and to believe in the principle of,

"...he follows along with and remembers all of the Buddhadharma; he knows the body is empty, false, and does not exist; there is nothing about it to be greedy for or concerned about..."

Ten Transferences Chapter
Avatamsaka Sutra

* * *

Two very unusual men stopped during lunch and wanted to rap. They were ashen-color and as lifeless as robot-automatons. The one who did all the talking had white pupils. The men were clearly not who or what they seemed.

"I studied Buddhism for two years," said one in a monotone, staring at us strangely. "It was called the Tibetan Book of the Dead."

* * *

A man came up with an offering and peeked in the car. "Oh, who's that!?" he exclaimed, seeing a picture of the Master.

"That's our teacher."

"What's his name?"

"We call him the Venerable Abbot of the monastery – no other name."

His face lit up with an incredible smile of joy and wonder. "How wonderful!" he finally said, after staring at the Master's photo. "How wonderful! Thank you." And he left.

> "I vow that all living beings who see my face or even hear my voice will fix their thoughts on Bodhi and quickly accomplish the Buddha-Way."
>
> One of the 18 vows made by the Master
> before the Buddhas at age 19 years

Heng Sure • October 31, 1978
The only certainty in the world is uncertainty

"Soap-Opera"

Parked beside a farm-field access road. A cyclone fence gate leads to Oceanside acreage full of brussel sprouts, pickers, and tractors. The tractors pull a fantastic sprout-stalk chopper and hopper that slices the crop, skins the buds, spits the pith, and shoots the sprouts into the waiting wagons. The wagons roll by every hour. I let my ear follow the sound once too often. An image of the driver appeared in my mind's eye. Watched it run from stillness to soap opera in that single thought. Like unwinding a T.V. melodrama, my mind concocted an instant fantasy. Saw the picker's family, then recalled my folks, brother, cousins, their folks – thoughts popping like sprouts in the hopper. The scenario swamped concentration. Saw my kin sharing a family farm; safe, solid, serene, living in a rambling estate compound. The story moved my heart to emotion; comforting, common, and completely a fairy tale.

Pain jabbed at my knees, woke me to the movie. I stopped the show in mid-reel with a dose of reality:

"Real life hurts, friend. Suppose the sprouts failed one year? Suppose the draft called your brothers, then a war killed them. What would you say to the sister-in-law widows? Would you gather in his kids? Who would cover if the credit union closed on your mortgages? Suppose Dad died young, would you have the guts to stick it out? Could you keep the kids happy down here on the farm? Suppose they got tired of the coast and itched for scouts and schools in San Jose? People fight, grow up, change, and die without notice; the only certainty in the world is uncertainty. The family fantasy has a happy ending only on the tube. In fact, there's not a single place of peace and happiness anywhere in the Triple Realm. This pipe dream is as bare of fruit as the sprout stalks the chopper strips and drops in the furrows. You ought to wake up and enter Samadhi, open wisdom, and speak the truth for people."

"The Bodhisattvas know the family life easily falls apart and in their minds they despise and forsake it. Amidst the family they feel no love or delight for it."

Ten Transferences Chapter
Avatamsaka Sutra

Returned to meditation with a new resolve to clear out the weeds of false thinking and truly own this investigation of the mind to the ultimate point. When I can see through it and put it all down, that very thought returns to the true home. In a single thought I can wake up from the dream-drama I've been sleeping through.

> "They vow that all beings leave the common, worldly home life and dwell together in the Tathagata's family."
>
> Ten Transferences Chapter
> Avatamsaka Sutra

Heng Chau • October 31, 1978
I can't remember yesterday

> "All the past, present and future are nothing but talk. All words and speech have no place to rely amid dharmas; all dharmas have no place to rely amid words and speech."
>
> Ten Practices Chapter
> Avatamsaka Sutra

Actually, today is Wednesday, not Tuesday, but I didn't find time to record yesterday until today. Now it is too late. I can't remember yesterday. So past thought is gone and can't be retrieved, present thoughts can't be stopped, and the future is still unmade. Thought after thought, passing through time and none of it's real or lasts – not the thoughts, not the times, not the thinker. Our words and ideas are like the wind which has no place it stops and abides. Time is just talk and amid talk there's nothing to rely on and no ground to stand on.

* * * * * * * *
November 1978

Heng Sure • November 1, 1978
The only force that can cut without harming

"Way-Virtue"

Out in the boondocks once again, contemplating the power of Way-virtue. In Chinese, it's two words *dao* and *de* (道德) sometimes translated as "the Way and its power" or "the Way and its attributes." Way-virtue is called "the only force that can cut without harming." Sages with fully-developed Way-virtue can effortlessly harmonize heaven and earth and wordlessly inspire people to change for the better.

North of Santa Cruz the traces of civilization grow thin and gradually fall away. Sprout fields, ocean coast and empty cliffs replace the shopping plazas, bus routes, traffic lights and power poles of the town. Cities discipline and order the countryside as cultivating Way-virtue regulates the body and corrects the mind.

When barbarian tribes entered ancient China's capital cities, they met for the first time – streets, walls, market squares, written words, and Imperial rulers. The vast harmony of a great civilization moved the Huns, the Tartars, the Mongols, each in turn to forsake their nomadic tribes and to adopt Chinese styles. The virtues of well-ordered society ultimately conquered and pacified the invaders without force or conflict of arms.

Good Advisors with Way-virtue transform people like exposure to Chang An subdued the barbarians. A sage generates a natural power and a bright light that compels admiration and a wish to imitate his conduct.

A young man made an offering of tomatoes and bread yesterday. Heng Chau placed the three tomatoes on the altar while the man watched wordlessly through the open door. His eyes swept the Sutra rack, the Dharma instruments, the incense burner. Then he saw the Master's photograph. His face changed, his eyes widened.

"Who's that?" he asked with a gulp.

"The Venerable Abbot of Gold Mountain Monastery," replied Heng Chau.

"Oh! Is he your teacher?"

His eyes glued fast to the picture. His entire world stopped; the Master's image completely captured his attention. Without reserve, the man drank in the photograph, looking at it first this way, then that way. No words were needed; we understood, and shared the experience of standing before true Way-virtue: a mixture of shame, respect, and joy. Shame for our personal shortcomings, respect for the power of Way-virtue, and joy to gaze upon a superior person.

> The Buddha is the world's greatly powerful Lord,
> Perfect in all merit and virtue.
> He brings all Bodhisattvas to dwell here
> And teaches them to become supreme heroes.
>
> Ten Dwellings Chapter
> Avatamsaka Sutra

Heng Chau • November 1, 1978
You will disappear by bowing to all living beings

Bowing steadily along on a clear day. Few people and light traffic expand the solitude and deepen the inner wandering. The mind feels washed clean by the brisk wind from the white-capped sea and the autumn sunlight. Bits and pieces of one's life, long buried and forgotten rise up into consciousness like a covey of quail flushed from hiding. And equally at random, with no apparent rhyme or reason, bits and pieces of Dharma suddenly pop into mind like green shoots of grass coming up through cracks in the sidewalk. They come from a lecture given by the Abbot months ago in L.A. and blend exquisitely with each rising thought and reflection, like form and shadow, like sound and echo:

> "Faith is the source of the Way, the mother of merit and virtue. Accomplishment in cultivation is the result of having faith... Samantabhadra saves beings. He doesn't seek fame and profit. He does good without it being known and universally transfers to all living beings...

> "In cultivation you want to gradually reduce food and drink to avoid ghostly visitations. The body is a huge bug, a big bacteria made up of 84,000 worms. You give all these little bugs too much food and drink and they grow and get fatter. The more they grow, the fatter they get and the more they want... Take the entire Dharma Realm as your body and dwell in empty space and the wonderful existence within true emptiness. No thoughts, no desires, no discriminations, is the wisdom of all Buddhas..."

A farm truck passes by; a seagull cries overhead and dives for the surf below. More memories rise and more Dharma pearls stringing an invisible necklace of meanings over some back-road of the mind:

> "...This world comes about only through the present fruition of past false thoughts... Everything depends on you. You say you have no good roots so you can't cultivate. But if you don't cultivate, you'll never have good roots... Any accomplishment will come about because of faith; any principle will be understood because of faith..."

I took a few notes from this lecture. We had no interview or specific instructions and yet these Dharma sprouts now appear as if secretly seeded in the deeper consciousness long ago. So fine and subtle they are as the traces of a bird in the sky and yet so true and real! It's said that the Buddhas' wisdom is that way; pervasive in the minds of living beings. But because of our deluded thoughts and attachments, we are unaware and cannot know. Every once in a while though, in a fleeting moment of stillness and letting go, we get a vision and behold the subtle distinctions of what is usually so blurred and hard to see; and then it's gone gain.

> Like pictures that are painted in the air,
> Like traces of the wind in empty space,
> The wisdom of the Muni is that way.
> Its distinctions very hard for me to see.
>
> Ten Grounds Chapter
> Avatamsaka Sutra

* * *

Contemplating the sun: big, bright, impartial, and generous, it shines on the land and sea, on rich and poor, on fields and meadows. No one is excluded, nothing is not warmed and nourished by its rays. Day after day, tirelessly supporting all that lives without one thought of seeking repayment. The Bodhisattva is the same way. He says, "Everything I do is for the benefit of all beings. I have long forgotten about myself. Everything's O.K." This is called "Transference."

> "Disciples of the Buddha, the Bodhisattva, Mahasattva again thinks: I should be like the sun which shines universally on everything without seeking repayment for its kindness... I vigorously cultivate the transference of good roots to universally cause living beings to attain peace and happiness."
>
> Ten Transferences Chapter
> Avatamsaka Sutra

* * *

Inside and outside are the same. The mind and the highway are non-dual. The road is just an extension of our thoughts and our thoughts mutually reflect with the road. Pain in sitting meditation comes from false thoughts and attachments. Pain in our lives comes from that, too. Everything is made from the mind and the mind is made of everything. Knowing yourself is enough; do not seek outside.

> Great with nothing outside;
> Small with nothing inside.

* * *

"Losing You"

The silence outside and long hours of solitary bowing subdue the body and soften the mind. At the end of the day one feels so mellow and empty, so peaceful and quiet that it's difficult to raise the voice and find the words.

I called Gold Mountain Monastery after bowing. Standing in the glass phone booth, looking out to sea, the soft Avatamsaka chant still echoing inside, absorbed in another world.

"Are you still there!?" asked the operator. "You are so quiet, I thought I lost you."

So did I, for a moment.

> "Bowing removes arrogance. With no self there is no pride. You will disappear by bowing to all living beings."
>
> Master Hua
> instructions en route

Heng Sure • November 2, 1978
Sailing the sea of suffering, crossing people over

"Guan Yin's Praise"

Heard about a new praise of Guan Shi Yin Bodhisattva in English that the Great Assembly now sings at the City of Ten Thousand Buddhas. Members of the Assembly translated the lyrics from the original Chinese praise sung for years and fitted them to a tune in the style of Western religious music. It's a major event every time the Dharma rituals and songs bridge the language between East and West. Translation of the Buddha's wisdom-treasures is holy work.

The Guan Yin Praise is a gem. Can't wait to hear the tune.

Bodhisattva, Guan Shi Yin
    is wonderful past gratitude.
Pure and clear are her adornments
    gained through practice ages long.
Sea-vast, a red lotus flower, fragrant
    rests beneath her foot,
Bay-curve of an autumn moon
    is in the crescent of her brows.
Everywhere and constantly
    sweet dews sprinkles from her vase,
In her hand a willow branch,
    through the countless autumns.
Prayers depart a thousand hearts;
    in a thousand hearts she answers.
Sailing the sea of suffering, crossing people over.

CHORUS
Namo Greatly Kind and Compassionate
    Bodhisattva of the Crystal Land,
Who dwells on Potola Mountain
    and observes the sounds of the world.

Heng Chau • November 2, 1978
It's as if we live in a house of mirrors

Dream: The Venerable Abbot was telling how the Pope had a vision of Guan Yin Bodhisattva somewhere in Europe. Guan Yin appeared suspended in mid-air in radiant colors. A number of people saw this and with the Pope, stared at and held the vision. But then they had the thought to call in scientists and the media. As soon as their minds left the vision, Guan Yin disappeared. Said the Abbot smiling, "Now, what do you all make of that?"

In fact, all the visions of the "Blessed Virgin" were really manifestations of Guan Yin Bodhisattva, but people didn't know and couldn't recognize her. It is said that Guan Yin's transformations are boundless and limitless.

> "Good Man, when I abide in this conduct door of Great Compassion I am always in the presence of all Thus Come Ones as well as universally appearing before all living beings... I manifest spiritual transformations to enlighten their minds and bring them to maturation. Or I transformationally manifest a shape similar to their own, dwell with them and bring them to maturity."
>
> Guan Yin Bodhisattva speaking to Good Wealth
> Entering the Dharma Realm – Avatamsaka Sutra

* * *

"House of Mirrors"

> "Buddhalands are not distinguishable. They are not longed for or loved; Only according to living beings thoughts do divisions appear to view, and therefore, in the world, all that is seen is different."
>
> Bodhisattvas Ask for Clarification Chapter
> Avatamsaka Sutra

We all look at the same reality, but no two people see exactly the same things. Divisions and differences appear not because of eyes, rather because of thoughts. Our minds filter and censor, distort and ignore according to our bias and bent. Psychologists call it "selective perception": the tendency to see what we prefer and to disregard the rest.

On the mundane level, a thought of fear at night turns a harmless rope into a poisonous snake. On the religious plane, a thought of doubt blinds one to the spiritual beings that surround us on all sides and fill up empty space. We only see the rocks, trees, mountains and dirt where other people see Buddhas, Bodhisattvas, devas, lotus flowers, and the seven precious gems. Some people see only one god, others see infinite gods, and still others see no god and nothing holy whatsoever. To one person the Buddha is merely a gilded icon from Asia; to another, the Buddha is the potential for perfect wisdom that lies buried within his own bosom.

Why so many differences? Karma. It's as if we live in a house of mirrors, some concave, some convex, others bent, tinted, twisted, and warped. Karma works the same way on our minds, shaping and bending them according to the words, thoughts and deeds we have committed with mouth, mind, and body. The worlds we inhabit and everything we see is conditioned by our karmic web. Karma is like a mirror and all that is seen and known is a reflection from our minds.

> It's just like a pure, bright mirror:
> Depending on what object stands before it
> The different images each appear; and
> The nature of karma is the same.
>
> The Bodhisattvas Ask for Clarification Chapter
> Avatamsaka Sutra

Also in the "Flower Store World" Chapter it says,

> From the power of living beings karma
> Are produced many lands...
> The mundane dharmas of the world are thus:
> The many kinds of views are each one different.

All the discord among religions, all the fighting among people and nations arise from the illusory differences we see darkly, through our crooked mirrors. If we could simply wipe away the accumulated dirt

and straighten our hearts, then everything we beheld would be pure
and adorned, just like the Buddhas see it.

> Within each and every thought
> Are created measureless countries,
> And because of the Buddha's awesome spiritual power,
> All is seen as pure, without defilement.
>
> Flower Store World System Chapter
> Avatamsaka Sutra

Heng Sure • November 3, 1978
Death does not honor Knighthood

"Goals."

The Venerable Abbot asked a new refuge disciple:

"Why do you want to become a Buddhist?" The disciple, a
carpenter, answered,

"Because I want to cultivate the Way to Buddhahood."

"Why do you want to do that?" asked the Abbot.

"Because there's nothing else to do!" came the firm reply.

Contemplating what is worth doing in the world, I counted the
blue-ribbon prizes, the status marks a person could attain:
Knighthood by the Queen, the Nobel Prize, Catholic Pope,
Supreme Court Judge, U.N. Ambassador, a long list. Thought then
of the personal power these people wield: U.S. President, General
Motors' Chairman of the Board, New York Times editors; then
envisioned the ability to benefit the world achieved by an Oxford
Ph.D., an M.D. from John Hopkins, and L.L.B. from Harvard Law.

These titles, degrees and honors testify to brilliant minds and rich
blessings. Suppose we rolled up every worldly trophy and gave all
those good roots to a single person. Although his merit and virtue
would be enormous, it could not surpass the supreme goodness in
the single thought for Bodhi, the decision to cultivate and achieve
Buddhahood.

Why? Death does not honor Knighthood. The president cannot sign a treaty with the Ghost of Impermanence. Skilled surgeons cannot remove their bad karma. Ambassadors, Nobel winners, editors, and doctorates, all arrive empty-handed at King Yama's bench. Kings stand in line behind beggars, noble and mean alike listen to the facts of their good and bad deeds as their karmic ledger is read.

> Good deeds make you rise, offenses make you fall.
> It has nothing to do with anybody else at all.
>
> Ten Dharma Realms

What is worth doing in our eye-blink of a lifetime on earth? Bring forth the great Bodhi resolve! "There's nothing else to do!" Buddhas alone resolve the One Great Matter, and leap free forever of the prison of birth and death. The ultimate achieved, the Great Hero work is done.

> "By bringing forth the mind, one can separate from the afflictions of karma and can make offerings to all Thus Come Ones. When karma and delusion are left behind and their continuity is severed, everywhere throughout the three periods of time, one is liberated."
>
> Merit and Virtue From First Bringing Forth The Resolve
> Avatamsaka Sutra

Heng Chau • November 3, 1978
The undependable bag of skin

"Back to the Natural…"

A young man stopped on his bicycle with a can of fuel. "You know," he said, "this is all new to me, and a lot of it goes in one ear and out the other. But since I've started meditating, eating meat feels really wrong. It's just happening that way by itself."

He cultivates the good without fatigue,
His quest intensifying for the Way Supreme.
Such, then, is his liking for the Dharma
That merit and virtue interact with meanings.

Ten Grounds Chapter
Avatamsaka Sutra

Practice and understanding mutually interact. The more you practice, the more you understand, and the more you understand, the more you like to practice. As soon as one opens a single door to the good, all the other 84,000 pure Dharma doors seem to open by themselves. It just happens that way, naturally.

* * *

Sitting in long, quiet periods of meditation is the hardest and most rewarding work I've ever done.

The body is contrary, unreliable, and unpredictable. It's forever breaking down and going bad. It likes bad habits and turbidity, resists the good and avoids hard work. The body is a loosely strung-together bag of skin and snot that is undependable. A dog is more loyal. No matter how good you treat it, the body always runs out on you. All living beings sing the "Skin Bag Blues." It's the song of the body and yet all living beings have the Buddhanature, and can become Buddhas if they can lay it down.

Lay down your bag of skin,
    leap onto the Supreme Vehicle.
This is the Song of the Skin Bag.
    Hearken to it, friends.

Venerable Hsu Yun

Heng Sure • November 4, 1978
May all beings share this deep, boundless joy

"Rain of Sweet Dew"

Big collections of knowledge appeal to the human mind: Encyclopedia Brittanica, China's largest literary encyclopedias that collected all written knowledge of science, medicine, commerce, literature, ritual, civilization, and nature under one cover; the Complete Shakespeare, the Oxford English Dictionary – comprehensive, complete, round treasuries, all that people have learned about life, the Earth, its inhabitants, their words, their ideas, their feelings.

Felt deep joy today as I recognized the Avatamsaka Sutra's greatness.

"Homage to the Flower Adornment Assembly of Buddhas and Bodhisattvas as vast as the sea."

I saw my eighteen years of education in the perspective of the Avatamsaka. The knowledge gathered over two decades of constant schooling does not measure up to a single grain of sand on the beach of the boundless Avatamsaka's wisdom-sea.

> It is like Sumeru, which spreads across the seas,
> Lowering retinue of peaks' high altitudes.
>
> Avatamsaka Sutra

The sutra's pages tell of pure, lofty heroes, their courage, their vows, their conduct; it explains the nature of the universe and reveals methods for cultivating the person and returning to harmony with all of creation.

A gentle rain fell today over the ocean-side fields and cliffs. Brussel sprout-pickers in yellow slickers moved across the gray landscape. The dusty, summer-baked plants and people alike delighted in the showering rain, just as the human heart is moistened and refreshed by the sweet dew of Dharma. May all beings share this deep, boundless joy and together return to our true home in the Avatamsaka's ocean-wide assembly of Buddhas and Bodhisattvas.

> I transfer this supreme good
> equally to all that live:
> May they soon accomplish Bodhi's fruit
> of never-ending bliss.
>
> Avatamsaka Sutra

Heng Chau • November 4, 1978
Possible, but easier by leaving home

A local doctor offers food and medicine and says, "the Avatamsaka Sutra really seems like quite the real thing!"

A nurse from a nearby medical clinic has put up Buddha images in the patients' reception room. She advises people to eat vegetarian food and to meditate.

"If more people would meditate, there wouldn't be any blood pressure problems," she says with authority.

> "He vows that living beings' only delight will be dharma bliss and the food of transcendence... so that their energy will be strong, their minds pure, and always happy. Their faculties sharp and clear, their internal organs full and solid; poisons will be unable to attack, illness unable to harm. Never troubled by disasters, they will be able to be eternally happy and at peace."
>
> Ten Transferences Chapter
> Avatamsaka Sutra

* * *

"Home"

A layman who bowed with us for a few days expressed gratitude and also reluctance to go back home and to his job.

"This bowing pilgrimage seems like my home, and my home seems just like a place to rest," he said. It's possible to cultivate the Way at home, but easier to accomplish the Way by leaving home. But most of all, cultivation is where your mind abides.

> "He vows that all living beings skillfully be able to transform and entice others. Without leaving the dharmas of the householder's life, they can speak the Buddhas' wisdom. He vows that all beings physically appear as householders, yet their minds constantly accord with the Buddha's wisdom in their dwelling."
>
> Ten Transferences Chapter
> Avatamsaka Sutra

The famous P'ang family is an example. Mr. and Mrs. P'ang and their son and daughter were all enlightened as householders. They accomplished the Way without leaving home and residing in the Way Place. However, it is important to note that they did not carry on like ordinary married people. They held the precepts immaculately, didn't drink wine or run around to plays and dances and the like. Mr. P'ang took all his wealth, piled it in a boat, and dumped it in the sea as an offer to rebuild the Dragon King's palace. After that, they lived in voluntary poverty and cultivated the Way purely and sincerely.

Heng Sure • November 5, 1978
The Western Land of Ultimate Bliss

"Soaring"

Laypeople Kuo Hsu and Kuo Pi join us for lunch. We unroll the plastic mats on a level shoulder amid weed stalks, barbed wire, and a deep irrigation ditch. Cars flow by on Sunday journeys, pickups, trailers, mobile homes, all of us on the road looking for the promised land.

The air is crystal clear, intense, the weather constantly changing. The laypeople's conversation turns to a favorite topic:

"The City of Ten Thousand Buddhas is alive. It's wonderful to be there," said Kuo Hsu. "A light and glowing energy fills every corner of the place," echoed Kuo Pi.

Kuo Chou, who is bowing with us this week, recently moved his home to the lay community at the City.

"Ever since the Master returned from Asia there has been a stepping up of the magic," he said. "The City is totally vibrant."

Our hearts soar aloft on news of our destination, the home of Buddhist disciples and sincere cultivators everywhere.

"You know," said Kuo Hsu, "there's no other way to capture the experience. The City of Ten Thousand Buddhas simply feels like the Western Land of Ultimate Bliss.

Heng Chau • November 5, 1978
Bang! Something hit the car

"Ch'an Trick and Treat"

We pulled off the highway and parked about 20 yards from the road behind some tall hemlocks. It was pitch-dark outside. We sat in Ch'an meditation in the car by a dimly-lit kerosene lamp.

"I can't, I can't, I can't!" cried my aching legs. "I can't sit for another second!" I was sleepy too, and just about to give in to weakness and uncross my legs. Suddenly the car shook with the impact of something hitting it broadside. Bang! The car shuddered.

We heard noises outside but couldn't see past the windows. It was a lonely, isolated campsite on the edge of a harvested brussel sprout field. Nobody around for miles. What was out there? What was coming next?! The adrenaline flowed and all senses went on alert. "So why couldn't I do this on my own without being 'tricked' into it by the loud noise and whatever hit the car?" I thought. Because I don't work up to my mind's capacity. By nature, I take the easy way unless I'm pushed… or scared. It was quite an eye-opener. I thought I had reached my limit but discovered that it was my thoughts that were limited. Basically, the mind is vast, measureless, and without limits, just like the Buddha.

> One should know that the Buddha and the mind,
> In substance and nature are inexhaustible.
>
> Praises in the Suyama Heaven
> Avatamsaka Sutra

Stepping outside with a flashlight to confront the "monster" that had moved my mind and slammed the car, I found a small, broken pumpkin lying next to the car. Someone tossed it from a passing car, probably. It was a Ch'an trick and treat. When conditions are right, even a rotten pumpkin can speak Dharma and help wake one from confusion.

* * *

The power of the mind and thoughts is inconceivable. It can destroy the world or create a Buddha. Good thoughts gather blessings and peace. False thoughts create offenses and attract unrest. No thoughts at all attain the Way and nurture everything under heaven. But "no thoughts, no mind" can only be reached after the anger and fighting cease within.

> "Don't fight so much in your mind. Why do we have war in this world? It is because everybody fights in their mind non-stop… contending, always seeking for one's self."
>
> Venerable Abbot in Hong Kong
> (September 26, 1978)

Put red dye into a pool and the water turns red. Our thoughts color the world the same way. They begin in the individual heart but never end there. There's no such thing as private thoughts. Just as the wind doesn't recognize fences, the mind also has no boundary and universally pervades. When a person resolves on Bodhi and brings forth a mind for the Way, the goodness and light from that thought spread swiftly throughout the entire world.

As a strong, swift wind
    whips along unobstructed,
So too, does the Buddhadharma
    quickly pervade the world.

Entering the Dharma Realm
Avatamsaka Sutra

* * *

"They give rise to happiness because they are mindful of all Buddhas. They give rise to happiness because they are mindful of all Buddhas' Dharmas."

Ten Grounds Chapter
Avatamsaka Sutra

Simple living clears the mind. Bowing to the Buddhas washes the soul. Now 1½ years of bowing, Ch'an meditation and the Avatamsaka Sutra. Every day the same. The flavor of desires lessens; the taste for Dharma grows. Watching our own faults and transgressions like the cat watches the mouse-hole. Returning the light even in sleep. No T.V. or radio, no books or papers, no movies or music. The sun and stars, the wind and rain as our traveling companions. Forms and sounds appear and fade. The heart is happy and knows peace in precepts, concentration, and in practicing wisdom. A picture of Amitabha Buddha and Guan Yin Bodhisattva suffice for conversation. Few words prevent disasters. In silence, learning to look within and contemplate the mind. Walking the high road, mindful of all Buddhas, happy in the Dharma. Going home again. In repentance and reform, going back home once more.

Heng Sure • November 6, 1978
The hundreds of dead clams I wear around my neck

"Clam-Karma"

We found a cache of plump brussel sprouts on the road Friday night. We didn't eat them on Saturday or Sunday, but they wouldn't leave my mind. Sunday evening I felt compelled to rinse and to sort the sprouts, tossing out dried and wilted ones. Why so much tender concern for vegetables? After meditating on it I saw that since we began bowing, I get uptight about perishable leftovers in the pantry. Until the food is eaten or passed on, I can't relax. The cause of this curious burden came clear today.

In 1972, I made bad karma by cruelly, carelessly killing living beings. The experience stung, and went deep, suppressed until today. That summer I took a week's vacation from theatre-workshop in Connecticut. With friends, I toured Swan's Island off the Maine coast. One afternoon at low tide, we dug a heap of clams and had a clambake, then carried home several hundred we couldn't eat. The clams were stacked alive in buckets, but no one tended them. The water splashed out, the clams dried up, making little sighs and whistles as they suffered and died.

The pails sat on the porch, at the workshop, forgotten. The clams continued to wheeze and die. Days later, someone threw the lot into the garbage.

Although I knew these poor creatures were in torment, I didn't bother to relieve their distress. Following the crowd, I let the clams suffer. Every day I passed the porch, saw the buckets and heard pitiful sounds, but I did nothing. Later I felt huge guilt and shame for my cruelty, so I buried the memory.

Now when fresh food appears, even though I no longer eat living beings' flesh, guilt moves me to ridiculous over-concern. I did not have to water the brussel sprouts, but bad karma from the past haunts my heart.

Just as I wrote this memory, Heng Chau began to sniff the air. He said he smelled rotting meat, a foul odor. Of course there is no meat in our car except for the hundreds of dead clams I wear around my neck.

"…A Bodhisattva must not involve himself in the causes, conditions, methods, or karma of killing, to the extent that he cannot deliberately kill any living creature. A Bodhisattva should always give rise to an eternally abiding mind of kindness, compassion, and filial compliance. Thus, he should devise skillful means to rescue and protect all beings."

excerpt from "First Major Precepts"
Brahma Net Sutra

Heng Chau • November 6, 1978
Polite begging, American style

Between Santa Cruz and Davenport, California

"They do not seek offerings from others but only give to other living beings… They have left the view of self far behind and have no thought of self."

Ten Grounds Chapter
Avatamsaka Sutra

"Do you need anything? Food, money…?" asks a man.

"Whatever people want to give us is what we need," I respond.

"Yeah, sure, of course," he says as if he understands an innuendo, or secret message in my response. (He's probably thinking: "Right, you need a lot of things, but you wouldn't think of asking; too proud to beg. Yeah, sure, I get it.")

"Here, hope this helps," he says, as he makes an offering of food and money.

Few people believe this answer: "Whatever people like to offer, that's what we like to get. We don't seek things." They see it as polite begging, American style. How else could you beg in a country where poverty spells laziness, lack of talent, or bad luck; where rugged individualism is stronger than hunger pangs and tattered clothes: "I may be cold and hungry, but I still got my pride."

But we mean it: what makes people happy, makes us happy.

"Straight Talk."

The ancients held that it is in the realm of thought that people truly express themselves. If merely in a thought, one harbors desire, anger, or scheming, then that is what we "say," despite our actual words. Children are valued for their "heaven trueness" (*tian zhen* 天真), but unfortunately, as we grow up, most of us lose this straightforward naïveté. Instead, we learn to use words as decoys to deceive and manipulate others. Not meaning what we say, not saying what we mean sets into habit, and soon words are rendered cheap and unreliable, and nobody knows what to believe or who to trust. But if the mind can be made straight, then without effort and quite naturally, the body will be proper and every word true.

Han Yu said that the mind is the root of humaneness, righteousness, propriety, sincerity, and wisdom. When the mind is straight, a glow of goodness is produced that flushes one's skin and shows even in one's back. The glow infuses the whole body and then, "the four limbs thus speak without saying a word."

In the Midwest there is a saying, "Practice what you preach." A Bodhisattva does just that. He speaks exactly as he practices and practices exactly as he speaks. Even when alone, in every thought and feeling, he is secured in the true and actual speech and in this way, he constantly benefits the world.

> He cultivates all of the paramitas,
> Far separates from flattery and deceit.
> As is spoken, so too does he practice,
> And is secured in true and actual speech.

> Ten Grounds Chapter
> Avatamsaka Sutra

Heng Sure • November 7, 1978
A parlor-conversation, a topic of debate

> "Bodhisattvas wear armor of vigor and grasp a sword of Prajna. They mow down the mad thieves of the six sense organs, seize the *yin* ghost of the six consciousnesses, and sweep out the defiled demons of the six dusts."
>
> Water and Mirror Reflections
> by Venerable Abbot Hua

How different from my college days' notions of Buddhism as a parlor-conversation, a topic of debate. The Buddha teaches earth-solid ways to save people's lives. Bodhisattvas use hard effort right here amid the same sense organs that stare at rosebuds, listen to news, taste buttered toast, and plan on trips to the beach. Vigorous cultivators armored against their bad habits, armed with Manjushri's wisdom-cutlass, sever out-flowing thoughts and guard the sense faculties from the dust that flows through them.

"Mow down the mad thieves." When the senses ask for light, the sword dices the urge to run out. Roses, news, toast, and beach tides can wait; birth and death wait for no one. "Seize the *yin* ghost." Six consciousness-fields discriminate good/bad, gain/loss, contact/emptiness. Not dividing, not choosing, not rejecting, we liberate gallons of wasted energy in each new moment of discipline.

"Sweep out the defiled demons." For example, give the ear a sound to fix on: "Namo Da Fang Gwang Fwo Hwa Yen Jing." Keep it busy listening to the pure names of Buddhas and Bodhisattvas or their mantras. Make it the ear's job to hold that sound. Investigate in stillness how empty and fragile the ear, how random and fleeting the impure noises that echo and pass on without cease. Trace the source of the dusty sound. Is it inside? Is it outside? Neither inside nor outside? Who's listening?

It takes a lot of asking to answer these questions but when we do, we can enter the pure and still Dharma-nature. Not an after-dinner bull-session! Hard work brings lasting liberation. Buddha-dharma puts the wisdom of eternity in our hands free of charge. Grasp it!

> Eyes, ears, nose, tongue and body,
> The mind, the will, and all organs of feeling.
> Are all empty, without a nature.
> They exist only from the discrimination of the false mind.
>
> Bodhisattvas Ask for Clarification Chapter
> Avatamsaka Sutra

Heng Chau • November 7, 1978
It will be something to look back on with nostalgia

Last week at the close of day as the sun set, a sleek Mercedes-Benz convertible glided up. A middle-aged, debonair bachelor-type flashed a salute to us, while his gaily-dressed escort watched from behind her sunglasses. It went like this:

"…So my partner on the ranch said he saw the monks out here bowing on the road, and so I said to Susan… This is Susan here," he says, reaching his arm around his date and pulling her into view.

"Susan is ah… well, Susan is my friend. My friend Susan. So I said, 'Susan…'"

"Hi," says Susan, softly, leaning over and peeking into the open car door with uplifted sunglasses.

"…so I said, 'Susan, we should go out and see the monks. After all, I don't imagine one will get to ever again see such an event in one's lifetime. It will be something to look back on with nostalgia.' So here we are!"

Susan lifts her glasses, leans over and peeks in to smile and softly say "Hi" again.

On the surface, we have next to nothing in common with this leisure-class vineyard playboy and his friend Susan. But underneath the appearances and past the surface trappings, one can feel deep affinities that seem to reach back through endless time and space to connect us. We sense this kinship with many people who come out – an unspoken, dimly expressed urge to put it all down and to follow their spiritual inclinations. Often, most visitors don't even know why they came out. They just have "this feeling" or "can't seem to get you out of my mind, so I just had to drive out and see for myself." Sometimes they feign interest in trivial aspects of the trip – our clothes, the weather, our diet – but behind the silly questions and nervous jokes are sincere hearts and deeply searching minds probing with every sense organ and hairpore to find the link and the likeness. It's as if this world were a huge masquerade. Behind the masks and disguises of kings, queens, clowns, ministers, beggars, cowboys, priests, and bandits, hide family and friends from the past, people we cultivated the Way with life after life.

> When offenses are not heavy,
>> one need not be born in the Saha World.
> When karma is not pure,
>> one cannot be born in the Pure Land.

It's said we are born as people to pay off debts of past karma. We want to leave home and cultivate the Unsurpassed Way, but our accounts aren't settled, and until the debt is cleared, we return life after life to make our payments. And in the process, because of delusion, we create more karma, incur more debts until we are completely enmeshed in a sticky net, stretching from beginningless time into the endless future.

"All living beings flow and turn following their karma amid the bitter, difficult places of birth, sickness, old age, and death... Moreover, living beings are bound in the net of love. They are covered with ignorance and defiled and attached to their existence. They follow it and cannot give it up… When the Bodhisattva sees this, he gives rise to a mind of great compassion and a heart of great benefit, and he wishes for all beings to attain liberation."

Ten Transferences Chapter
Avatamsaka Sutra

So it's said,

> The sea of suffering is boundless,
> But a turn of the head is the other shore.

And yet sometimes it's so hard to just turn the head around and look for the other shore. We "follow it and cannot give it up."

Today, a sleek Mercedes convertible pulled up. "Hi, Heng!" shouts a familiar-looking man. "Remember me?"

"Yes," I say. It was the vineyard playboy who came out with his "friend" Susan, for nostalgia, last week.

"Listen, Heng. What you say to my taking a few color photos of this? Oh, ah… This is Toni… um, ah, Toni is my friend, yes, my friend Toni."

"Hi" says Toni, softly peeking over her sunglasses.

"Anyways Heng, I was thinking…"

Heng Sure • November 8, 1978
I was the drowning man

"Ears! Ears! Ears!"

The Venerable Abbot's words took me by the ear, their meaning hard to miss: lion's roar of good Dharma. The Master's instructions at Gold Wheel last month:

"Listen! Listen! Obey! Obey!" he said.

"The eyes contemplate shapes and forms
     but they don't exist within.
The ears hear dusty sounds,
     but the mind does not know."

He could not have been more emphatic, as if this verse were a life-boat to rescue a drowning man. Following the teachings this month, I realize I was the drowning man! I investigated my listening habits and found my ear gate standing wide open, the energy constantly flowing and mixing with dusty sounds: voices harmonizing in morning recitation, discriminating the different whines and roars of VW buses, Volvo sedans, Harley Davidson and Honda motorcycles, to ocean tides, bird songs, and wind in the power lines. My ears are too busy and they drain my energy and rob me of the fullness of self. Thank you, Shih Fu. I will listen (to my self-nature) and climb aboard your compassionate lifeboat of instructions.

"Return the hearing and listen to the self-nature, until the nature accomplishes the Supreme Way."

Shurangama Sutra

Heng Sure • November 8, 1978
We are, by nature, spiritual beings

Dear Shr Fu,

There is an ineffable feeling of completeness and security in the life of a left-home monk. Having given up private home and personal relationships, the left-home person is at home in the world at large. His companions are all beings everywhere. His refuge is peaceful dwelling with the Supreme Knight, the Buddha, the wisdom-lore and the Enlightened Ones of the Sutras, and the selfless, pure, "field of blessings" Sangha members. Has there ever been any greater happiness and peace than this?

Several weeks ago I witnessed a wonderful story unfold which I've called "The Monk and the Militants". We were bowing in Santa Cruz when a reporter for the local college paper came up to interview Heng Chau. She was interested in our work and our vows. She was surprised that all our material needs come from free-will offerings.

The next day, after lunch, we bowed across Branciforte Creek and the reporter appeared again. She looked apologetic and flustered. Another student stood beside her, a hostile expression on her face.

"I feel embarrassed to ask you these questions, but I have to ask anyhow," the reporter said. The questions were all about politics and economics. They were pointed questions, and the language was angry, resentful, full of jargon and political rhetoric. It was clear that the reporter had been under attack by political classmates at school. They had pegged Buddhism as parasitical and exclusive and *san bu yi bai*[2] as an elitist and frivolous exercise, of interest and of benefit only to members of a rich, white minority in society.

---

2. Three Steps One Bow

The militants did not pick their opponent well. Heng Chau's answers left the students speechless: the reporter speechless with delight, her angry friend speechless with dismay. Heng Chau is not politically ignorant or naive. Rather he is experienced at the political-consciousness parlor game. Before he left home to become a monk he was a Doctoral candidate in the highly competitive History Department at the University of Wisconsin. He cut his political teeth during the red-hot sixties, the era of marches, sit-ins and conscious-ness-raising confrontations. It was precisely his disenchantment with the ineffectiveness and the narrow scope of the political answer to the world's problems that led to his discovery of Buddhism. In the Buddhadharma he found real solutions to the suffering that all people undergo. He left the home-life to study and practice the Dharma full-time as a monk.

Here are the questions and answers given that day as the monk met the challenge of the militants:

Q: What is the racial and class background of the members of the Sino-American Buddhist Association?

A: We come from the class of all living beings. SABA is truly international. The Buddhadharma cuts across all divisions of class, race, sex, age, nationality, ethnic and economic backgrounds. It is the direct mind-to-mind language, the teaching of all beings, the teaching of the heart. It is the true classless origin of human beings. No one in SABA thinks in those divisive categories any longer.

Q: How can you avoid the reality of "those categories?"

A: It's all made from the mind. If you want to see the world as rich and poor, black and white, have and have not, then that's how it is. But if you take a step two inches to the left or two inches to the right or look over your shoulder, then it all looks different. If you are open to all possibilities, if you turn your head all the way around, then you approach the Buddhist view. Buddhism is the teaching of the mind and all its states. Both have no beginning and have no end.

Q: How can you feel comfortable taking the time to make a pilgrimage like this? Third World people have more primary concerns, like filling their bellies. Your pilgrimage is possible only in a country where everyone gets to eat his fill. Only then are you able to sit around and think of transcendental bliss.

A: No one who understands people could say that the only concern of any person or group of people is filling their bellies. That's just a handy label that rabble-rousers use to identify "the Third World" as they call it. In fact, Third World people are *people*, not bellies and mouths. They think of birth and death, where they came from and where they are going. All people think about it. We just returned from a trip through Asia and we visited some back-water places, where the Third World lives. People there met the Buddhadharma with an overwhelmingly positive response, as strong and as enthusiastic as anywhere in the U.S.A. Why? Because Buddhism is the language of the heart. Everyone recognizes it. It transcends the simple concern for a full belly. Buddhism is our original home. The rest is superficial.

Q: How are you adding to the world's production? Living like soft parasites in a safe monastery, how are you helping anyone?

A: People at Gold Mountain Monastery and the City of Ten Thousand Buddhas, and at the International Institute for the Translation of Buddhist Texts are deeply concerned with the suffering of beings everywhere. We believe that we must,

> Truly recognize your own mistakes,
> And don't discuss the faults of others.
> Others' faults are just my own;
> Being of one substance with everyone
>   is great compassion

But we don't just talk about it. So we eat just one meal a day. Some of the monks eat just one bowl of food per day. Why? Because there are people in the world who do not get enough to eat every day. We add to production by not being greedy and by decreasing consumption.

We do not solicit anything. All that we have and use are offerings given freely. We do not use money for food. We get our vegetables from what the markets throw away, or we grow it in our fields. We live on the scraps of the U.S.A. Any money that is offered is used to build Way-places and to print books. No one holds private property, it all belongs to the church. Our clothes are not bought. We recycle the clothes that other people no longer want. We are not concerned with stylish appearances. There are no water-beds at our way places. Most of the monks and nuns and even some of the lay people never lie down – they sleep sitting in meditation posture. We don't turn on heaters in our monasteries, no matter what season it is. We do nothing for name or for gain. We do not lead personal lives. The monks and nuns are celibate, they believe in eliminating all selfish desires. Now this is genuine revolution. Our Three Great Principles are these:

> Freezing to death, we do not climb on conditions.
> Starving to death, we do not beg.
> Dying of poverty, we do not scheme.
> We accord with conditions but do not change.
> Unchanging, we accord with conditions.
> These are our Three Great Principles.
> We give up our lives to do the Buddha's work.
> We rectify our lives to do the Sangha's work.
> Our business is illuminating principles,
> So that our principles are revealed in our practice.
> In this way we carry out
> The pulse of the Patriarchs' heart-transmission.

When we follow these principles, we truly help the Third World and all living beings. The answer to the world's suffering is not simply to give the Third World what the U.S. has. Rather we must turn our

abundant blessing into merit and virtue through hard work and cultivation of our own natures. It's said that

> To receive suffering is to end suffering.
> To cash in blessings is to exhaust blessings.

The Buddhadharma teaches that the reason the world is in a
mess is because our minds are a mess. If we want to clean up the
world, we must first purify our own minds. We do not tell other
people to wash their dirty clothes. Buddhists do their own dirty
laundry. All of the problems in the world come from selfishness and
the desire for self-benefit. The heart of Buddhism teaches us to have
no self.

"Now if you have no more questions I'll get back to work
bowing," said Heng Chau, and that ended the interview.

> "In this way, they tend toward true, real principles and
> gain entry into the profound place that is without wrangling."
>
> Avatamsaka

Part II.

On Sunday afternoon, Heng Chau told me the story of his
encounter with the students. He said, "I gave some thought to my
answers and there was much more I could have said but that was not
the time or place to go into depth. I would explain the principles of
compassion and cause and effect. These two principles really
expanded my own mind from my former materialist and divisive
political views. My thinking used to be really narrow. It was purely
intellectual. The materialist view is one-dimensional, it divides the
world, it's based on fighting. Either side of the coin, capitalism or
communism, is a dead end. There's no heart there. People are not as
simple as mouths and bellies and greed for wealth. We are, by nature,
spiritual beings.

"That's what lead me to change my mind. I looked into my own
heart and realized that there was more inside than concern for my

own benefit. How could I assume that that's all there is in others? Buddhism is based on kindness, compassion, joy and giving. It includes everyone, no one is excluded. Great compassion is grand and magnanimous; great division is petty and full of hatred. And, *everyone* has the Buddha nature."

What does our teacher say about class? He says:

> All beings are my family,
>   all the universe is my body.
> Empty space is my school,
>   the invisible is my name.
> Kindness, compassion, joy and giving
>   are my functions.

"After you hear this truth, who could ever be satisfied with class struggle and washing others' dirty clothes?" Heng Chau asked.

"I understand now that cause and effect determines the worlds that we live in. If we waste our blessings and don't cultivate merit and virtue, then even if we have wealth, we can lose it in this lifetime. If you do nothing but exhaust your blessings and follow greed, then in the next life you will certainly come up short. On the other hand, people are sunk in poverty this life because in the past they stole, wasted resources, were stingy and dishonest. This is what's really going on beneath the surface of the materialistic world.

"It's not difficult to see beyond the purely political view of the intellectual," said Heng Chau. "It's got no heart to it. Within it there is a really arrogant and superior attitude towards people. The basic assumptions are that poor people are worse off than rich folks and won't be happy until they have what the wealthy have and want. If you see the world that way, then that's how it is: a blend of greed and guilt. If the Third World does not want what we have, then how does it make us feel about our excess? Are two cars and a color T.V. and living the good life really our righteous share?

"In Asia I heard many people, particularly older people, say that as their countries 'modernized' and people moved closer to big cities, they all got more nervous as life got less simple. There was no time to enjoy life anymore. All people knew about was chasing the buck, desires grew and then simple things, simple thoughts no longer satisfied people. Families began to break down, headaches and problems increased as soon as First World culture was imported.

"What's more, the Buddhadharma faces squarely the big matter of birth and death and its suffering. Poor people embrace the Dharma because they see the emptiness of life and the universality of suffering up close. They aren't cushioned from it the way the 'better half' is," said Heng Chau.

"The turning point in the encounter with the students came when I explained the actual practices of the members of SABA. Up to that point the interviewers assumed that we were just students, too, wearing funny clothes and playing the same political game. They assumed that we ate the same food, listened to the same music, danced to the same rhythms. When they heard about the bitter practices of SABA's 'Dharma-revolutionaries' the conversation quickly became very real. Great compassion is such a wonderful heart. As soon as you include all beings instead of dividing them up, discrimination and hatred just shrivel up," Heng Chau said. "Like the Master told us in L.A., once you grasp any of the fundamental Buddhist principles, then there's no one you can't win over in debate. Who can refuse to stand inside the peace and happiness of the Buddha's light? The Buddhadharma is truly the highest of all teachings. It is 'without sophistry,' it 'goes beyond words and thoughts'. It's inconceivable!"

Disciple Guo Chen (Heng Sure)
bows in respect

Heng Chau • November 8, 1978
Institutionalization

> "All living beings are confined in the prison of the world. They endure all kinds of bitter suffering."
>
> Ten Grounds Chapter
> Avatamsaka Sutra

We bow past prisons and prison road gangs repairing the highways or fire crews on leave from jail to fight forest fires. All are under lock and key, guarded and watched every minute in every move. We bow past mental hospitals, old folks' homes with bars on the windows, reform schools and correctional facilities all full of people who have lost "the skillful means of liberation."

There is a disease called "institutionalization," where after too many years of confinement in an institutional setting, people cannot handle freedom. They become so well-adjusted to internment that their biggest fear is being let out. They actually dread the thought of release and view freedom as a fate worse than death.

From the enlightened eyes of the Buddha, this world of ours is a big prison and all living beings suffer from "institutionalization." Within the three realms of existence we take impurity as purity, a false self for our true self, what is impermanent as permanent, and suffering for bliss. And worst of all, we bring it all on ourselves and become so inured, we cower in a cold sweat when the Buddhas and Bodhisattvas offer us true freedom.

> "They do not respect the King of the Ten Powers. They do not know to repay the kindness of the Bodhisattvas. Doting on their attachments to dwelling places, upon hearing that all dharmas are empty, their hearts know terror and alarm."
>
> Ten Conducts Chapter
> Avatamsaka Sutra

Ignorance says, "You need lots of good food, the more the better. Fame is necessary for a healthy self-image. Sex is as important as food to your well-being. Wealth makes life bearable and frees you from worry. Sleep is good for the body and sharpens the mind. You only go around once in life, so grab all the gusto you can get!"

"…they themselves bring on their own worry and fear. The heavy shackles of greed and desire bind and restrain them."

Ten Grounds Chapter
Avatamsaka Sutra

One and one half years of bowing and simple living say otherwise: "Good food spoils the palate and disturbs the mind. With plain vegetarian food, the mind grows sweet and calm, the body strong and peaceful. Without fame, there is no fear of a bad reputation. Wealth is a hornet's nest of worry and weight. The more you have the more troubles follow you. Sex harms our health and steals away our inherent wisdom. Too much sleep leaves you dull and stupid. We don't go around in life just once, we go around ceaselessly, and the more gusto we grab for, the deeper we sink in the sea of suffering." There is a curious paradox: only when we put it all down and stop grabbing for all we can get, do we get everything we could ever want.

"He sees all beings are obstructed by the prison of existence and he feels sympathy. He sees that all beings have lost the skillful means of liberation, and he feels sympathy."

Ten Grounds Chapter
Avatamsaka Sutra

* * *

On silence…

> The wonderful principles of the Buddha-dharma
>   originally were not spoken.
> After awakening, even one word is too many.
> Only because living beings are confused
>   and so heavily obstructed
> Does the Buddha come with skillful means
>   and talk and talk.
>
> verse by Venerable Abbot Hua

Silence is an expedient, a means to an end, not an ultimate goal in itself. We close the mouth for a time in order to listen to our minds. When the mouth inside the mind is silent, then the mouth outside can speak without error.

A visiting layman said to us yesterday, "Every time I open my mouth, I break the rules and cause problems. I am going to shut up!"

Silence has a use, so do words. To be constantly talking is against nature, but to be constantly silent falls into a useless, dull kind of emptiness. The practice of silence is a temporary Dharma-door to quiet the mind's chatter. When the mad mind stops talking, then the Bodhisattva, at the proper time and without timidity, extends a vast and long tongue to proclaim the wonderful Dharma and benefit living beings.

> Their speech is harmonious and pleasing,
>   devoid of what is coarse and rude.
> They speak at the proper time and also without fear.
> They penetrate the meaning
>   and practice according to Dharma.
> Far removed from stupidity and confusion,
>   their minds do not move.
>
> Ten Dwellings Chapter
Avatamsaka Sutra

"Dragons and Tigers"

Bowing and meditation today: body full of fire like a dragon, mind wild, pacing like a tiger. Had a dream last night that I had let a powerful tiger out of its cage and was trying to wrestle it back into submission. In the dream I was putting many women behind locked doors to protect them from the hungry cat.

The ancients described desire as fierce tigers and mighty dragons, that if left un-caged, could tear one to shreds. But if men can subdue the white tiger and women can slay the red dragon, then they can live forever.

> "Immortals possess the trick for subduing dragons and slaying tigers. They know the heavenly skill of 'returning to the root, going back to the source.' Therefore, they live forever and do not die."
>
> from Lao Tzu's Classic of Purity and Stillness

"Home Again"

> Deeply bowing to the Buddhas,
> Sitting long to still the mind;
> Pain and loneliness come riding but,
>   losing interest in my bidding.
> Pass me by again,
> Pass me by again.
> Close the doors, unroll the Sutras,
> Roam the magic wisdom sea;
> Single lamplight's flickering vigil
> Stays the darkness, cleaves the middle, to,
> Bring me back again,
> Bring me back again.
> Happy alone, original home,
> Bring me back again.

November, 1978
South of Santa Cruz

Heng Sure • November 9, 1978
Returning the light to illumine within

D.M. Chau has a practice of physically returning the light from all six sense organs. First, he pins eyes to nose, then nose watches mouth, ears listen to tongue reciting. Taste and touch senses return to stillness and the mind focuses on the center of the body, the *tan t'ien* "cinnabar field." He contemplates in sequence, "eyes, ears, nose, tongue, body, mind," and gathers the energies back and down to a single center. Then he lets them all go in the next instant and begins the practice once more. It's mental *kung fu*, a concentration technique that unites the body and stills random thoughts.

Reversing outflows is the work of Sages. The Buddha perfected this mind-body skill and escaped the turning wheel of birth and death. He recognized the undisciplined mind as the biggest leak of all, and came up with a way to stop the outflow. What happens when "the light" returns completely? I can't say, but the Sutra explains that everything we experience in the world is projected from the mind. The sun and stars, mountains, houses, cars, fear, love, hunger, our bodies, and all people, are like illusions, like tricks of vision, as ephemeral as a rainbow. All Buddhas say it's so. But using the Dharma method, anybody who can take charge of his six sense gates can "light up the mind, and see the nature." There's no other secret to seek. Constant, vigorous work can liberate our lives from endless aeons of suffering.

> He does not seek forms, sounds, smells, or tastes,
> Nor does he seek wonderful sensations of touch;
> But only to save all living beings
> He constantly seeks the supreme, victorious wisdom.
>
> Ten Transferences Chapter
> Avatamsaka Sutra

Heng Chau • November 9, 1978
Outgrowing milk, pain and death

Childhood advertising jingle said,

"You never outgrow your need for milk!"

Dream: A beautiful demon grabs me. I stiffen and shout, "No, no!" The demon transforms into a vicious, furious animal and attacks. I yell, "Master, Master, help me!" and then recite lines from the Shurangama Mantra loudly into the charging demon/beast's face. The demon freezes, the dream stops, I wake up saved.

Why this dream? Because before falling asleep I gulped down a glass of warm, sweet milk. I rationalized the indulgence as an expedient to hasten recovery from a cold. However, the real motive was desire, and that one thought of greed while awake, instantly manifested as a savage demon in sleep. Perhaps this is why the Shurangama Sutra advises cultivators of the Way to avoid dairy products: they increase desire and tie up karmic affinities with animals. You do outgrow your need for milk, it seems.

* * *

While meditating I reached a point where I felt I couldn't go on. The mind, will, and every muscle wanted to quit. I looked up and saw the Master's picture hanging in the car and got inspired to be patient and hang on a little longer. So I let go and hung on. In a little while the pain passed, followed by a vision of sitting next to the Master in a cool, shaded, quiet room.

* * *

The Buddha Amitabha is always here. The Buddha Amitabha doesn't come or go, isn't near or far, big or small, inside or outside. When my mind is that way too, then I will meet Amitabha.

"…and in a single thought instant he will be reborn in the Land of Ultimate Bliss. Arriving there, he will see Amita Buddha."

Universal Worthy's Conduct and Vows Chapter
Avatamsaka Sutra

* * *

"Dream Talk."

Strange dream last night:

We were led to a scaffold for hanging. There were ten of us. Our "crimes" were political. We were being sacrificed in a political play for power by a puppet government. I thought it was just bold posturing, a joke. But when the rope was thrown around my neck I knew it was for real. No one was smiling. One hundred yards away a dozen bodies were still slowly swinging from an identical scaffold. Our hands were tied behind our backs.

One could feel the tension in the drop door under our feet ready to release. Below were 15 feet of empty space to fall into before our necks snapped at the end of the coarse hemp rope. "Hey," it hit me hard, "I'm going to really die!"

An indescribable shock and panic filled every inch and cell of my being. The world stopped. The whole of my life condensed into a superficial, half-forgotten day-dream. Only the moment was real. And the moment was death.

They pulled the release. It jammed. But we could feel the bolts turn and the levers wiggle and click in the soles of our bare feet. I started to recite "Namo Guan Shi Yin Pu Sa, Namo Guan Shi Yin Pu Sa" over and over. Suddenly, a warm flow of peace and calm filled me. Everything was still and smooth. Death? "Oh, I'll just keep reciting right through the hanging and see where I come out next," I said to myself, cheerfully and unafraid.

Then I woke up. A dream? Maybe. But it felt too real. When alive, death seems far away and like a dream. But when facing death, life becomes the illusion. Cultivating the Buddha-dharma is for real. It is the only thing that matters. The rest is dream talk.

* * *

We bowed into Davenport, California. A large cement plant, a sprinkling of houses and a lone gas station. Strong winds from the Northwest drove grit and dirt into everything: the car, our bodies, the food, our lungs, and filled the air. Truly, outside and inside are not different. The wind was speaking Dharma; there are no boundaries.

No body or mind inside,
No world outside.
No self or others, contemplating freedom.
Not formed or empty, seeing the Thus Come One.

Kuo Chou decides to stay on with the pilgrimage a bit longer. The bowing dharma gets sweeter over time and soon begins to feel more like home than home itself.

Heng Sure • November 10, 1978
Bowed into a labyrinth of defiled thoughts

Mind wandering, pondering the karma that puts one person behind the wheel of a dump truck, another riding the sprouts wagon; one person cultivating the Way in a monastery, another reading tickertape in a marketing firm, another tending patients in a mental health.

Followed the state and left my center of concentration. Emotion rose and turned into desire. I bowed on and entered a labyrinth of defiled thoughts. Felt moved by a sudden, heart-filling urge to give kindness to all men, to make people happy. I called the feeling compassion. It was, in fact, impatience, a thought of desire to run out and vent the pressure of hard cultivation before the gathered energy transformed into wisdom. Bodhisattvas' great compassion is impartial to all beings, cool and selfless, based on respect and born of flawless precepts and genuine Samadhi-power.

In Singapore, a cultivator asked the Venerable Abbot about genuine Great Compassion.

Question: "Shih Fu, what does real compassion mean? I don't feel it entails just being 'nice' to people, because that often is false."

Ven. Abbot: "Of course, compassion is not mere external show of kindness. The latter falls easily into the realm of artificiality. Compassion arises on its own as you understand more. As you grow up, it flows out from your self-nature because you are able to really see."

Heng Chau • November 10, 1978
We are now a bowing parade

Laypeople from L.A. arrive to spend the weekend doing three steps, one bow. At night, wrapped up in blankets and hooded sweatshirts, they sleep in their cars.

With the addition of four more people, we legally qualify as a "parade," a good-nature policeman informed us this morning. He watched the slow process of a half-dozen, long-robed pilgrims rising and falling devoutly along and assured me,

"But don't worry, we'll overlook the parade-permit law this time. You're a special case," he said with a wide grin, as he pushed back his blue hat and scratched his head.

Getting colder as the winter rain clouds gather and thicken in the northern skies. At night, the howls of hungry coyotes echo as we chant and read from the Avatamsaka by an oil lamp. May all who hear and see be filled with Dharma bliss!

> "He vows that all beings obtain the wisdom body and that they be nourished and filled with happiness by the flavor of the Buddhadharma."
>
> Ten Transferences Chapter
> Avatamsaka Sutra

Heng Sure • November 11, 1978
I wouldn't miss coming out here for the world

"Heart Of Giving"

Lunch on Cement Plant Road, Davenport, California.

Dharma Protectors from Pacifica arrive at the same time as a family of laypeople from L.A. The autumn wind bites through our clothes. Caught by a sudden 10-degree drop in temperature with nothing but barbed-wire pastures and hills on every side, we settle on a cattle-path off the highway. The hand-bell chimes the offering chant, but nobody can hear it over the shrill wind. Sycamore leaves knocked from above by the rain, plaster the tofu and rice pots. The laymen scramble to put rocks on the napkins and recover the rolls as gusts scoop food from the plates and send it rolling down the cow path. Sand and grit season the orange juice and peanut butter.

Shivering and sniffling as we sit between parked cars, words give way to gestures and sign language – the wind snatches away sounds as they leave the tongue. Eucalyptus berries spatter on the Plymouth's roof like bongo drums. Food doesn't warm the belly; the rain chills the bone.

Cross the barb-wire and enter the pasture to exercise. Slap arms windmill-style, see the cattle tracks, and hear, on the wings of the November gale, the lonely howls of a coyote pack across the hills to the East.

Rejoin the gathering of Dharma friends, see their bright faces, runny noses, and gentle good humor. Nobody complains. The spirit of giving transforms trials and tests into unexpected discoveries of inner strength and self-awareness.

"I've never been so c-o-o-old in my life," said one of the laypeople between chattering teeth. "But you know, I wouldn't miss coming out here for the world. Our experiences since drawing near to the Triple Jewel have opened up a whole new life for my family."

Her words said it for us all, a feeling difficult to describe but deep and right in the heart.

> "Disciples of the Buddha, when Bodhisattvas give away their bodies, they bring forth humble minds, minds like the earth, minds which patiently receive a host of suffering without changing or retreating, minds which serve living beings without weariness... peacefully dwelling in good roots, they vigorously, earnestly offer up their service."
>
> Ten Transferences Chapter
> Avatamsaka Sutra

Heng Chau • November 11, 1978
Withered sprouts and sterile seeds

"The Davenport Arhat: Withered Sprouts and Sterile Seeds..."
Davenport, California

Since Big Sur I've been itching for a chance to go into seclusion. But instead of solitude we found ourselves surrounded by people: well-wishers, hecklers, newsmen, and old friends. Then came a Dharma-tour of Asia where thousands of people daily drew near the Master and our delegation, hungry as bees for honey to hear the Abbot speak Dharma and to receive the nectar of his kindness and compassion.

Upon returning to the U.S.A. and the coast highway pilgrimage, I decided to put it all down and see how far I could go in my meditation. For the last ten days I did a mini-Ch'an session on my own, using the station wagon as my makeshift cave-on-wheels.

I worked hard at subduing body: pushing past their aches and noise, going beyond thresholds of pain and tedium, ignoring the clock. At the end of ten days I began to experience a state of total oneness with everything – incredibly blissful and still. Self-satisfaction crept in, followed by greedy attachment to the bliss and quietude. Soon, I wanted only to enter my tranquil cave. I didn't wish to see or to talk with people. I lost interest in answering questions, bowing, cooking, writing. In short, unaware, I was ready to forsake my Bodhi-sattva vows to dwell in the "fixed wisdom and ultimate stillness" of the Sound-Hearer Vehicle. The Buddha rebuked these fixed-nature Arhats as "withered sprouts and sterile seeds" within Buddhism.

> "They had peacefully dwelt in the Sound-Hearer's fruition; and obtained fixed wisdom. From the truth of non-existence, constantly dwelling in the reality-limit and ultimate stillness and quietude, they were far removed from great compassion. They forsook living beings and dwelt in their own affairs."
>
> Entering the Dharma Realm
> Avatamsaka Sutra

They were selfish and small-minded, caring nothing for other beings. When it was time to eat they opened their mouths; when it was time to sleep, they closed their eyes.

Just as I entered my placid cave-state on Friday, a car full of devout laypeople arrived, planning to join the pilgrimage for the weekend. I didn't want to get up from meditation or to step outside the car to acknowledge their arrival or to receive their offerings. I felt imposed upon, and grew irritable. Anger and aloofness rose inside, coupled with a wish to withdraw into my cave and "cling to my still emptiness and Dhyana-bliss."

That night I had the following dream: a selfish, haughty aristocrat driving a plush, expensive, European car, refused to stop to let people cross the street. He was totally cut off from humanity, locked inside a little castle-on-wheels, oblivious, and unconcerned with the world. Enraged, I stepped in front of his car, forcing him to stop while I escorted the people safely across the street. The snobbish baron was furious with me. He jumped out of his limousine and crushed a small car with his foot. He was huge and powerful, Titan-like, and incensed that he was made to yield and to show concern for others.

We wrestled and debated, at first with principles and words – I quoting Sutras, he quoting worldly philosophers and advocating laissez-faire, self-interest "every man for himself," and "survival of the fittest." Words gave way to fists and soon we were locked in hand-to-hand combat, fighting all the way up to the oak-paneled trophy room/library of his castle. End of dream.

"In worlds in the ten directions he does not give rise to thoughts of self-seeking and grasping what belongs to self. He does not discriminate at all regarding all worlds. He does not produce defiled attachment to any state."

Ten Transferences Chapter
Avatamsaka Sutra

Interpretation: I caught this demon-state by attaching to the bliss of my meditation "cave." The arrogant, snobbish aristocrat was a being I created from my thoughts. He symbolized clinging to Ch'an bliss and turning my back on others.

"He raises up great vows and never forsakes living beings."

Avatamsaka Sutra

Prior to the laypeople's arrival, I got a warning in the form of a vision of my teacher. The Master appeared in my meditation state and said: "The Bodhisattva vows not to become a Buddha or to perfect his own enlightenment until all living beings get enlightened to Buddhahood. The Bodhisattva liberates himself by liberating others. And until his vows to save and take across all beings are fulfilled, he doesn't leave the world, nor does he attach to the world. His body dwells in the world yet his mind has gone beyond. Benefiting others is first and foremost. Wandering high and far comes second." Unfortunately, I ignored this timely advice and clung to my Ch'an state. The laypeople arrived, I was turned, and failed the test.

Bodhisattvas accomplish Buddhahood by teaching and transforming living beings and by making offerings to all Thus Come Ones. Why? Because living beings and Buddhas are one, not two. All Buddhas take the heart of great compassion as their substance. That is to say, "being one with everyone is called great compassion." Because of living beings they give rise to and express compassion. From compassion and kindness the mind for enlightenment is born. And because of the resolve for enlightenment, they accomplish Buddhahood. That is why,

> "If a Bodhisattva accords with living beings, then he accords with and makes offerings to all Buddhas. If he can honor and serve living beings, then he honors and serves the Thus Come Ones. If he makes living beings happy, he is making all Thus Come Ones happy."
>
> Universal Worthy's Conduct And Vows Chapter
> Avatamsaka Sutra

By benefiting living beings, one walks the Bodhisattva path to Buddhahood. By only benefiting oneself, one walks the Self-ending Arhat path back to the turning wheel. Hence they received the Buddha's scolding for being "withered sprouts and sterile seeds." In contrast to,

> "By benefiting all beings with the water of great compassion, one can realize the fruits and flowers of the Buddhas' and Bodhisattvas' wisdom... Bodhi belongs to living beings. Without living beings, no Bodhisattva could perfect unsurpassed, proper enlightenment."
>
> Universal Worthy's Conduct and Vows Chapter
> Avatamsaka Sutra

In all, I learned an important lesson. By going off on my own and seeking self-accomplishment, I stepped outside my instructions and trampled on my vows. I put myself on a tangled by-path by forsaking the roots and grabbing the branch-tips. The roots are the Bodhisattva vows. The roots are all living beings, and it's only by watering and nurturing the roots that one obtains the fruits and flowers of sagely wisdom.

I should trust my teacher, keep my hands and heart on my vows and attach to nothing. Bodhisattvas benefit others without weariness, without a thought of self. Time to leave my "Arhat cave" and get back to work.

> Inside and outside, in all worlds
> The Bodhisattva attaches to nothing.
> He does not give up his career of benefiting living beings.
> The Great Knight cultivates this kind of wisdom.

Ten Transferences Chapter
Avatamsaka Sutra

Heng Sure • November 12, 1978
In time they'll come around

"Positive Stroking"

Scolded Heng Chau this morning and told him to learn the bell-rhythm for a ceremony-praise. My tone of voice was bullying, whining. Heng Chau smiled at the bantam-rooster belligerence and pointed out the fighting attitude behind my words.

"These old, bad habits are bound to rise in the heat of smelting. Cultivation uncovers the garbage we need to purge in order to change and to renew. The treatment center I worked in for emotionally disturbed children used behavior modification methods. The methods boil down to this: ignore behavior you want to decrease and reinforce behavior you want to increase." said Dharma Master Chau.

"I'm ready to give up the whining, bully habit. It's hardly the conduct of a Bodhisattva," I said. "But how do you go about making an actual change?" I asked.

"When you don't support what's wrong, the negative traits go away by themselves. First of all, base yourself in a heart of kindness and of patience. Then identity the behavior you want to change, every time it appears. Point out the alternative, open the new road. When the negative stuff rises again, ignore it. Stroke the positive, most importantly, don't label the person, in this case the living beings inside your mind, as right or wrong. Don't reject them because they misbehaved in the past. Patiently praise the positive. In time they'll come around," said Heng Chau.

"I should for the sake of one living being, in every country, in every world of the ten directions, pass through inexpressible, inexpressible aeons to teach and transform and bring him to maturity. In this way for a single being, so too will I act for all beings, never feeling fatigue, nor abandoning them and taking leave."

Ten Practices Chapter
Avatamsaka Sutra

Heng Chau • November 12, 1978
Too much was just enough

Bowing reflection in the early dawn: all sickness comes from greed, anger ushers in all disasters, and ignorance gives birth to the myriad sufferings.

Good health and long life are the blessings of morality. In Samadhi, every day is happy and heaven and earth know peace, and, when wisdom opens and lets go, it fills up the universe and all the suffering is over.

"He vows that every living being attain the measureless light (of wisdom) that universally radiates the Proper Dharma of all Buddhas."

Ten Transferences Chapter
Avatamsaka Sutra

Yesterday, offerings of warm clothes and bedding arrived. "Oh, this is too much, too much! It's as hot as mid-summer," I thought, and fretted. Basically, there was no problem, but I went ahead and made one and tied myself up in knots of afflictions, fearing the burden of too many things.

Overnight, it turned bitter cold. The "too much" clothes and blankets were just what was needed. The only excess was my hang-ups and worried thoughts. The clothes and bedding were just right.

Truly "everything is okay." It is the mad mind that makes trouble. Subdue and overcome the mind and all problems vanish.

> When thought stirs, the ten thousand matters come up;
> When thought stops, the myriad matters vanish.
>
> Ch'an Verse

* * *

"Hell of Boiling Excrement"

Dream: A group of the most-advanced minds in the field of human psychology meet with an enlightened Master and some Sanghans in a small apartment. The psychologists are pushing beyond the frontiers into the unknown regions of the mind via direct, personal experience and drug experimentation. The leader is young, bright, and dedicated. He is the intellectual scion of one of the big-names in modern psychology.

The sage off-handedly describes a "state" where, "...as the sun rises it shines through the hole in the center of a bright orange, unmoving cloud. The light illumines everything and pervades everywhere..." The leader jumps up from his chair, all excited, and says, "You are describing the central vision of the highest state achieved from the use of an ancient drug – a drug that promises to break down the wall between body and mind, man and the cosmos. It produces an awareness of the total oneness of all things and ends all schizophrenia." He adds, "All splits in the human psyche are dissolved by this drug."

The psychologists are very excited. They had heard of such a drug and this "state," but had been unable to find or reach it themselves. They thought it was maybe just an ancient myth.

The sage is playful and smiling. He quotes verbatim, the key paragraph from the leader's latest thesis and simultaneously we all see the paragraph in our minds. "How could he have known!?" the leader asks, amazed. The Master goes on to quote the ancient name for the drug and the modern chemical derivation. The psychologist is totally beside himself by now.

> "Those who crave intoxicants will descend at death into the Hell of Boiling Excrement, and in succeeding lives be stupid, having lost their seed of wisdom. Intoxicants cause madness and confuse the spirit, affecting one as would a deadly poison. Therefore the text says, 'It would be better to drink molten copper!' Take care not to violate this precept against taking intoxicants."
>
> from The Shramanera Vinaya

[Note: "Intoxicants" refers to all intoxicating substances including: alcohol, marijuana, opium, depressants (unless medically prescribed), hallucinogens (LSD, peyote, mescaline, etc.), narcotics, stimulants ('speed,' amphetamines), inhalants (glue, etc.), tranquilizers, tobacco, and so forth.]

The old Master continues, "Oh, sure, that drug is no big deal. It isn't ultimate. Besides, few have the samadhi power to not be turned by its states. If you take it you are certain to catch a demon." People are on the edge of their seats and their minds. The Master then makes a gesture of ripping away something covering the heart with his hand. Everyone understands this wordless message: "Tear away all coverings over your true mind. This is total freedom and ultimate wisdom. Get rid of all marks, sweep away all Dharmas."

The old Master then speaks straight from the heart: "The highest state and realization is within your own nature, not outside. Cultivate precepts, samadhi, and wisdom. Investigate the Buddha-dharma, not drugs. When you attain genuine skill, then this drug you are seeking will be rendered quite useless and seem foolish to you. You will naturally have gone far beyond and entered wisdom deep as the sea. This is my wish for all of you." End of dream.

Heng Sure • November 13, 1978
A blend of circles and squares

"Standing Meditation"

Looks like nothin', sure ain't nothin'. This martial exercise stills the body outside, but moves the internal-energy in a way swimming, skiing, or three non-stop sets of tennis never could.

Standing meditation's posture is a blend of circles and squares: spine straight, arms encircled, outstretched, entire body relaxed, head erect, eyes focused eagle-like, on distant horizon, thoughts emptied, breathing natural and effortless. After standing, one feels invigorated, glowing with light, not winded and drained as after calisthenics or western-style sports. Standing gathers energy instead of dispersing it; it disciplines the boy, subdues the mind, and prolongs life. Sure ain't nothin'!!

Standing meditation is the final basic exercise we practice after doing the *tai ji* set every day. It's part of the traditional Chinese "soft martial arts" system. But soft means not mushy or feeble; soft means internal, yielding, cracking, vibrant, flowing, strength of water that can overcome and wash away hard granite mountains.

Standing meditation is called "the universal post" because the body must be aligned as straight as a lightning rod. It takes a trained, certified teacher to transmit and to correct the posture. Once I found "the spot" after months of patient coaching from Heng Chau. It felt like I had plugged in to a universal electrical outlet – kerzatz! went the energy.

Last month at Gold Wheel, the Venerable Abbot stepped on to the back porch while we practiced standing on the temple driveway. He playfully mimicked the standing pose, nodded his head and walked around, with his arms outstretched. Later, the Venerable Abbot spoke about standing meditation:

"The principles are the same as cultivation," he said. Somebody who can penetrate this *gung fu* can enter samadhi.

Hearing the Master's approval gave our standing meditation a big boost and increased our understanding of the parameters of cultivation.

Bit by bit we're learning that when the mind is concentrated, without scattered, extraneous thoughts, then everything one does is part of proper concentration and proper reception.

"When one connects, all connect," says the proverb, and we're finding it true amid our myriad practices.

> "All of these Bodhisattvas used various understandings, various paths, various doors, various entrances... as expedient means to enter into the sea of the Buddha's spiritual transformations."
>
> Entering the Dharma Realm
> Avatamsaka Sutra

Heng Chau • November 13, 1978
The dust motes that settle day by day

Listening to my thoughts come and go like the ebb and flow sounds of passing cars. I don't know where they come from or where they are going. Like the cars, thoughts pass without pause and leave no trace.

> The strength of the mind and what it thinks
> Gives birth to all kinds of dharmas.
> They quickly pass away without an instant's pause.
> In thought after thought, that's how it is.
>
> The Bodhisattvas Ask for Clarification Chapter
> Avatamsaka Sutra

At the end of day we sit in meditation in the back of the station wagon. The setting sun slants long shafts of light in the windows. The incense smoke curls, mixing gladly with the dusty air. There is something very peaceful and liberating about sitting quietly in a still and empty place, watching dust motes float and turn in a still and empty place, watching dust motes float and turn in a beam of sunlight. The still and empty place is our true mind, the clear sunlight is the Buddha's wisdom, and the dust motes are useless thoughts that settle day by day.

Heng Chau • November 13, 1978
Just try your best to die

Dear Shr Fu,

Today the Master and a bus-full of bright-eyed Dharma friends came from the City of Ten Thousand Buddhas to give the bowing monks "a little gasoline" as the Master put it. How did we run out of fuel? I ran out of fuel by looking at women. Then I got sick. When the Master stepped down from the yellow dragon bus he started whisking away our obstacles and afflictions. "I heard from Kuo Chou you were sick. I asked him if you had died. He said no. So because you haven't died yet, I have come to see you. If you had died, I wouldn't have come. Do you understand?" The Master's strange words went straight to my heart. Finally, I understood. This is the whole story.

I should have left home the first time I came to Gold Mountain Monastery almost three years ago. I had returned to my true home and knew this was where I belonged. But I couldn't put down my selfish desire. So I turned my back on enlightenment and reunited with the dust. As a layman the purity and happiness I experienced at Gold Mountain was soon exhausted every time I went back home. Soon after I got all afflicted and hung-up, trying to act like a cultivator at home. I was trying to cultivate the Way and romance at the same time. It didn't work. At the peak of this self-inflicted crisis, with my girlfriend threatening to leave, I called Shr Fu expecting sympathy. The Master wasted no words or phony emotion. "So!? So she leaves. Good. No one is dying are they? Don't have any false thoughts or attachments." The Master warned me to be careful and act according to principle. I did not listen. I just couldn't cut off my desire and so things got worse and my "sickness" drained my spiritual strength.

When I left home, the Master remarked, "I believe you can leave home and cultivate the Way because you have put down your girl-friend. Be vigorous and advance!" Then Shr Fu addressed all the monks present informally and kindly, "You can't be sloppy or casual, especially now in America. This is the only way Buddhism will be established in the West. Most important, don't attach to women... that is the most important example for you to show America. You can't be too close to women or too far away or you're wrong. You are all my precious jewels. I won't sell any one of you. Don't waste your light-treasure!" Did I understand? No.

In the beginning of the bowing pilgrimage my false thoughts about women brought a hornet's nest of troubles. Bad dreams and demons, harsh weather and hassles all came because of this *mau bing* (sickness) of mine I believe. For example, in Santa Barbara, while false thinking about an old girlfriend, a lemon flew off of a passing garbage truck and hit me in the jaw, sending me to my knees. I said to myself, "Just a coincidence. If it really hit me because of my mind for women, then if I keep on thinking about them it should happen again." So I went on wondering if my old girlfriend had found another man and ZAP! Another lemon hit me square in the back, knocking me down again! Later the Master said, "Those sour lemons were from your sour thoughts about your girlfriend. Now that you know that your false-thinking isn't okay, don't do it any more." Did I understand? No.

In Malaysia I couldn't subdue my eyes or thoughts and got turned upside down. But this time my fuel reserves of merit and virtue were used up. I got so sick as a result of scattering all my energy by false thinking about women I nearly died. Shr Fu saved my life and brought me back from King Yama. While I was bedridden in Malacca, I saw clearly as never before, in my dreams and waking thoughts, that sexual desire is the root of birth and death. The Master would come to my bedside, rub my head and recite mantras, at the critical times, breaking the fever and purging toxins. All the while he kept smiling and asking, "Good, good. Did you die yet? Are you going to die?" In Singapore and Hong Kong the cause and effect of my false thinking and getting sick was uncanny and undeniable. Less than an hour after my mind would move I would become sick. The Master kept saying, "Sick again? Good. I hope you die soon." Did I understand? I thought so. But habits are stubborn and my ignorance deep. It is hard to "die" even when you try your best. Never again I vowed, never again would I run out to beautiful forms.

When we returned to the U.S., Heng Sure and I began bowing near Santa Cruz. We went into town to contact the police and inform them of our journey. Surprise! The cop was a woman. I got turned and started smiling and rapping with her in the course of conducting our official business. That night I took ill again. Either my mind for women was going to die or I was. It now was clear to me that *all* desire was at root just sexual desire. Running outside one's own nature and seeking anything is death – the slow death of outflowing. Literally, the blessings and wisdom of the original nature dribble away until all that is left of one's bright Dharma jewel is dog shit. It is just like it says in the Avatamsaka:

> Moreover, living beings are bound in a net of love.
> They are covered over with ignorance
>   and attached to their existence.
> They follow it and cannot give it up.
> They enter into a cage of suffering
>   and do the deeds of demons.
> Their blessings and wisdom are exhausted
>   and they forever harbor doubts.
> They do not seek the place of peace and tranquility.

They do not know the path of escape,
    and without rest they turn
On the wheel of birth and death.
They constantly bob and sink in the suffering mud.

I've had a lot of time while slowly recovering in the back of the Plymouth to reflect on my "sickness" and how to get well. What I took for happiness in the world is really suffering; and what I once thought to be suffering (cultivating) is really happiness. Things aren't always what they seem. So it says,

"I do not seek the unsurpassed Path for myself, nor do I cultivate Bodhi Practices in order to seek the states of the five desires or the many kinds of bliss in the three realms of existence. Why? Of all the happiness in the world, there is none which is not suffering…"

Avatamsaka Sutra
Ten Transferences Chapter

That is straight talk! In my heart, in ways no words could express, I now know this is so. This is what the Master meant when he asked when I was going to "die". His words were full of compassion and wisdom. It is the false mind that runs outside after desire that must die to cure the sickness of birth and death. The Master's words were the finest of medicines. "When your mind for women dies, then you can be free. If you can't kill it then you'll always be locked up in a cage. Do you understand?"

"Yes, Shr Fu," I answered, "I tried to, but I didn't quite pull it off."

"I'm a lousy teacher. I can't teach and transform my disciples. All I can do is talk unlucky talk and say I wish they would die," said the Master with a kind smile.

I write to tell the whole story so no one will think the Master's words were inauspicious. I am a lousy disciple. Even after the Master saved my life, I can't manage to "die". So, Shr Fu and all our Dharma friends braved the cold and rain to bring a little "gas" to the bowing monks. "Try your best," grinned the Master as everyone climbed back aboard the bus. A storm that had been gathering suddenly broke up and the sun shone down on all of us. I was so grateful I wanted to cry. Truly we are *all* one heart bowing to the City of Ten Thousand Buddhas! Then I had this thought, "Just try your best, Kuo T'ing. Don't cry, just die."

Like Bodhidharma liberated the bird in the cage, the Master has shown me a way to escape from the cage. But mistaking what's before my eyes I have flown back in mistaking the cage for a palace. No more. The beginning of returning to health is to know that you're sick. To be reborn in the Way one must die to the world.

Peace in the Way,
Disciple Guo Ting (Heng Chau)
bows in respect

Heng Sure • November 14, 1978
Like sleepwalkers, lost in dreams

"In the Movie"

On the plane coming from Asia I peeked at the in-flight movie. My mind has changed. I used to be a big cinema fan. How come I never noticed how phony the whole motion-picture trip is? The films on the screen were so hokey! The actors looked stiff and unnatural; bored, even. The story was gimmicked, unreal, unimportant. To enter it took a huge gulp of faith from the audience. On both sides of the screen the experience was total make-believe.

> Whether false or unreal,
> Whether false or not false.
> Mundane and world-transcending
> Are only the prattle of false words.

The Bodhisattvas Ask for Clarification Chapter
Avatamsaka Sutra

Realized then that we common people must look like actors in a film when a Sage sees us through unattached, enlightened eyes. We must look like sleepwalkers, lost in dreams. Like puppets following the script of our habits we obey the cues of our karma, follow our desires, and bind ourselves in costumes of afflictions and thoughts. The Sage must experience a rare sorrow to know life in the Triple World is only a play and see us taking the show as real.

"...And here we are, dreaming within a dream, having returned on our vows to do the work of the Buddha."

Venerable Master Hua

Heng Chau • November 14, 1978
Let it all drift by

"Crossing Over Afflictions"

When I become worried, angry, jealous or uptight, I reflect, "Afflictions have no door, you yourself enter them. Simply let go of the angry and jealous mind. Throw out the worried, uptight thoughts. Cast off the false and the true returns by itself. Cut through the net of coverings with a single swing of the wisdom-sword and free the Bodhi-mind!"

"It is in order to cut through the net of all afflictions and to purify the nature of All-wisdom that he brings forth the Bodhi-mind."

The Merit and Virtue From
First Bringing Forth the Mind Chapter
Avatamsaka Sutra

Then I tell myself: "No matter what state appears, good or bad, bitter or sweet, don't mix or get afflicted. Value your energy, and store it in a deep pool. Take kindness and compassion as your food; take joy and giving as your function. What's worth a second of worry or doubt? Such a waste, jealousy and anger! Lay your troubles down

and let it all drift by. Gently roll along, sing this lullaby to the Buddha
in your mind.

> Namo Guan Shi Yin Pu Sa,
> Namo Guan Shi Yin Pu Sa.

Take it as it comes, leave it when it goes; as the flower drops a
petal, as a pine tree droops a cone.

Heng Sure • November 15, 1978
But the curtain always fell

"Real Theatre"

Used to enjoy acting in high school theatre productions.
Bringing imaginary characters to life let me expand my mind and
seek a true self. Portraying people born from playwrights' pens, I
dared let go of my adolescent hang-ups and absorb myself
completely in the make-believe roles. Within the "safe" limits of the
script, I was free to enter the character's personality and to explore
his relationships. I could drop my habits and inhibitions, and briefly,
find a new identity in the fantasy world on stage.

But the curtain always fell, the spotlights dimmed and died, the
applause stopped. All alone after the show, I faced the uncertain
reality of "who am I really?" once more. No matter what play or the
role, acting never lit up the true heart. Pretending to be somebody
else ultimately was as meaningless and as empty as the dusty coats on
the costume rack. Attaching to the false people I portrayed on stage
postponed and obstructed the growth of the true person within.

> All disciples of the Buddha in this way know:
> The nature of all dharmas is always empty and still.
> There is not a single dharma which can be created,
> And just like all Buddhas, they awaken to "no self."
>
> Ten Transferences Chapter
> Avatamsaka Sutra

Reviewed the lessons of the theatre this week while bowing and discovered a satisfaction and joy difficult to describe. Acting spotlighted a need all people share: to develop a true self, to find our original face. But only the Buddhadharma reveals the ultimate truth: there is no self to find. All dharmas are empty and false. The personalities we create in our "real" lives are as illusory as the characters I portrayed on stage. Left-home Buddhist disciples face the truth and cast off all traces of individual ego: name, possessions, family ties, credit ratings, phone listings, distinctive clothing, jewelry, and personality props of all kinds. Bhikshus shave their heads and retire from the stage of the world. Adorned with the precept sash and following ancient rules of deportment, cultivators take the Dharma as their original scripts, and Bodhisattva's practices as their basic directions. Teaching and transforming living beings with kindness and compassion becomes their eternal living theater.

And most satisfying of all, upon enlightenment, the light of wisdom penetrates the curtain of forms. Bodhisattvas reunite with all creation. They leave discriminations of self and others far behind, like faded cloaks on the costume rack. The boundaries of the stage vanish. Roles, curtains, actor and audience merge into one great, level, equal, illusory reality.

> "Bodhisattvas should contemplate that all dharmas are like illusions, like dreams, like shadows, like echoes, like the moon's reflection in water, like images in a mirror, like flames, like transformations; therefore, they are all level and equal."
>
> Ten Grounds Chapter
> Avatamsaka Sutra

Heng Chau • November 15, 1978
Transforming the multi-headed serpent

Subduing the mind of desire is like severing one of the heads of Hydra (a nine-headed serpent in Greek mythology, slain by Hercules. Each head, when cut off, was replaced with two others unless the wound was cauterized). Reduce desire in one area and it rears up twice as strong in another. Cultivation becomes a war of attrition, a slow, painstaking battle of backbone over greed. With practice, the multi-headed serpent is subdued; with patience, each wound is cauterized and forever closed. Our teacher told us:

> Principle fights with desire; only practice decides.
> And patience is always victorious.

The Master stood by the highway as diesel trucks went roaring by, sucking up and slapping our long robes and sashes with their wind. Behind us, yellow rain-slicked farm crews harvested brussel sprouts in the early morning, dew-wet, green fields. The Master went on:

> "If you can cut off your mind of desire, then you'll be free. If you cannot, then you'll never escape from the cage."

Although the Master says "cut off," he really means "change," for cultivation is an exercise in transformation, and patient remodeling. Purity cannot be forced. Force is against the Way. Cultivators don't put down others, they put down the self. They don't seek purity. They simply do not let desires and false thoughts disturb it, because the nature is already pure and needs no cleansing. Sending desires away, the mind and spirit of themselves return to purity.

And so it is right within the world that we learn to transcend the world. We are taught to purify our minds and cultivate good roots in the middle of a busy marketplace, on a jet plane, amid the din and clamor of the traffic jams, rush hours, and all worldly dharmas.

"Bodhisattvas intensely and diligently cultivate all good roots which then become accomplished... through not abandoning all worldly matters, yet accomplishing the way of world transcendence."

Ten Grounds Chapter
Avatamsaka Sutra

Heng Sure • November 16, 1978
Seagulls can fly, but they are not free

"Wings"

Seagulls aren't free. Cultivators are truly free. Osprey and pelicans can fly but know only the liberty of the air. Cultivators cast off the chains of body and mind and soar to ultimate freedom, freedom from birth and death.

We had a regular lunch guest this week: a one-legged herring gull showed up promptly every day at eleven for bread crumbs. We moved up the coast a mile per day; the one-pin gull tracked our progress and swooped down on the Plymouth, beak open, eyes bright, unafraid. Heng Chau tossed him moldy bread crust and apple cores while reciting the Great Compassion Mantra. The bird got nourishment for both body and soul at once. We got a Dharma-lesson on independence.

Contemplated the gull's state: bound in feathers, stifled by a walnut-sized brain, deaf to Dharma-speech, short one leg, he has very few choices. The gull is a slave to survival. He eats, calls, mates, and dies. He can't hold precept; he's unable to give, unable to meditate. Result: in this life he can earn no blessings, no wisdom, and no freedom.

Some people feel that freedom comes from doing as they please. "I don't bow to no man," says the western maverick. Other people see bowing as un-American, as slavish idolatry. It's come clear to us that the path of discipleship itself is a brand-new idea in the west.

What makes people noble and different from seagulls? We can worship the Tao, we can give ourselves up to the Holy and the Pure, and we can humble our minds before true disciples. The more we dare let go our selfish "me-centered" thoughts, the closer we come to true independence. Returning our lives to the Buddha, bowing to the Dharma, and offering our hair, clothes, and habits to the Sangha's disciplined order may look at first like voluntarily clipping our wings. But karma is the ultimate cage. Until living beings cut off thoughts and empty emotions, our karma pins us to the wheel of rebirth; we are no freer than the crippled gull, which gobbles our breadcrumbs. The measure of our freedom is how much of ourselves we are able to surrender.

And only a person who is fully in charge of his life can truly give himself away. Taking refuge with the Triple Jewel opens the door of the big cage. By returning our lives as disciples, by holding precepts, practicing Ch'an meditation, and opening wisdom, we escape our worldly shackles, and fly free of birth and death. Our precept sashes are wings of liberation.

> No karma and no affliction,
> Without possessions or a dwelling place,
> They neither illuminate nor practice anything.
> They travel in level equality through the world.
>
> The Bodhisattvas Ask for Clarification Chapter
> Avatamsaka Sutra

Heng Chau • November 16, 1978
The Dharma is also spoken with deeds

Note with money left on the car by two elderly people: "Gassho. A small gift from a couple of Zen Buddhists. We thought it might help for gasoline for the car."

* * *

"Making Living Beings Happy"

The Master and a busload of good Dharma-friends drove out from the City of Ten Thousand Buddhas. They came to cheer us up and to lift our sagging spirits. Singing songs and serving food, amid laughter and Dharma talks, they chased away my lingering case of the flu and brought joy to body, mind, and soul. The Master leaned over during lunch and told us,

"You know, quite a few of the Assembly are sick themselves and should be in bed, but they wanted to come out anyway to cheer you up. They got up at two o'clock this morning to prepare food and offerings to bring you."

After they left, Heng Sure and I sat on the open car tailgate, back-to-back, staring blankly out across the long fields to the sea. Our pens lay frozen in our hands. No words, no thoughts. Just full of gratitude and happiness. Finally we shook our heads to break the spell of being left speechless, smiled an unspoken grin of thanks, and went back to bow. The Dharma is spoken with words; it is also spoken with deeds. Today, the ninth vow of Samantabhadra (Universal Worthy) was skillfully explained: according with living beings. By making living beings happy, Bodhisattvas are making all Thus Come Ones happy. Without fatigue or a thought of self, they use the heart of great compassion to constantly honor, serve, and protect living beings. In this way they perfect the making of offerings to all Buddhas. The magic of Dharma-friends is truly rare!

With all advisors good and wise who aid me.
By explaining Samantabhadra's deeds,
I vow to always congregate together.
May they never be displeased with me.

Universal Worthy's Conduct and Vows
Avatamsaka Sutra

Heng Sure • November 17, 1978
A simple bamboo cup of rice

"Confucius Praised Him"

The Ancients were people like us who explored their minds. They faced states, turned obstacles and tasted the same joys and fears that have come to cultivators throughout time. It's thrilling to walk the same road, to step into the path of the worthy ones of time past. The pages of classics and Sutras spring to life and the voices of Sagely teachers resound as they exhort their disciples to diligence and sincerity. The texts record the questions, answers, and methods of Masters and the difficulties we meet every day. How often have I found strength in this realization: "Not only am I meeting resistance in seeing through my pretenses, Confucius' disciples did too! The Way is timeless. Seeing the Nature and lighting up the mind has always been the toughest challenge of a lifetime. I'm not alone in my attachments!"

Two passages in Mencius encourage me on to be diligent in subduing food desire. Mencius scolded Le Cheng for attending the assembly purely for the good eats and drinks. I know how ashamed the disciple felt. "I would not have thought that you, having learned the Tao of the Ancients, would have acted with a view for eating and drinking," said his teacher. Le Cheng experienced difficulty when he faced the animal nature in his own person. Taming desire was hard for the ancients too.

But some found the strength to truly put it down:

> "The disciple Yen, in an age of confusion, dwelt in a mean, narrow lane, having his single bamboo cup of rice and one gourd dish of water. Other men could not have endured this distress, but he did not allow his joy to be affected by it. Confucius praised him."

Mencius

Heng Chau • November 17, 1978
The nine contemplations of the body

"Monkey Mind"

Bowing, copying out the sutra, and sitting long in meditation are becoming more vital than food and sleep. Little things we once performed so casually and unaware, such as eating, talking, driving to town for gas, drain energy and scatter the magic. But once out on the open highway, next to the rolling hills and vast sea, the energy renews itself. Bowing repentance and reform, sitting in quiet stillness, the magic returns. Trying to quiet my restless mind is the hardest and most rewarding work I've ever done. Truly, the mind is like a monkey.

> "The mad mind is like a monkey. The monkey is always looking for something to do. If you haven't any work to give it, it runs off East and West. If you give the mind some work to do, such as reciting sutras and holding mantras, then it will strike up less false thinking, and the money won't run off."
>
> commentaries to the Avatamsaka Sutra
> by Master Hua

Just when the monkey is subdued and the magic's in the making, the tests arrive. This morning a woman approached me while bowing. She put money before me, then stood in front of me waiting for a response. I immediately sensed this was not above board. Her manner and energy were improper. I recited mantras and also waited. She left, but then returned later with food and began bowing next to me. Again I didn't directly look at her or converse. I continued to recite mantras to resist her compelling, drawing out power. My eyelids fluttered under pressure, but the monkey did not run off, and soon the woman left.

* * *

A family from San Luis followed our car half-way across town, waiting for us to stop, so they could make an offering. They finally caught us hosing the dust and seagull droppings off the Plymouth at a local coin-op carwash.

"We saw you back in San Luis, our hometown, and are so happy to see you're still at it and looking so good. We support your purpose one hundred per cent and only wish we would do more than donate some groceries. Our hearts are with you all the time though. It's a good thing you are doing for the world," said the father as he loaded our car with bags of groceries. They were on their way to a family outing: mom, dad, grandma and grandpa, and too many kids to count. They spotted us on the freeway, followed for an hour, and then sent the children to buy food offerings when they saw us stop at the carwash.

"Good luck. We're with you all the way. Hope we didn't disturb your concentration." They smiled, waved, and drove away.

* * *

"Portrait of a Master"

We are situated on a high cliff overlooking the sea. Sitting down for lunch, I look up at a small framed picture hanging in the window. It is a picture of the Master at age nineteen. The glass frame is filled with a reflection from the tall swaying grass, dry brush, the blue sea and empty space. I can't see the Master's image. An ineffable joy and understanding comes through me. A big smile and the thought, "That is a Master! No name, no face, no self. Not different or apart from all things."

"He spoke the Dharma of all Buddhas' level non-duality."

Entering the Dharma Realm
Avatamsaka Sutra

* * *

"See It Clearly"

"If you are attached, you can't be liberated. This means you have to put it down in order to be free; as long as you can't put it down, you won't be free. How do you put it down? You must see right through it; see it for what it really is. Then you can put it aside. If you can't see through it, you won't be able to put it down."

Venerable Master Hua

See through what? See through forms. In Chinese, the character for forms and sexual desire is the same. Before coming upon the Buddha-dharma, I used to imagine my body or that of a beautiful woman I was attracted to as rapidly going through old age, ill health, and death. I could visualize all the gory details based on my hospital orderly days and memories of the morgue. I don't know why I envisioned the body decaying and going to worms. The contemplation arose spontaneously, as if to put things in perspective. Far from morbid wallowing, the reflection left me clear-headed and seemed to put me back in touch with my true self.

Today I found these contemplations in Sutras and Shastras: they are almost identical to the homemade contemplation that I fashioned on my own. Perhaps I was just remembering a Dharma I had heard long ago and was not really coming up with anything new at all. Plato said that learning is just remembering, and an ancient author wrote, "In the Tao, the only motion is returning."

"As you look at the most beautiful woman, you realize that eventually she will die, she will get old."

There are Nine Contemplations:

– Time faction. When that lovely woman dies, her body will first swell up.

– The body will turn a mottled green color.

– It will start to rot.

– It will break open and discharge blood.

– It will discharge rotten flesh and pus.

– It will be devoured by birds and beast and insects.

– Its remains will be in a dismembered condition.

– Finally, it will be nothing but a skeleton.

– It will eventually turn into ashes.

The body is basically impure. Male or female, it's just a filthy form and not at all different from a leaking bag of garbage. Seeing it clearly, then what is there to lust after and want to embrace? The Avatamsaka also has a contemplation for seeing through the attachment to the body:

"If the body were pure conduct, then we should know that pure conduct would not be wholesome, would not be Dharma; that it would be turbid, stinking, evil, and impure; that it would be disgusting, contrary, mixed up and defiled; that it would be a dead corpse an ultimately, a heap of worms."

Brahma Conduct Chapter

Contemplating the body in this way reduces desires and chases confusion. Cultivation takes on new interest while an attractive and comfortable body loses all its meaning.

Heng Sure • November 18, 1978
He resolved the great matter all by himself

Contemplated the Buddha's independence as I bowed, all alone between the cliffs and the sea. Felt an invigorating thrill in the heart, as brisk as the breeze off the white caps. Enlightenment is a 100-percent do-it-yourself challenge. But cultivators rely on the Buddha's spirit of fearlessness and renunciation as guides on the journey out of the Triple Realm.

"They vow that living beings set themselves on the independent throne and attain sovereignty within the Dharma."

Ten Transferences Chapter
Avatamsaka Sutra

When the Buddha sat beneath the Bodhi Tree he had only his skill and determination to rely on. He applied effort and resolved the great matter – birth and death – all by himself. Cultivators depend on nothing outside the mind. Yet we do have the Buddha's example of courage; further, we have the Sagely advice of a Good Advisor. In this way we are more fortunate than the Buddha himself – our models of heroic independence lead us out of fears and attachments all the way to the source of our minds.

Heng Chau • November 18, 1978
The seeds do not know each other

"Seeking the Buddha's great wisdom, he cultivates great renunciation."

Ten Grounds Chapter
Avatamsaka Sutra

It's clear that progress through the stages of meditation, at the bare minimum, means no desire. Desire and wisdom are mutually exclusive. We can't have both. Renunciation makes room for the light of wisdom. The loss is small; the gain is great.

Today all was quiet, no one for miles. Then suddenly, four people joined us at once. There was a young bohemian-hip couple, bedecked in clothes from ten different countries and time periods; Ray, a leathery, one-eye fifty year old sawmill worker; and Stephen, a living-on-a-shoestring photographer from a "teeney-weenie newspaper in a small town few people ever heard of."

As disparate as we were on the surface, there was that much likeness underneath. Everyone felt a coming together of deep and distant paths. As we stood together on the side of the highway, there was a familiarity that spoke of strong affinities.

It seems nothing happens without previous causes and conditions. Whether good or bad, auspicious or ill-fated, when the time is ripe, all the loose strands find each other and reconnect as if out of empty space. Karma is just that way.

> It's like the seeds planted in a field:
> The seeds do not know each other,
> Yet they naturally grow forth by themselves.
> And the nature of karma is the same.
>
> The Bodhisattvas Ask for Clarification Chapter
> Avatamsaka Sutra

With body, mouth, and thought we plant seeds in life after life. Some are good, some are bad, some are a little of both. The seeds do not know each other, and yet when conditions mature, the seeds grow forth and united to produce a harvest. Ray had been thinking about stopping for three weeks. Stephen, the journalist, said he couldn't shake the thought for two weeks to come out and do a story. The young couple acted on an impulse while driving by. Each person a different seed growing by itself, yet at exactly the right moment, we all found ourselves sharing the same field, and part of the same crop.

Heng Sure • November 19, 1978
The dangerous roads of birth and death

"Murder Capital"

The gentle, wooded mountains just to the East are known in the sensational journals as "murder capital, U.S.A." Numerous hatchet slayings, shotgun massacres, missing persons found dismembered and stuffed in grocery sack: these woods hide such horrors. The Santa Cruz-Ben Lomond Mountain forests carry a queer energy that fosters violent death and keeps the scandal sheets in business. Only the unwary hitchhike these roads any more; college students pair up at the student union ride-boards before traveling north from Santa Cruz.

We heard the stories for years in the Bay Area news, and knowing our journey carried us through "murder capital, U.S.A.," we could only shrug and bow on in faith, three steps at a time. We've found that a straight mind is the only safe refuge in the world. Thoughts of anger and harming transform a quiet highway into a nightmare alley. Kind and compassionate thoughts gain the protection of Bodhisattvas and good spirits.

A passage from the Avatamsaka opened my mind to the actual state of the Saha World. There's not a single safe road to be found anywhere outside a purified mind.

As we think, so do we receive our retribution. The road outside is mapped by the mind within.

> "All living beings are within the dangerous roads of birth and death, and are about to fall into the hells, animals, and hungry ghosts. They enter the net of evil views. Confused by the thick forest of stupidity, they follow deviant paths and practice inverted conduct. Like blind people who lack guides, roads which do not lead to escape, they think lead to escape."
>
> Ten Transferences Chapter
> Avatamsaka Sutra

The Sutra tells it straight: most of us not only walk perilous roads, but do so blindly. With each step, we create offenses that jeopardize body and life. We break the rules, follow passions, fight for nickels and dimes, and listen to bad friends who steer us onto dead-end paths and lull us into the dream sleep of confusion.

> "They enter into the states of demons and are seized by evil bandits. They accord with the demon mind and become far removed from the Buddha's will."
>
> Ten Transferences Chapter
> Avatamsaka Sutra

Who walks these dangerous roads? My parents, brothers, friends, and neighbors. Every being within the Triple Realm, including the gods in the heavens, turn their backs on the Buddha's will and fall into the hands of bandits with each defiled thought. This is the original murder story, too true and too painful for even the seamiest scandal-sheet to print. Only the fearless wisdom-eye of the Avatamsaka dares reveal the actual "murder capital" of the Saha world: the afflicted mind of living beings.

Bodhisattvas read the road map and fully informed, wise to its dangers, risk the peril in order to guide beings safely through the dense forest.

"I should pull them out of such danger and difficulty and cause them to dwell in the fearless city of all wisdom."

Ten Transferences Chapter
Avatamsaka Sutra

Bodhisattvas say to murderers and victims alike both inside and outside his mind,

"Do no evil, offer up good conduct, and purify the mind. Cut off desire and cast out love. Seek the Buddha's high road; it's right within the mind."

Heng Chau • November 19, 1978
Every one of us by nature is alone

"Breakthrough"

Feels like I've been climbing a long, tall mountain struggling for every inch of ascent against gravity, oxygen, and my own inertia and frailties. Pushing to reach an invisible summit of the psyche, and to conquer this mountain of desire and grasping attachment that ties me to the ground.

"He vows that all living beings reach the peak of the earth, that they attain All-wisdom, ultimately get the ten powers, and break through the summit of the desire realm."

Ten Transferences Chapter
Avatamsaka Sutra

For as long as I could remember, I thought I needed a mate, a partner, in order to be happy and complete. Yet no relationship ever brought happiness or felt complete. Last night in meditation I reached a place I always feared I couldn't bear to face: I saw that every one of us by nature is alone.

"No-dwelling is the basic nature of human beings."

Sixth Patriarch Sutra

A gate inside my mind gave way and opened. A huge smile that came all the way from my belly, filled my face and heart. I was happy beyond words. The mountain I labored to scale was a single, confused thought, lodged in my own mind, a single grain of sand that weighed down like the earth itself on my spirit. When the thought let go its hold, the sunlit, snowy peak appeared. Breakthrough. I wanted nothing and knew contentment.

"He who has once known the contentment that comes simply through being content, will never again be otherwise than contented."

Lao Tzu

Sitting in the open door of the car, silently looking out at the vast sea and the tall trees on the distant hills. A few hours of daylight remain, judging by the sun. The long ribbon of coast highway stretches and fades to a hairline trace of the far cliffs across the bay. Many miles to go before reaching the City of Ten Thousand Buddhas. But that's somewhere many tomorrows from now and just yesterday seems already so far away. Right now is all I need to make me happy.

Retired deep in the mountains,
Dwelling in a still place,
Secluded far on a lonely cliff beneath the tall pines,
I stroll and sit in quietness,
    a monk at home in the wilderness,
Filled with stillness and peace,
    living in true lightheartedness.

                      from Song of Enlightenment
                      by Great Master Yung Chia

Bowing reflections at the close of day: Buddhism takes us back to the root and returns us to the source. The source is without a mark of self or others, totally unattached and liberated. The root is our original nature: the Buddha-mind. Thus our natural home is enlightenment and our true family is the Thus Come One's household. This family embraces all things and includes all beings. It is only natural that we would want to return to our roots and go back home.

"He vows that all beings leave the common worldly home-life and dwell in the Thus Come One's family."

                      Ten Transferences Chapter
                      Avatamsaka Sutra

The ultimate act of filiality is leaving home to cultivate the Way. By going beyond the bonds and limitations of the common family we mutually free each other to return to our original, pure nature. Leaving home is a heroic deed that can liberate boundless beings. Liberation begins with one's own family and doesn't end until all beings everywhere reach the Buddha Way.

"He vows that all beings liberate themselves from the bond of the family life and that they enter the Buddhadharma which is not a family dharma, and that they cultivate pure conduct."

                      Ten Transferences Chapter
                      Avatamsaka Sutra

Heng Sure • November 20, 1978
An illusory heap of wrong ideas

"Personality"

Been watching personality habits rise and return for years now.
In the stillness of bowing and Ch'an the mind's patterns jell and crys-
tallize like a photo print in the fixer-tray, the way the black and white
contrasts rise gradually on the blank paper. In my mind the rising
patterns seem to be living beings, like play characters, or people in a
novel. I've identified seven different personalities that appear in turn
within. Are they real? It's hard to tell. The mind's states are infinite
and subtle. The Buddha teaches that the personality is made of
illusory heaps of wrong ideas, called skandhas.

> The realm of all beings is within the three periods of time.
> All beings past, present, and future
> > are within the five skandhas.
> All skandhas take karma as their basis.
> All karma takes the mind as its basis.
> The dharmas of the mind are just like illusions.
> All the mundane world is the same.
>
> > Praises in the Suyama Heaven Palace
> > Avatamsaka Sutra

Recently I began to label and name my inner characters just to
keep track, and to gain some control over my personality.

I've got an ego-shadow I call the Kid, and one called the Cop.
There's a doctor-image, a wizard, a critic, a knight, and a star-politi-
cian. They have strengths and flaws, entrances and exits, dislikes,
limitations, and favorite styles. What are they? False thoughts. My
attempt to use consciousness to understand and to enter the
Buddha's wisdom is a dead-end expedient means, like adding a head
on top of a head. The only result is sure to be increased attachments
and deeper confusion in the long run.

"When the Bodhisattva Who Contemplates At Ease was practicing the profound Prajna Paramita, he illuminated the five skandhas and saw that they are all empty, and he crossed beyond all suffering and difficulty."

Heart Sutra

I suspect my mind attaches to the skandhas and creates the lineup of phony people inside just to avoid directly facing the truth that the entire world is empty and false. The ego-label scheme is a clever system of psychological inventory but in the light of true wisdom, it's puny and false and one more obstacle to entering genuine concentration. Why do I run from wisdom's proper view? Why do I refuse to walk the bridge that "crosses beyond all suffering and difficulty?"

The dharmas of the three periods
    and the five skandhas,
When named, bring the world into being.
When they are extinguished, the world is gone.
In this way, they are only false names.

Praises in the Suyama Heaven Palace
Avatamsaka Sutra

Because the names, labels, and familiar dharmas of the world are comforting, attachments and false thoughts in turn chain me to rounds of rebirth. But the personality depends on and dotes on his mind, like a child clutching his threadbare security blanket. Slowly, bit by bit, the dharmas of wisdom reveal my attachments as illusions, and show the personality as the bars of a cage, confining me to the prison of the Triple World.

"Do no false-thinking! With no thoughts there is no mind. With no mind there is no dwelling. With no dwelling there is no attachment. And no attachment is wonderful beyond words."

The Master delivered this teaching with the fearless Lion's Roar as we left Gold Wheel to begin our journey. The words haunt the mind, echoing, ringing, urging me to leave the narrow cave-dwelling of consciousness and enter the sparkling, sunlit world of the Buddha's wisdom.

Heng Chau • November 20, 1978
The old Plymouth fool

Coast notes… The ocean is impartial, like the Way. Seagulls are greedy like animals. Raining for two days solid. The car leaks oil out and leaks water in. The Plymouth is twenty-two years old, well past mandatory retirement for cars, and entitled to relax and naturally fall apart if it chooses. But it seems to have a mind of its own to see this pilgrimage through to the City of Ten Thousand Buddhas, come what may: summer droughts, winter typhoons, mud slides, forest fires, mountain detours, and beatings from flying beer bottles and angry pick-up trucks. It simply takes things as they come.

The car is constantly speaking Dharma. People pepper it with eggs, rotten tomatoes, even rocks and bottles, but it just lets them bounce off or dry up. Rammed or battered, it just goes back to sleep. It's sun-bleached, rusty, dented, and scraped outside, but the engine runs like a jewel and has power to spare. We fill its belly with crude-oil and cheap gasoline to keep it running at night and it defies the wind and rain like the fir and cypress trees. It saves its energy and gives no one any afflictions, like the Old Fool, intent on gaining the jewel within the wonderful and perfecting the Way.

> The Old Fool wears second-hand clothes,
> And fills his belly with tasteless food,
> Mends his clothes to keep out the cold,
> And thus the myriad things of life,
> According to what comes, are done.
> Scolded, the Old Fool merely says, "Fine."

Struck, the Old Fool lies down to sleep.
"Spit on my face, I just let it dry;
I save my strength and energy
    and give you no affliction."
Paramita is his style;
    he gains the jewel within the wonderful.
Know this news and then what worry is there
    of not perfecting the Way?

Maitreya Bodhisattva verse

Heng Sure • November 21, 1978
Concentration and sincerity

"Fire From the Sun-Pearl"

Steady rain for two days at Ano Nuevo. Our world is damp. Moisture hangs in the air, fills space, wet inside, wet outside. To the East, brown hills have turned dull gold. On the roadside, dried bushes and herbs have gone green.

Sunshine broke through clouds this morning. Within minutes, it sparked a dramatic turning: the wet haze heated and flashed – transformation – the world began to dry out. The moisture gradually evaporated from our sleeping bags, our slimy clothes, and our skin.

"When your concentration reaches the ultimate point of sincerity, then there can be a transformation."

Venerable Abbot Hua

Concentration transforms ignorance to wisdom in the same way. The pure water of precepts washes clean turbid emotions and undisciplined habits. The bright sun of Ch'an meditation heats the precept water to steam. Patient meditators wait with vajra-willpower until the process reaches a flash point – transformation – light and ease, clear seeing. A feeling of cool, proper energy fills the heart.

Sincerity is vigor; vigor is single-minded focusing, no extraneous thoughts. Stilling the monkey mind takes ultimate sincerity and crystal-clear focus. At that ultimate point, the Dharma of Ch'an concentration acts like a magnifying glass – the ancient Chinese name for it is "a sun-pearl," to bring the transforming fire to flame.

> Like a person with a magnifying glass (sun pearl),
> Who fails to focus on the tinder:
> The fire will never come to flame;
> And the lazy one is also thus.
>
> The Bodhisattvas Ask for Clarification Chapter
Avatamsaka Sutra

Heng Sure • November 21, 1978
The truth is right within the false

Venerable Master,

> The mother of heaven and earth
>   is said to be born from the Tao.
> The sun and the moon are both bright,
>   moving in their orbits.
> So it is with the basic substance
>   of all in creation:
> It is infinitely wonderful.
>
> Ch'an Master Hua

This poem came alive today, Shr Fu, as the sun rose on the rain-soaked coast. It's been raining for two days at Ano Nuevo. Everything in our world is damp. Moisture hangs in the air, saturating space without boundaries. It's wet outside the skin, wet inside our bones. The dusty hills have turned to dull gold, the sagebrush and the tall grasses have exploded in green. Everything is happy with the rain.

This morning the clouds blew away and the sun appeared. At nine a.m. there was a turning point; a transformation happened. The wetness began to flash, change, and disappear. You could see and feel the *yin*-moisture stage of the weather cycle reach its extreme and suddenly, dryness was born. Soon the water vapor left our slimy clothes, our sleeping bags, and the puddles on the ground.

Birth and change, *yin* and *yang*, happening all by itself, wonderful to see. All in its proper time. Nature is patient, the Tao contains all things.

Cultivating the Way has been called the great reversal. "Go towards the good," says the Master. "Return the light in every thought. Change your bad habits from evil to good. Find out your real self." This is what all Buddhist Sutras tell us. Because one who walks the Way turns back the energy that used to flow out in bad habits, soon the accumulated light will reach a flash-point. Like the sun transforms the wetness, the resolve to go toward the good and the practice of returning the light will carry one surely on to a new high road. There will be a birth of wisdom, a change of darkness to inner-light. The dross metal of the body transforms into vajra, the selfishness of false-thoughts transforms into the universal lamplight of Great Compassion. Birth, change, returning, transforming.

"If you want to find what's really true, don't look for it apart from the false," said the Master in Kuantan, Malaysia. "It's right within the false that you find what's true. And you have to be very, very patient."

"How do you find the false within the true?" asked a layman.

"Diamonds come out of the earth, don't they?" answered the Master.

The keys seem to be patience and faith. The three necessities for the Pure Land are Faith, Vows, and Practice. Faith can mean not pushing the Way, not forcing and seeking results overnight. The magic of the weather change at Ano Nuevo was in its perfect, effortless timing. It happened slowly and completely all by itself, wet changed to dry, *yin* changed to *yang*, all in perfect harmony. As the poem says, "The sun and the moon are both bright, moving in their orbits."

Even though we took a lot of wrong roads before we began to practice the Dharma, once we recognize our faults and resolve to change, we step inside the orbit of Enlightenment. Patiently, faithfully, "making tracks for the good, one step at a time," as the Master says, will certainly bring about the Great Reversal.

Now it's raining again and the autumn wind is whistling past our tin-roofed, four-wheeled Bodhimanda. Soon the sun will rise and the whole cycle will move on in its orbit. From empty space there is birth and change. "Infinitely wonderful."

Disciple Guo Chen (Heng Sure)
bows in respect

Heng Chau • November 21, 1978
Next 60 thoughts, use extreme caution

"Dangerous Road Ahead: Saha World"

We live in the southern continent Jambudvipa, of the Saha World which is located on the thirteenth tier of the Flower Treasury world-system. The nature of the Saha World is suffering. And so it translates from Sanskrit as, "to be endured," because there is so much suffering that living beings find it hard to endure.

We are born in a stupor of confusion and die in a muddled dream. Unless we meet a Good and Wise Advisor who shows us how to wake up and escape, the brief interval between birth and death passes in vain. When babies are born into the Saha we are happy and celebrate. When people die and leave the Saha we are grieved and mourn. Isn't this confusion!? Not knowing where we came from, unaware of where we are going, birth and death toss us back and forth like a cork at sea.

How easy it is to fall into this sea of suffering! It's just like the narrow ribbon of highway that clings to the steep mountains and sheer rocky cliffs of Big Sur. The road sign at the beginning of the Big Sur Highway reads: "Dangerous Road Ahead. Hazard. Frequent Rockslides. Not maintained at night. Next 60 miles use extreme caution."

The sign could have been posted on every single road in this world, outer and inner. The inner road is our attitudes, views, thoughts, and attachments which pave our way through life. Earth Store Bodhisattva says that,

> "I see that almost every motion and stirring of thought of the living beings of Jambudvipa is an offense... They are like a man who becomes confused, loses his original home, and mistakenly enters a dangerous path."
>
> Earth Store Sutra

Our minds are extremely dangerous roads. Big Sur's highway had no shoulder – only 100 foot cliffs that plunged into the jagged rocks and the deep sea below. The inner road we travel is just that narrow: an error in cause and effect is a misstep that could send us head-over-heels from the inner highway into the evil destinies far below. No joke.

> "All living beings are on the dangerous road of birth and death, and about to fall into the hells, animals, and hungry ghosts... They are like blind people who do not have a guide."
>
> Ten Grounds Chapter
> Avatamsaka Sutra

The only safe road is the Tao's great highway. It is broad, and easy, but requires a Bright-Eyed guide to find it and to get us started. Perhaps we should have cultivated the Way sooner, but on the mind ground, right now is the same as always, so how could it ever be too late? What rare and magic luck then, to meet such a guide, a true Good Knowing One, who can lead us out of the dangerous roads of our minds and safely across the wilderness of birth and death!

"We are like a confused person who mistakenly enters a dangerous road, but then encounters a Good Advisor who leads him out. He does not enter that road again... The Good Knowing Advisor takes him by the hand, leading him off the dangerous path so that he avoids the evil poisons. They reach a good path and he becomes happy and at peace."

Earth Store Sutra

Heng Sure • November 22, 1978
Oh, I have slipped the surly bonds of Earth

"High Flight"
Big lumber mill on the hill to the East. Private plane landing strip between the highway and the sea to the west. On this quiet Sunday, a man in a pickup unlocks the chain-link gate, wheels a small flying machine from a hangar, fuels up, pre-flights, and takes off into the sky.

The plane circles, roars, and sets out North towards San Francisco. Recalled the poem "High Flight" I used to recite as a child: "Oh, I have slipped the surly bonds of Earth..." Remembered the exhilaration of flying, suddenly to be riding the wind lighter than air, freer than clouds, swifter than falcons.

Bowing to the ground every three steps would seem the exact opposite of "slipping the surly bonds of earth." But cultivating the Way enables ordinary people to leap over the Triple Realm, climb to Sagehood, and experience freedom and ease of spirit beyond imagination.

"...I put out my hand and touched the face of God," concludes "High Flight." Cultivators empty the mind of self, enter vajra-like concentration, and then, unhindered by airplane, can realize the Buddhas' wisdom and make their constant reality the supreme liberation of the Buddha-dharma.

If one holds the mind like vajra,
With deep faith in the Buddha's foremost wisdom,
Knowing that the mind-ground lacks a self,
One can hear these Dharmas most supreme.
Like pictures that we painted in the air,
Like traces of wind in empty space
The wisdom of the Muni is that way:
Its distinctions very hard to see.

Ten Grounds Chapter
Avatamsaka Sutra

Heng Chau • November 22, 1978
And for a thousand miles, all is calm and clear

Storm cleared this morning. Fresh winds from the sea blew away the clouds, leaving blue skies, the deep turquoise sea, and distant green hills sparkling in the crisp, autumn air.

Bowing and Ch'an meditation blow away inner storm clouds, leaving a soft and pliant body, a firm will, and a calm, clear mind.

His heart and will are soft and flexible,
All his faculties clean and cool.

Ten Transferences Chapter
Avatamsaka Sutra

The nature of people is basically clear and pure like the sky, but the floating clouds of false thought cover the self-nature so that it cannot shine. Above the clouds the sun, moon, and stars shine as brightly as ever, but below the clouds, darkness blankets everything. Yet if a wind suddenly comes up and scatters the fog and clouds, there is lightness everywhere and the world comes back to life. Meeting a Good Knowing Advisor and cultivating the Way is the same way: suddenly a wind blows up and scatters falseness and confusion. And for a thousand miles inside and out, all is calm and clear.

The heart calm,
All worries go away.
The mind still,
Heaven has no clouds.

* * *

"The Host"

Ice dissolves the water,
Water turns to snow.
Sun of wisdom always shines,
Dark clouds come and go.

Afflictions change to Bodhi,
Buddhas come from ghosts.
Ten thousand transformations,
The mind alone is host.

Heng Sure • November 23, 1978
Flying through stone walls and mountains

"Flying the Spirits"

As a child I loved to read about flying, delighting in stories of the Wright Brothers' first take-off Kitty Hawk's sloping dunes, and Leonardo Da Vinci's clever gliders. I dreamed of leaving the ground, and soaring high, free of all impediments. I flew from my favorite reading chair at home with Lindberg's Spirit of St. Louis, St. Exupery's Night Flight, the biplanes of the Lafayette Escadrille, Major Chennault's Flying Tigers, and rode the wings of war-time fliers of the Royal Air Force, Army Air Corps, and Luftwaffe, right up to the days of jets and rockets. I flew the skies of my mind and spirit as I read the exploits of daring men in flying machines.

Lost interest in flying during high school when the reality dawned that progress in aviation was controlled by the martial mind, that the magic of flight had become inextricably bound up with weapons, with thoughts of harm and destruction, and in space travel, with intense greed for conquest of nature and control of other planets. The original pure impulse to cast off the bonds of gravity and explore new realms, free of earthly dust became a tarnished dream, a naïve, fanciful notion. I stopped reading books about aviation and forgot my wish to fly.

Then the magic of the Buddha-dharma entered my heart. In college I read descriptions of the Buddha's psychic powers and immediately the embers of my early love of flying first aflame. Recognized the interest in flight was only a branch of a deeper tree, rooted in a wish for ultimate liberation from suffering of all kinds. This wish occupied a very pure and special place in my heart of hearts, and emerged as the resolve to leave the home life and cultivate the Way.

Bowing today beside steep cliffs above the ocean. A trio of intrepid hang-glider pilots is sailing aloft on the coast breezes, wheeling and cutting empty space like seagulls. This passage from the "Ten Grounds" Chapter of the Sutra came to mind as the gliders circles overhead, and I marveled at the mysteries of the mind, the original lighter-than-air spacecraft. When purified and rectified according to the Buddha-dharma's methods, the mind can fly free of all bonds whatsoever and realize a state of unattached, limitless, liberation beyond imagination.

> "Disciples of the Buddha! This Bodhisattva obtains limitless powers of spiritual penetrations… He goes through stone walls and obstructive mountains as if they were space. In the midst of empty space he travels in full lotus just like a bird in flight… His body is free and at ease even up to the world of Brahma."
>
> Avatamsaka Sutra

More wonderful still: Bodhisattvas regard the ability to fly as quite ordinary, the way an astronaut might take for granted a commuter flight on a 707. What's truly remarkable is the Bodhisattva's selfless vows to enter all paths of rebirth and transform countless bodies to stand in for living beings and endure suffering on their behalf. This is flying the heights of the spirit!

Heng Chau • November 23, 1978
A real man doesn't lean on anything

"Dead at Sixteen, Buried at Sixty"

When I was 18 years old I realized that the desire to marry and to raise a family was motivated by fear and insecurity. It was a reaching out in desperation for a small and cozy world I could control and feel important in. The urge to marry and mate came on the heels of suddenly standing face-to-face with the big, cold, cruel world and by contrast, my own insignificance. This was the time of graduating from high school. All one's friends, almost overnight, found themselves thrust out of the familiar family nest to factory jobs, foreign wars, college, corporation punch-clock anonymity, traveling salesmen, and the open road. The urge to regress and to grasp was knee-jerk swift. But I also recognized that if I ever hoped to be a whole and free person, I would have to stand on my own two feet. The feelings of fear and insecurity were strong, but false; the longing of freedom and enlightenment was stronger, and more true.

Fortunately, I went to a school where the boys and girls were separated. The young women were taught by nuns; the young men by Christian Brothers. The Brothers were young, bright, idealistic, and dedicated. We looked up to them and idolized their righteous energy: a rare blend of scholarship, athletic prowess, social commitment, deep spiritual introspection, broad-minded compassion for all mankind, and an unmatched sense of humor.

Brother Louis quoted Shakespeare and G.K. Chesterton over lunch, and tossed the football with us after school. Destined for the pro's, turned down athletic fame to become a Christian Brother. Nobody could catch his bullet-pass, match his generosity, or stand up to his Irish temper when we triggered it by not acting like gentlemen. Brother Louis' pet peeve was "going steady." We should see young couples walking home from school holding hands and then disappearing on weekends to their narrow world of "each other only." He would shake his head and say,

"Talk about chicken-shit! That's called selling out and biting the dust."

Brother Peter, the principal, would smile and agree. A concert pianist and Ph.D., he could run the hundred in 10 seconds flat and had a face you couldn't look squarely at and tell a lie to.

"A real man, a genuine person, doesn't lean on anything. Whatever you can't do without will keep you from being free," he would say.

Brother Lawrence played guitar and sang Spanish folk songs to us that he learned while doing missionary work with young people in the Bluefields of Nicaragua. Active in Civil Rights and the ecumenical reform movement, he began our Sophomore English class with a challenge.

"This year we are going for depth. We are going to take a good look inside ourselves and find out who we are and what we are doing in life. The unexamined life is not worth living. Socrates said, 'Know thyself.' That's what we are going to do, okay?"

Brother Lawrence could always be found in the middle of a group of young men sitting on the school green or in the gymnasium bleachers, engaged in a lively bull-session. The topic would turn to dating and going steady. You could hear Brother Lawrence's fearless, probing voice crescendo:

"Those guys are just too pitiful. All tied down and locked into a rut before they even get a taste of their own potential. They die at sixteen years old, but don't get buried until they're sixty!"

Teachers like these made it easier for us to swallow our fears and temporary loneliness and go for the long distance run: seek out ultimate truth and discover our true selves. Often now, while bowing,

I look back on their guidance and inspiration with a deep sense of gratitude and a wish to repay their kindness. They were truly good friends and a gateway to Buddhism for me. They spoke the Dharma of the bliss of leaving home and helped keep my mind open so when I learned of the highest liberation – the Buddha's independence – I was able to respond to the challenge of cultivating the Way.

> "He vows that all beings give up their wives and children, and accomplish the foremost bliss of leaving the home-life… He vows that all living beings obtain the ultimate place and accomplish the Thus Come Ones' independence and wisdom."

Ten transferences Chapter
Avatamsaka Sutra

* * *

"What do you want? Tell us and we will go buy anything you need or want. Just tell us and we'll make an offering," says a visiting layperson.

"We don't want anything. Our needs are simple. Whatever you want to offer is what we want," answers the monk.

> They delight in Dharma's true and actual benefits,
> And do not love the reception of desires;
> They reflect on the Dharma they have heard,
> Far free from the practice of grasping.

Ten Grounds Chapter
Avatamsaka Sutra

Layperson #1: "They're just like their teacher: they don't want anything. Then whatever you bring them, that's what they want."

Layperson #2: "All monks are like that."

Layperson #3: "Nooo…! Only some are that way nowadays. The Buddha encouraged all his disciples to be that way, but… well, not everyone really is."

It is difficult not to seek self-benefits, but in the long run, it is a lot easier on everyone.

> They have no greed for benefits or offerings,
> And only delight in the Buddhas' Bodhi;
> With one mind they seek the Buddhas' wisdom,
> Concentration undivided, with no other thought.

Ten Grounds Chapter
Avatamsaka Sutra

Heng Chau • November 23, 1978
We should all go to America and investigate Dharma

Dear Master,

It says in the Avatamsaka:

> "According to what living beings practice in their minds, the vision of kshetras follow suit."

I have found this to be really the case with dreams.

"Vow Power."

The Buddhadharma is vast and great, without bounds or distinctions. So are the Bodhisattvas' vows:

> "He further makes great vows, vowing within all worlds to achieve Anuttarasamyaksambodhi without leaving the place of the tip of a single hair; in every place of a hair tip to make appear being born, leaving home, going to the Way place, accomplishing Proper Enlightenment, turning the Dharma Wheel, and entering Nirvana... in thought after thought, in accord with the minds of living beings to display the accomplishment of Buddhahood... With a single sound to speak Dharma and cause all living beings to be delighted at heart – vast and great as the Dharma Realm, ultimate as

empty space, exhausting the boundaries of the future, throughout all numbers of kalpas without cease."

Avatamsaka Sutra
The Ten Grounds Chapter

In May of 1977 when we began from Gold Wheel Temple in Los Angeles, the Master noted in a lecture that all of us had been together with Vairocana Buddha in the past investigating the Buddhadharma. And way back then the Master said we should all go to America and investigate the Dharma there. "So now we are here together to fulfill our vows. Causes and conditions in the past create a strength of togetherness here, now, that stays through all circumstances. From limitless kalpas past, our conditions with one another are deep... Everyone is Vairocana. All around you, in front, behind, all around you is the Buddha. The pure Dharma body of the Buddha fills up all places."

All living beings are deeply related and connected. Who can say where we have been in the past or will be in the future cultivating the Way and fulfilling the vows of Bodhisattvas. Nothing is fixed. What we can see isn't always real, and what is real we often cannot see. The Master ended that lecture with this remark, "In the midst of a dream, we are all here doing the work of the Buddha."

Peace in the Way,
Disciple Guo Ting (Heng Chau)
bows in respect

Heng Sure • November 24, 1978
It doesn't hide away and fail to shine

"It's Just Like the Sun"

Book-beating preacher attempts to turn us: "Why are you doing it? I mean, with all the things to do in the world, all the ways to spend your life, it seems like an awful shame to hide yourself away behind silence and this bowing business. I really can't see it benefits anybody."

The Avatamsaka answers eloquently:

> "It's like the sun that appears in the world. It doesn't hide away and fail to shine because there are people who have been blind from birth and cannot see it."

Ten Transferences Chapter
Avatamsaka Sutra

Frosty morning, breath-steam puffing from chattering lips as we bow down and recite, waiting for the rising sun to break over the clouds to the East and thaw our frozen mitts. Sutra warm in our hearts:

> "It's also like the sun, which does not fail to appear because Gandharva's cities, Asura's hands, Jambudvipa's trees, craggy mountain peaks, precipitous valleys, or clouds of dust, fog, smoke, or other objects try to cover and block its light."

Ten Transferences Chapter
Avatamsaka Sutra

"And the Bodhisattvas are the same way," the Sutra concludes. Once cultivators stand even briefly in the bright rays of the Buddha's wisdom-sun and feel the warmth of that pure light within, they never fail to shine and never stop cultivating.

Heng Chau • November 24, 1978
As strong as the pull of gravity

Winter winds, hoary frost in the morning, seasonal cold rains beginning. Laypeople bring offerings of warm clothes, flashlights, rubber boots, two pairs of strong canvas shoes to last the winter, and a single line of advice and encouragement from the Master:

"Do a really good job of cultivating the Way."

We are a few miles south of Ano Nuevo Point. Open country, long quiet days of bowing and just being.

I've been using these two verses from the "Ten Transferences" Chapter as an inner map. I silently contemplate as we bow along the open road, through gravel, sand, and empty space:

I do not rely on form, I'm not attached to feelings.
I am not turned upside down by thoughts.
I don't do actions,
I don't seek consciousness,
I forsake the six places.

I do not dwell in mundane dharmas,
My joy is in leaving the world.
I know that all dharmas are like empty space,
They come from nowhere.

Avatamsaka Sutra

* * *

"They bring forth the mind for Bodhi in order to completely know the heart's delights, afflictions, and habitual energies of all living beings."

The Merit and Virtue From First Bringing
Forth the Mind – Avatamsaka Sutra

* * *

One can feel the rip-tides of afflictions and bad habits pull us back again and again as we try to swim to the other shore. Lifetimes of accumulated pride, doubts and deviant views, encrusted layers of torpor, restless inattention, jealousy and laziness are as strong as the pull of gravity, as automatic as our pulse and respiration. They clog the heart's delights and exasperate the soul. Yet,

> What is of all things most yielding
> Can overcome that which is of all things most hard.
>
> Lao Tzu

Water is soft and yielding, yet it can eventually wear down the hardest rock. In the same way the will for Bodhi, like water, gradually overcomes the strongest habit energies and toughest afflictions. Bodhi gets its way simply through enduring. Its power lies in patience, faith, and a constant attitude of non-contention. And because Bodhi never contends, it always wins. Because it bears down with the strength of kindness and the righteousness of the Proper, the hard and resistant surrender and have no way of altering it.

As afflictions and habit energies grow thinner, our blessings and virtue fill out and grow fat. Bodhi accumulates in small increments of self-improvement, and in inches of reclaiming what is true. And sometimes the clouds of karma part, a beam of sunlight shines through, and for a moment we get a brief vision of what it must be like to constantly dwell in the bliss of Bodhi. Seeking nothing, nowhere relying, all grasping and worry gone. Alone without a self; in oneness, not alone. Traveling through all words saving living beings without a single thing being done.

> No karma and no afflictions,
> Without possessions, or without a home.
> Not illumining or practicing anything,
> In level equality, they travel through the world.
>
> The Bodhisattvas Ask for Clarification Chapter
> Avatamsaka Sutra

Heng Sure • November 25, 1978
A brand new world

Overflowing with a rare, inner excitement. The ageless words of the "Ten Practices" Chapter continue to flush out unexpected responses from the darkest caverns of my mind. Like bears breaking out of winter hibernation, the hairy, scary ideas and habits of deepest consciousness are startled awake by the light of the Avatamsaka's wisdom-sun. Blinking and stretching, these murky, unexamined thoughts emerge from their caves.

The world they meet this year is brand new: body vigorously bowing in respect, mind repenting of selfishness and greed, mouth holding to a vow of silence. My spirit cradles and cherishes the phrases of wisdom from the Sutra like a dragon delights in his precious pearl.

> His mind is purified and it is never lost,
> His enlightened understanding is decisive.
> His goodness increases and grows,
> The net of doubts, turbidities,
>   he completely leaves behind.
>
> > Ten Grounds Chapter, "Fourth Ground"
> > Avatamsaka Sutra

Heng Chau • November 25, 1978
The incense stick must be wet

> "Expediently proclaiming in the stillness of Samadhi."
>
> Ten Dwellings Chapter
> Avatamsaka Sutra

Ch'an meditation notes:

Legs: "I've had it. I'm quitting."

Bodhi-Will: "Go ahead. I'm staying."

Knees: "I can't take another second; I'm going with the legs."

Bodhi-Will: "Fine, go ahead. I'm going to see what's on the other side of pain."

Hips: "He's crazy. There's just more pain on the other side of pain. I can't bear it."

Bodhi-Will: "You're all a bunch of spineless wonders. A little pain and you freak out. Be patient. Laugh. Don't get nervous."

Mind: "The incense stick must be wet. It should have burned out long ago. Better check the clock, too. What's for lunch tomorrow? I'm really sleeping. Don't force it. How do you get 'Light ease'… If you keep this up, for sure you'll go crazy…"

Legs, knees, hips and back: "He's right! The mind's right. Oh, we're all going to die or go crazy. Ohh…"

Bodhi-Will: "You all can do what you want. No one ever died from pain or a little hard work. It's all empty. Bear what you can't bear. Take what you can't take. Be patient and you'll make it through the gate. Be brave! Be strong! Don't waste this chance to go where you've never gone before. Chase the demons, find the Buddha! Only work harder, never retreat!"

Stomach: "Next time you plan to sit long don't drink apple juice or prune juice before."

Bodhi-Will: "Okay, everything's okay. Don't be so nervous; don't get nervous. Let go of everything inside; don't chase after anything outside. Easy does it, okay?"

Skinbag: "Okay. Besides, what's a little suffering compared to All-wisdom?"

> With the wondrous merit and virtue
>   from many kinds of meditation,
> They skillfully cultivate
>   the unsurpassed, foremost karma.
> Never forsaking all practices supreme,
> They fix their thoughts on accomplishing All-wisdom.
>
> The Merit and Virtue From First Bringing
> Forth the Mind – Avatamsaka Sutra

* * *

"Harmless"

We leave Santa Cruz and cross into San Mateo County. A carful of youths cautiously lets go a volley of rotten eggs and soda-pop cans from a safe distance. Both fall wide of the mark. They leave in a hurry and the quiet, still, and empty nature of all dharmas returns; it always returns. At some point all conditioned dharmas seem like dreams and like shadows. There is a special space we sometimes discover after a long day of bowing, a place of peace and serenity apart from all appearances where it is easy to be patient and everything feels harmless.

> They understand that dharmas are harmless
>   and they are always able to endure;
> They know the dharma-nature is apart
>   from appearances, and they perfect vigor.
>
> Ten Grounds Chapter
> Sixth Ground, Manifestation
> Avatamsaka Sutra

Heng Sure • November 26, 1978
Drowning in the whirlpool of birth and death

Bowed all day in downpour. Long hours of standing among deepening puddles, counting bows in place. Watching handprints indent the road-shoulder mud. They fill with rain and reflect the somber sky, five fingers and a palm full of clouds. Listening to the roar of raindrops on the plastic parka hood. Water trickles into collar, soaks armpits, fills rubber gloves, sloshes with every bow, like scuba wet suit. Mind complains of dreary monotony. Have to hustle to keep sagging spirits afloat. Challenged myself to do the hard work of self-discipline. Level all states: rainy, sunny, silent, deafening, soggy or dry, only our efforts in cultivation and nothing else carry us out of the sea of suffering.

> "All living beings revolve in the whirlpool of birth and death, they toss and turn in the river of love. They are carried away by the galloping flood and have no leisure to contemplate."
>
> Avatamsaka Sutra

These lines from the "Ten Grounds" Chapter provided a raft and transformed self-pity to light-hearted gratitude. What matters after all? Ending birth and death. Cultivation means owning our lifetime, devoting every second to resolving the one great matter. It's clear in contemplating that there's not a moment to waste. Right now, all living beings are "drowning in the whirlpool of birth and death." Only determined vigor in cultivation can ford the torrent. "The leisure to contemplate" is the greatest gift one can give oneself.

At day's end washed the mud from head, elbows, knees, emptied water from inside the gloves. Packed soggy shirts into clothes bin and gratefully folded legs into full lotus in the dry snug harbor of the Plymouth. Sat and contemplated the Buddha's sweet Dharma-rain.

Like the earth that is unmoving,
Like water that benefits,
In this way are living beings transported.
May I ride upon the carriage.

Entering the Dharma Realm
Avatamsaka Sutra

Heng Chau • November 26, 1978
The teacher and the sutra as one

"He can universally cause one to behold the sea of
Dharmas of all time."

Entering the Dharma Realm
Avatamsaka Sutra

The Avatamsaka Sutra and the Master's instructions have begun
to jell the mind and come alive in the belly. For a long time they were
like riddles or disassembled puzzle pieces. Now each word of the
Avatamsaka "strings together deep crystallizations of wonderful
meanings," and every instruction from our teacher leads us into an
ocean of Dharmas. The teacher embodies the Sutra; the Sutra
describes the teacher. And together they both arouse and reveal the
knowledge and vision of the Buddha latent within our own minds.

"He can universally open and explain the wonderful
meanings of the Great Vehicle."

Entering the Dharma Realm
Avatamsaka Sutra

Without the Sutra and a Good Knowing Advisor, I would be
wandering in a spiritual wasteland, forever cursing the darkness. To
repay this debt of kindness only seems natural and right. Today while
bowing, this vow came forth:

"I vow in body, speech and mind to completely merge in
substance and nature with the Avatamsaka Sutra and the Flower

Adornment Assembly of Buddhas and Bodhisattvas. I vow to always and everywhere protect and propagate it for the benefit of all living beings."

"He can universally encourage one to bring forth the conduct and vows of Universal Worthy."

Entering the Dharma Realm
Avatamsaka Sutra

Heng Sure • November 27, 1978
The spiritual quest of Thomas Merton

Thomas Merton, the contemplative and author, wrote in his autobiography about a period of self-exploration before he took up the monk's robe. A group of seminary colleagues rented a rambling house in the country and settled in to search their souls. They sat in all-night bull-sessions, kept detailed journals of their insights and confusions, squeezed countless cups of tea from a single teabag, and pushed their mind to exhaustion. The group made an earnest effort to solve the big questions: "Who am I? Where am I going? What is life all about?" Their methods were hit-and-miss, they lacked a teacher and their efforts failed to produce real fruit.

Merton's companions fell away from the spiritual path. Merton persevered; he trusted his heart, endured the hours of doubt, followed the sparks of faith, and became a monk. After years of inner questing, he began to investigate Buddhism. His writings built a new bridge to ancient spiritual disciplines for many eager Westerners.

Today in America, people bow to the Buddha, sit in Ch'an meditation, recite mantras, hold precepts, investigate the Buddha's discourses, and cultivate ascetic practices. There are now native Buddhist monks and nuns ordained in the orthodox traditions on Western soil. If Father Merton and his companions had met the methods and disciplines available to Buddhists from beginningless time to regulate the body and to purify and unlock the mind, how much richer their lives could have been, how much more satisfying their spiritual search. How lucky we all are now!

> Head, eyes, ears, and nose, tongue, as well as teeth,
> Hands and feet, his marrow,
>   his heart and blood and flesh –
> All such things as these renouncing
>   he does not find difficult.
> Only a chance to hear the Dharma
>   he counts as most difficult.

Ten Grounds Chapter
Avatamsaka Sutra

Heng Chau • November 27, 1978
They all looked ten years younger

"The City of Clear Light"

The City of Ten Thousand Buddhas is hundreds of miles away, but we can "see" it. We see it in the eyes and on the faces of people who have just come from there. Yesterday a family stopped who had just spent the weekend at "the City." They were full of light, peace, and happiness. They all looked ten years younger than when we saw them three days earlier. So obvious was the contrast!

The Buddha's City implants purity and instills a lightheartedness in whoever visits. Just as riches adorn the house, so does virtue adorn people. When Buddhas and Bodhisattvas use their merit and virtue to decorate people, the result is dazzling. These people looked like red-cheeked, innocent children after their Saturday night bath. Only they were glowing from the waters of Bodhi and flushed with the radiance of kindness, compassion, joy, and giving.

It is said that the countries we live in are transformationally manifested from the vows and spiritual strength of Buddhas and Bodhisattvas so as to benefit and teach us. The City of Ten

Thousand Buddhas must be the transformation body ("country body") of measureless Thus Come Ones. It puts out a clear light whose wonderful decorations can be seen for miles and are reflected in the faces of all who visit or dwell there.

> Some kshetras put out a clear light
> Composed of the "apart from defilement jewel."
> Many kinds of wonderful decorations,
> The Buddhas make them fully purified.
>
> Flower Store World Chapter
Avatamsaka Sutra

* * *

Bowing thoughts: just forget about self and seeking for self. There's too much work to do. Help and support living beings everywhere. Do only good and constantly purify your thoughts. Be a great person and in 10,000 ways bring kindness, compassion, joy, and giving into everything you do. Make people happy and free. Do a good job of cultivating the Way. What could compare to the pleasure of seeing someone first bring forth the resolve for enlightenment!?

> I should be a good garden for all beings.
> I should reveal the joy of Dharma for all beings.
> I should give the thought of happiness to all beings.
> I should cause all beings to have happy thoughts.
> I should cause all beings
>   to gain the Buddhas' enlightenment.
>
> Ten Transferences Chapter
Avatamsaka Sutra

* * *

Sometimes our own thoughts and the words we read from the Sutra at night seem to touch each other. Some days our steps seem to travel along an invisible Avatamsaka highway under our feet. And there is no better feeling on earth than when the Sutra, the world, and the heart connect.

Seeking all the various sutra books,
Their minds never weary or fatigued,
Well can they understand their drift and meaning;
And make their practices accord with the world.

Ten Grounds Chapter
Avatamsaka Sutra

Heng Sure • November 28, 1978
No Buddha ever achieved Bodhi outside of the rules

"The Rules"

Young disciple stopped to offer a bag of vegetarian spring rolls on his way home to the hills of Campbell from the City of Ten Thousand Buddhas. He said,

"Saw an article in Time magazine this week that confused me. A western businessman on a flight from New York to Los Angeles sat next to a high Lama in purple robes. The Lama ate the beef stew that came for lunch without any hesitation. The businessman questioned him about it – he asked the same question I would have asked had I been there:

"'Aren't Buddhists supposed to be vegetarian?' The story relates that the Lama winked, smiled, and said, 'Only the strictest Buddhists don't eat meat.'"

"The question bothered me all week," said Kuo Ch'en. "I intended to ask the Ven. Abbot about it this weekend. Funny thing, it was as if the Master knew my thoughts. Before I could ask, he delivered the answer in his Saturday afternoon lecture. He said, 'Buddhas start out as ordinary people on the road to enlightenment. It's only because they learn the rules, respect the pure precepts, and hold them perfectly that they soon enter samadhi and open great wisdom. Precepts are the foundation of Buddhahood. No Buddha ever achieved Bodhi outside of the rules. And the rules stress kindness and compassion, not killing, or harming, and not eating any living being. This is basic,' the Master said.

"So when I reviewed the Lama's answer, I realized why there are so few Buddhas in the world. It's because so few people are willing to follow the rules. Hearing the Master's words always seems to strip away my ignorance. I get a big recharge in my resolve to cultivate every time I visit the City. I realize that I've to really work hard just to be worthy to take refuge with the Triple Jewel and have the chance to take the precepts," said Kuo Ch'en.

> When living beings receive the Buddha's precepts
> They enter the Buddha's position.
> When their state is identical to great enlightenment,
> They are truly the Buddha's disciples.
>
> Brahma Net Sutra

Heng Chau • November 28, 1978
The stars and planets orbit without hurry

"Take Time"

> "Living beings toss and turn in the river of love. They are carried away by the galloping flood and take no time to contemplate."
>
> Ten Grounds Chapter
> Avatamsaka Sutra

Screeching red-tail hawks, the inexorable sounds of the sea, an occasional falling tree in the woods, blend in unobstructed with the soft chanting and slow bowing. Each night the stars and planets orbit in their measured way, without rush, unhurried. The rhythms of nature seem tentative, almost thoughtful in contrast to the harried and frantic pace of man. The black river of asphalt we bow along pulses with the same fast and frenzied vibrations day and night, whether L.A. rush hour or state park wilderness. The cars always move at the same whining, bewildered rpm's. And we people drive our bodies and minds like our cars. Soon they break down unless we take time to stop and consider, take time to calm down and cultivate.

> "They give rise to happiness because they can cause all living beings to take time to cultivate and purify all wholesome dharmas to (their) universal perfection."
>
> Ten Transferences Chapter
> Avatamsaka Sutra

A thousand miles of highway bowing is easy, but doing only good is hard. Speaking wonderfully and speaking well is easy, but doing no evil is truly hard. Going along with the crowd and flowing with dust is easy, but offering up one's conduct according to the teachings is hard. Finding others' faults is easy, but purifying one's mind is most hard. Doing what's easy always leaves a bitter after-taste; doing what's hard tastes sweet indeed.

* * *

> "Good Man, a Bodhisattva is like a great cloud, because he lets fall limitless, wonderful Dharma rain; He is like a timely rain, because he causes all the roots and sprouts of faith of living beings to increase and grow."
>
> Entering the Dharma Realm
> Avatamsaka Sutra

Since the Abbot's last visit, the pilgrimage has changed and grown. Things have become smoother outside and more quiet and deep inside. We both feel refreshed and revived, as if a timely rain fell to nourish our roots of faith and Dharma-sprouts.

Material needs of food, clothes, water, and the like seem to take care of themselves, freeing the energy to go within and explore the mind ground. We are both discovering new territories of the psyche and body. Personal attachments daily wear thinner: rubbed away by time and the ever-pressing highway reality of impermanence; erased by the Dharma and the heightened awareness of no-self and non-attachment that living outdoors brings. A falling leaf tells all.

> Secluded at the roots of trees,
> And guarded well by deities,
> He lives in true devotedness;
> Nor covets any dwelling place.
>
> And when the tender leaves are seen,
> Bright red at first, then turning green,
> And then to yellow as they fall;
> He sheds belief once and for all in permanence.

from "Ascetic Practices"
The Path of Purification.

The more we can leave behind and stand alone, the deeper we enter the vast oneness of all things. Far from the loneliness and cold estrangement our hearts feared from letting go, a wonderful, warm, fullness and peace of mind greets us at every turn and with every show of faith. It doesn't pay to worry. Being here and now, true in every step, takes care of everything. A concentrated mind is like the wind: at ease and unobstructed.

> Bodhisattvas inhabit the world, yet
> They are not attached to any dharmas inside or out.
> Like the wind which travels through
>   the skies with no obstruction,
> The Great Knight's concentration is also like this.

Ten Transferences Chapter
Avatamsaka Sutra

Heng Sure • November 29, 1978
Refugees were pushed back to sea

We sat on a sandy ledge, above the lapping Pacific waves. The highway boomed with Thanksgiving traffic. A laywoman spoke, her grief barely controlled:

"Nine hundred people in South America took poison and died together. Boats full of Vietnamese refugees were pushed back to sea and not allowed to land. It's happened often now. The boats all sank. The Master says these are major disasters. He's going to find a way to bring the refugees to the City of Ten Thousand Buddhas and give them a place to live in peace. We thought you'd like to hear this news."

"The Bodhisattva Mahasattva sees living beings imprisoned and in the dark, bound in stocks and fetters, their bodies tied and chained, never at peace, surrounded by much misery, without kin or friends, to take them in or save them, naked, exposed to the elements, starving, poor, suffering beyond endurance. Seeing them, the Bodhisattva gives up all his wealth, his wife, children, and retinue, even his own body in order to rescue these beings from their prisons."

Ten Transferences Chapter
Avatamsaka Sutra

Heng Chau • November 29, 1978
Drinking the water of faith

"To Know Which Way the Wind Blows…"

A young disciple of the Abbot stopped. His heart was heavy and saddened with bad news: over nine hundred people committed mass suicide in South America, and the mayor of San Francisco along with a supervisor were assassinated.

"People are really feeling down and confused," the young man told us. "Nobody knows why. They are asking: 'What's wrong with us? Are we bad people that such tragic and horrible things could happen among us?' Everyone is asking why."

As we listened to this new, I found myself drawn to a passage of Sutra I often contemplate while bowing and listening to the troubled sounds of the world:

> "Seeking the states of the five desires and the many kinds of pleasures in the three realms of existence is the cause of all disasters that occur. The hells, hungry ghosts, and animals, King Yama's region; all animosity, hatred, conflict, slander, insult, all of these evils are caused by greed and attachment to the five desires."
>
> Ten Transferences Chapter
> Avatamsaka Sutra

The five desires are food, fame, wealth, sex, and sleep. Small and personal sufferings and disasters differ only in degree from large-scale sufferings and collective tragedies. The underlying, root cause is the same: greedy desire. The karma of the insatiable quest for the pleasures of the five desires returns as the retribution of disasters, wars, injury, and loss. Just like an epidemic: the virus itself is identical and tiny, but the misery it can cause is widespread and massive. In the same way, each person's personal diet quickly spreads and mushrooms until it threatens to wipe out the entire world. And so,

"The Bodhisattva contemplates the mundane world in this way and he reduces his greed for the flavors of the five desires. He thinks: I should be a regulating Master for all living beings. I should act as a general for the troops, and uphold the torch of great wisdom to show the path of peace and security and cause living beings to leave dangers and difficulties."

Ten Transferences Chapter
Avatamsaka Sutra

"Bodhisattva" means "enlightened being." He is enlightened to the truth of the total, inseparable, oneness of all things, great and small. And therefore he recognizes the path of world peace and security begins with the ground right under his own feet. By reducing his greed for the flavors of the five desires, he imperceptibly, but actually, reduces the dangers and difficulties of all that lives.

"He knows what is distant lies in what is near. He knows which way the wind blows. He know how what is minute becomes manifest, and such a one will surely enter virtue."

Confucius

What is "distant" is the world, the nation. What is "near" is the person. The "wind" is the influence, and the source from where it blows is his own virtue, his own person. He knows which way the wind blows and so he purifies his heart and straightens out his mind, and thereby mends the world.

* * *

"On Faith Alone"

At a gas station on Highway 1, south of Pigeon Pt.

Monk: "Got any water?"

Attendant: "For drinking or the radiator?"

Monk: "For drinking."

Attendant: "Well, sort of. Over there by the door. It looks bad and it tastes bad, but it won't hurt you."

This is the only water station for miles. Long stretch of barren coastline. No fresh-water creeks or streams, only salt water from the sea and a muddy soup that trickles up from a few wells. I fill our empty plastic jugs from a faded red hose. The water looks like the rusty sludge in our car's radiator. When it sits for awhile, the water turns ochre color and an inch of mineral deposits and sediment settles on the bottom. We drink it on faith.

> With faith one is not attached to any state of being.
> Far apart from all difficulties one becomes untroubled.
> Faith has no turbidity or stain, it purifies the mind.
> Faith eradicates pride, it is the basis of respect.
> Faith is the primary asset of the Dharma Treasury.
>
> Worthy Leader Chapter
> Avatamsaka Sutra

We run on faith; it is our primary asset. To people who pass, our lives may appear totally insecure and unpredictable. Our car should be in a museum; the weather, food, our clothes, come as they please. We constantly meet strangers and suspicious characters face-to-face without weapons, locks, or a house with nearby telephone for protection. It all looks so out of control and yet we don't see it that way.

Good luck or bad luck is a matter of choice, not chance. One of the basic tenets of Buddhism is belief in cause and effect: like cause, like results; similar results have similar causes. Good deeds bring good retributions, evil deed bring evil, as surely as planting corn and melon seeds yields corn and melons. The immutable workings of cause and effect are the natural law. We are learning to respect this law because no one breaks it and gets away. Faith eradicates pride because karma is king and has no feelings, makes no exceptions, and never forgets. It treats everybody equally; there are no specials, no favorites, and no "number ones."

Even after a hundred thousand aeons
The karma you have created is not forgotten.
When the proper conditions combine,
You still have to undergo the retribution.

Sutra on Cause and Effect
of The Three Periods of Time

Bodhisattvas have faith in cause and effect and so they don't fear results, they only fear causes. They carefully plant good causes in every deed, word, and thought. Then in the future they are "apart from all difficulties and become untroubled," because they rest in faith that "as you sow, thus you reap." The things that happen to us in daily life are the harvest of past deeds and have nothing to do with fate, god, luck, or accident. Blessings fall without strain like ripe apples; offenses follow like shadows and no effort can avoid them. So it says,

Families that do good enjoy good fortune.
Families that do evil are plagued
  by early deaths and many disasters.
The retribution of good and evil
Follows us around like a shadow.

Ancient verse

Is the water safe to drink? Is the station attendant trustworthy and a friend? It depends on our karma. If we merit drinking bad water, getting poisoned, or cheated, it is because we planted those seeds in the past. If we don't get sick from the water and it turns out the man did not mislead us, that too is our retribution. Either way we receive exactly what we deserve. Karma is very scientific and exact. Besides, there is no other water for miles, and even if there were, we should still be within the reach of karma and drinking it on faith alone.

Heng Sure • November 30, 1978
Issued an order to my mind

Decide: to settle by giving victory to one side, to give judgment. To come to a resolution. From Latin: to cut off.

Some people are decisive, some are wishy-washy. Ch'an practice cuts through the confusion of choice and delivers the mind to single-pointed concentration, free of duality's weary dust.

> Those who do not live in the single Way,
> Fail in both activity and passivity, assertion and denial.
> To deny the reality of things
>   is to miss their emptiness.
> To assert the emptiness of things
>   is to miss their reality...
> Do not remain in the dualistic state.
> Avoid such pursuits carefully.
> If there is even a trace of this and that,
>   of right and wrong,
> The mind-essence will be lost in confusion.
>
> "Have Faith in Your Mind"
> by Ch'an Patriarch Seng Ts'an

To help to renounce the habit of discriminating rights and wrongs, goods and bads, shoulds and shouldn'ts, I wrote orders to my mind to startle into wakefulness the fuzzy habit of endless indecision:

1.Decide what you value!
Own your choice.
Invest your life.
Use your energy.
Fill every second with concentration.

2.Take a loss.
Go light.
Go without.
Let it be – be content!

3.Be decisive!
Choose, then say no to the rest.
Liberate your mind from the endless back and forth.
Indecision is greed!!
Hoping for more benefit,
Seeking ever to climb, to improve, to increase.
Nothing in the world is ever perfect or permanent.

Heng Chau • November 30, 1978
A true cultivator turns states instead

Rainstorm and heavy winds. Squalls from sea pound coast road.
We bow in yellow rain slicks and rubbers. Chilled to bone, happy and
free.

> "Because they want to cause all beings to live together
> with cultivators of a single purpose."
>
> Ten Transferences Chapter
> Avatamsaka Sutra

Dream last night: An American Dharma assembly. Young-
hearted people cultivating together, informal, natural and sponta-
neous – yet serious and disciplined. Abbot asks us to talk: "Just talk
natural and how it really is. Don't be fancy or phony."

We gather on the go in campers and mobile homes, outside, city
and countryside. Everybody very vigorous and sincere in making
Dharma match up with practice, down to where they put their shoes
and what they eat. Col. Sanders comes up with a load of fried
chicken as a test and they chase him away. MacDonalds' hamburgers
are lying on tables untouched. People are doing lots of exercise,
meditation, and helping others. Simple and true, the essential flesh

and bones, no heroes or stars, and the emphasis is on practicing ultimate Dharma and becoming Buddhas.

> "He vows that all living beings become disciples of the Buddha and follow the Buddhas in practice. He vows that all living beings in the Buddhas' Way-place produce a thought of themselves as a Buddha which cannot be destroyed. He vows that all beings always be disciples of the Buddha and be born by transformation from the Dharma."
>
> Ten Transferences Chapter
Avatamsaka Sutra

"Get rid of all attachments, don't rely on any dharmas, and sweep out all marks," some says. "All that counts is what's inside, what's yours in the heart past words and thought." The air is charged with the great Bodhi-resolve.

The whole atmosphere is one of everyone changing fast and deep with a lot of sweat and humor. Exhilarating and scary, but the only honest thing to be doing. Wilderness trekking while sitting in the Ch'an furnace.

In the background we can hear a hit song play on a radio while people water their lawns and watch the days pass by.

> "He vows that all beings accomplish the supreme Sangha jewel and leave the ground of common people to enter the assembly of worthy sages."
>
> Ten Transferences Chapter
Avatamsaka Sutra

* * *

"Missed the Bulls-Eye, Don't Blame the Target"

> Truly recognize your own faults,
> Don't discuss the faults of others;
> Others faults are just my own...
>
> Venerable Abbot Hua

A scattered and unsettled person came out to bow. He was noisy, fidgety, and erratic. Before long I found myself becoming as scattered and frustrated as the visitor. I immediately sought to pin the blame on him and thought, "When this person leaves then everything will be calm and peaceful again." But a stronger, wiser voice inside counseled, "When you return then everything will be okay again. Your mind moved, not the visitor. A true cultivator turns states instead of being turned by states."

A cultivator corrects and regulates himself at all times and does not seek from others. He does not blames others or seek their approval. He does not curse heaven or grumble against people. He returns the light to illumine within, knowing that everything he encounters comes from what he does. And so he has no complaints towards others; all blame he takes on himself.

> "In archery we have something like the Way of the superior person: When the archer misses the center of the target, he turns around and seeks for the cause of his failure in himself."
>
> Confucius

* * * * * * * *

December 1978

Heng Sure • December 1, 1978
The wind was simply the wind

Bowed in a windstorm today from 8 A.M. to 5 P.M. My mind goes wild in the wind. It turns me the way nothing else can do. Wind chills the skin, tightens the nerves, obstructs even-mindedness, narrows the eyes, and dims clear, inner seeing. When it blows strong I have to dig deep for patience. It's a personal hang-up – Heng Chau enjoys big breezes – finds them refreshing and invigorating. But windy weather is my test. From the first hard gales outside Point

Mugu in Southern California, through the 100-miles-per-hour gusts on the Mesa, from Big Sur's power-winds that lash like a dragon's tail, right up to this blinding, deafening, daylong blow, the coast winds have been a Good Advisor.

The wind tests patience, requires vigor, and challenges concentration. It puts teeth in the resolve to bear all states. I can't idle along in neutral when the wind kicks up. Watching my mind run for shelter inside, I can review basic security habits. The ego ducks into harbors it considers safe and drops anchor in the bay of familiar thoughts. When reality gets too real my mind takes shelter in fantasies.

Pushed to the edge of strength by the wind today I found myself daydreaming inside. I smelled plates of chocolate chip cookies, felt the warmth of a fireplace hearth, tasted a mug of steaming cocoa with marshmallows, just as if I held it in my hand. I heard the T.V. jingle from Mickey Mouse Club and the Bugs Bunny cartoon shows. Temporary insanity? No, just a real-life lesson in faulty mindfulness.

> "He vows that living beings leave all distinctions that come from being moved from mindfulness and enter the unmoving wisdom ground of level equality."
>
> Ten Transferences Chapter
> Avatamsaka Sutra

All states are mind-made. A concentrated mind returns all dharmas to level equality. As long as I pick and choose among good and bad states, the ego survives, stuck to its attachments, limited by likes and dislikes that exist only within my thoughts.

Today just before sunset, battered and weary, for an instant I was able to let go my wish to control the weather. I focused on the sound of the bowing recitation and forgot the pouting, whimpering, fantasy-making ego. I said to myself, "Let it go. Let the wind be."

The single thought of patience and contentment suddenly silenced the roaring breeze. The sense-pictures of cozy refuges and safe harbors vanished. Everything was okay. The wind was simply wind, not an enemy, not a test, not an obstacle to happiness.

Heng Chau • December 1, 1978
It will have to be repaid with fur and horns

"A Single Grain of Rice"

Some laypeople brought out a food offering this morning. I casually let slip a remark to Heng Sure that the donors didn't seem very sincere. Such a shameless remark was gossip and showed arrogance. It violated precepts prohibiting false speech, slighting beginning students of the Way, accepting offerings with a mind in violation of the precepts, and discussing the faults of the Four-fold assembly. Loose speech also broke a personal vow not to speak any words that would cause others to lose proper mindfulness. I have vowed only to speak words that reveal the Proper Dharma and increase the Bodhi-resolve.

> "I resolve that I would rather swallow glowing hot iron pellets and streams of raging flames for a hundred thousand kalpas, then ever swallow with a mouth that has violated the precepts, the myriad flavors of food offered by a faithful donor."
>
> from "The Thirty-Sixth Minor Precept"
> in the Brahma Net Sutra

As soon as I ate the food offering, I got violent stomach cramps. I bowed in repentance and admitted this retribution was my due for bad mouth karma. Truly, all disasters come from the mouth! I promised never to err like this again, and then sat in mediation to do two mudras that relieve illness, from the Forty-Two Hands and Eyes dharma. The pain and cramping stopped immediately and I was able to continue the pilgrimage. It's said,

> "A single grain of donors' rice is as heavy as Mt. Sumeru. If one receives it, but does not cultivate the Way, it will have to be repaid with fur and horns."
>
> Buddhist Saying

One can receive offerings only if one is purely holding the Precepts, otherwise it's an offense. If one accepts a donor's kindness and then does not cultivate (i.e. breaks precepts), the offense karma, even for as little as a single grain of rice, merits retribution of rebirth in an animal's body. If all I incurred was a temporary illness, it was due to the power of repentance and reform and the kindly mindfulness of the Buddhas and Bodhisattvas.

* * *

Clear skies, cold ocean winds, open countryside and quiet days that pass as quickly as the clouds.

"Weathering"

> Winter rains, bones complain,
> Shoulders huddle from the winds.
> Nature's in Samadhi;
> Always fair within.
>
> Desire gathers demons,
> Anger beckons foes;
> Everything's okay, when
> Inside doesn't know.
>
> Patience under insult,
> Bearing loneliness and pain;
> Patience within patience
> Weathering all rains.

Heng Sure • December 2, 1978
The lesson of the hoe and brussel sprouts

"Sprouts of Greed"

Last year at this time I stumbled across a garden hoe, half-buried and rusting in a desolate field. I thought it could be well-used in a garden at the City of Ten Thousand Buddhas. Regardless of the intent, the tool was not given to me. I broke a precept by stealing it. Later, I discovered it belonged to a local farmer.

Returning the hoe to its owner became a lengthy comedy of errors. My cultivation was obstructed for weeks. One can't break the rules and hope to make progress in the Way.

Today the road was dotted with brussel sprouts blown by the windstorm from produce trucks. Heng Chau is our commissary supply agent but he didn't gather sprouts today. At lunch my greed for flavor ran high — I was hungry for a bowl of plump, steaming, brussel sprouts, and asked Heng Chau why he had passed them by. His reason: yesterday the Caltrans crews sprayed the gutters and drains with weed-poison. Heng Chau ruled out the sprouts on the chance they might poison us like weeds. I yielded to his wisdom.

Later, while walking to the bowing site, I saw beyond the irrigation ditch, a broad field the pickers had just harvested. The choppers had missed thousands of brussel sprouts. They lay in heaps, rotting in the sun. I crossed the ditch for a closer look, picked up a stalk, and calculated that in ten minutes I could gather enough sprouts to feed us for two weeks. Then a warning bell rang in my ear. "The hoe! Remember the Bodhisattva Precepts":

"A disciple of the Buddha must not steal by himself, encourage others to steal… any other beings' valuables and possessions including such objects as small as a needle or a blade of grass…"

extract of Second Precept
Brahma Net Sutra

A greedy voice inside began to protest, "Oh come on, that's stretching it. No one wants these sprouts. They're left here for no good purpose. It's wasteful."

A wiser, cooler voice responded:

"Use your wisdom. Suppose you fill your bowl with sprouts pulled from a farmer's field. Suppose someone asks you where they came from? Will you admit you took them without permission or will you lie and break another precept? How will those sprouts taste? Are little green plants worth the loss of precept-spirits and protectors?"

I dropped the sprout like a hot coal and hustled out of the field. That was a test!

"The Bodhisattva protects and upholds the pure precepts. He is unattached to forms, sounds, smells, tastes, and sensation of touch, and he explains them for others in this way as well."

Ten Practices Chapter
Avatamsaka Sutra

Heng Chau • December 2, 1978
The Senate passes a bill to protect the Sutra

Dream: We are attending a Senate sub-committee hearing. They are passing a bill to protect the Shurangama Sutra and restore the Shurangama Mantra in its original form. Pure Sanghans testify and verify the authentic version. It's almost too late however. Even the Chairman and newspeople can't remember or repeat a single line after hearing it. Some kind of mental block exists and hardly anyone can concentrate. Human communication and thinking have sunk to the level of T.V. commercials and advertising jingles. The Committee passes the bill as a token gesture. It's a time of a popular and widespread spiritual awakening. (The U.S. is a world leader, having blended Eastern and native traditions solidly into mainstream culture. A Texas politician, for example, gives a supportive speech expounding on the Sanskrit origins of the mantra like it was Daniel Boone – Abe Lincoln Americana.) But people's minds have been stunted and dulled by a trend for "easy, new, quick, and instant" in everything. The Mantra is being slowly killed by abbreviation and abridgement. People's minds, words, and views function just like T.V. and only a small handful can still distinguish deviant from proper.

"The Shurangama Sutra breaks up the deviant and reveals the proper. It smashes all the heavenly demons and those of externalist paths, and reveals the innate human capacity for right knowledge and right views. But when the Buddhadharma is about to become extinct, the very first sutra to vanish will be the Shurangama Sutra. So if we wish to maintain and protect the Proper Dharma, we should investigate the Shurangama Sutra, come to understand the Shurangama Sutra, and protect the Shurangama Sutra."

Venerable Master Hua
in commentary to Shurangama Sutra

* * *

In all worlds without an equal,
In a place which cannot be overthrown or conquered.
For Bodhisattvas he constantly praises it.
In that way he teaches them never to fall back.

Ten Dwellings Chapter
Avatamsaka Sutra

A cultivator's only defense against falling back is a concentrated mind, pure precepts, and bringing forth a resolve for Bodhi that cannot be overthrown or defeated. Once the resolve for Bodhi is expressed, comes the hard work of clearing the inner land and building a Bodhimanda (lit. place of enlightenment, plot or circle of the Way). The Bodhimanda is the monastery or temple outside, but even more important, it is the temple within: the straight mind and pure thoughts. The straight mind is just the absence of seeking and selfishness. Pure thoughts occur by themselves when defilement is cleansed away. Guarding the six sense organs of the eyes, ears, nose, tongue, body and mind keeps the Way-place clean, and when all is clean, the spirit comes to dwell.

The highest *gung fu* is the gathering back and regulating of these six roots. Subduing oneself, in thought after thought, is the Bodhimanda (lit. diamond throne of enlightenment) The Bodhimanda outside is the full lotus posture (vajrasana); inside it's proper knowledge and views, or simply, no desires. This is the true "place which cannot be overthrown or conquered," because the deviant cannot overcome the proper. Therefore it's called "diamond throne" or "vajra," and represents the fullness of merit and virtue.

> The Buddha is the world's Lord of Great Strength.
> Endowed with all merit and virtue,
> He brings all Bodhisattvas to dwell amid this.
> In this way he teaches them to be victorious heroes.
>
> Ten Dwellings Chapter
> Avatamsaka Sutra

The work of the great hero is to conquer himself, and in so doing, reunite with the Way. But conquering oneself is accomplished with patience, faith, and gentle renunciation, not with hard force and uptight repression. In this way, the soft overcomes the hard, the yielding conquers the resistant, and the work of the great hero is gradually brought to perfection: the merit and virtue of all Buddhas.

Heng Sure • December 3, 1978
C'mon wind, blow my attachments away

"Out On The Breeze"

Bodhisattvas leave attachments behind like snails leave shells. Cultivators leave attachments by letting go the ideas the ego needs to survive. The number one notion to disown: the Ego itself. The Ego exists in thoughts of me and mine: who am I? Who will I become? My identity, my self, lives only in the ideas, plans, hopes and desires I attach to. Suppose I simply let those thoughts go and stop planning ahead for myself? I might not exist!

The bittersweet catch: until I risk letting go the thought of gaining anything from cultivation, I chain myself to the desire realm. The fear of not getting free creates the very attachment I most long to be rid of.

Bowing in this endless windstorm stirs up the deepest fears; it blows the covers from attachments I'd rather not face. Letting go of the Ego's prized thoughts is the work of a Great Hero. Nothing ventured, nothing gained, but a humbling, painful insight into my brittle, useless ego-defenses. Truly,

> To conquer others requires strength.
> To conquer oneself is harder still.

> Lao Tzu

The reeds and sage-bushes whip and wave. Flexible, they withstand the wind's push by yielding, by letting go. C'mon wind, blow harder, blow these foolish, tired fears out into the whitecaps and foam; hang my attachments out on the breeze.

> "This is the Bodhisattva's transference… so that all beings can be completely certified to unobstructed, unattached, liberated wisdom."

> Ten Transferences Chapter
> Avatamsaka Sutra

Heng Chau • December 3, 1978
We have all been together with Vairochana Buddha

"A Golden Thread Of Vows"

This morning I remembered that I am part of a large assembly of Dharma-friends and fellow cultivators who made vows long ago to do the Buddha's work to the ends of future time. I vowed to do a bowing pilgrimage with another Dharma Master this time perhaps. Others vowed to translate Sutras, teach in schools, raise money to build Way-places, or put the Bodhimanda together, brick by brick, in every future world. Some vowed to leave home, others to be laypeople; some vowed to be men, others to be women. Together we ride these deep vows to protect and propagate the Proper Dharma and use our bodies and lives as vast offerings to all Thus Come Ones and to every living being.

> I vow to always meet Thus Come Ones face to face.
> And the hosts of disciples that circulate around them.
> I'll raise offerings which are vast and great,
> Untiring to the ends of future aeons.
>
> Universal Worthy's Conduct and Vows Chapter
> Avatamsaka Sutra

Whenever I neglect or drift away from these vows my life runs amok. When I hold firm to my vows and let things happen naturally and forsake the worldly trappings, my life grows light and happy and by itself, returns to the Buddha, the Dharma, and the Sangha. Vows are like a golden thread within our hearts. A fine delicate filament of faith, and none of us ever feels right or truly ourselves until we learn to trust and to follow it. We follow this thin golden thread until it widens into the broad, dazzling highway of the Tao itself and leads us home again. Just give this golden thread of faith room to grow and the power of vows takes care of the rest.

At the beginning of the pilgrimage the Abbot observed one night,

"All of you in the past have been together with Vairochana Buddha. We have been together investigating the Buddhadharma. And way back then I said we should all go to America and do it. Now we are all here to fulfill our vows.

"From limitless kalpas past our causes and conditions with one another are deep. They create a strength of togetherness that endures... and in the Hall of Ten Thousand Buddhas you can make vows, so in the future we can all become Ten Thousand Buddhas to protect ten thousand peoples... In the midst of a dream we are all here doing the Buddhas' work."

* * *

"The Right Road" – Gazos Creek, CA.

A young couple from the East Coast stopped and watched the bowing.

"I've been kickin' around, looking. I'm 24. I know there is a supreme path but it's hard to find the right road," said the man. "Buddhism huh? Maybe we'll be seeing you again. Thanks."

They drove off in an old car stuffed with all their belongings.

> "I will lead those who have lost their way to the right road."
>
> Universal Worthy's Conduct and Vows Chapter
> Avatamsaka Sutra

* * *

"Just like the Whales..."

A man who had seen us back in Big Sur stopped to offer support and share some thoughts:

"Well, this pilgrimage must be a great way to get to enjoy the coast. Have you seen the big whales?" he asked, looking out to sea. "Every year they migrate hundreds of miles."

"We pretty much keep our nose to our minds."

"Umm. Any troubles?" he asks.

"Only what we make for ourselves. People treat us like we treat them." I answer.

"That's a good way to look at it. I really admire your dedication. I saw you back in Big Sur and it made me stop and think a lot... You know," he added, looking out at the ocean, "the whales are really dedicated too, like you."

Whales follow deeply ingrained instincts. They migrate because it is in their nature and they could not have a thought of turning back. Bodhisattvas follow deep and sincere vows. They cultivate for Bodhi because it is in the nature of all living beings to seek enlightenment. Once they resolve their minds on Bodhi, they could never have a thought a turning back... just like the whales.

> "Following in accord with nirvana's still, extinct Dharma... they only head for Bodhi and never once retreat."
>
> Merit and Virtue From First Bringing Forth
> the Mind – Avatamsaka Sutra

* * *

Tai ji quan provides strength to do the Buddha's work. It's an expedient dharma that helps gather back the six organs, to "go back to the root and return to the source."

When I left home I gave my martial arts skills to the Buddhas as an offering, and with a wish to benefit others. I would like to see the martial arts return to the Buddhadharma where they belong.

> "He wants to make his own body into the foremost of stupas and universally make everyone happy."
>
> Ten Transferences Chapter
> Avatamsaka Sutra

Heng Sure • December 4, 1978
The wind has frozen my head!

> "Once the Bodhisattva attains the Ground of Happiness,
> he leaves all fears behind."
>
> Ten Grounds Chapter
> Avatamsaka Sutra

This windstorm has teeth! Now it's bitten through our last refuge, the Plymouth. Meditated long last night, bare-headed in a cold wind. The draft blew in through the crack in the tailgate door. After an hour I felt a pain across the forehead and a line of chill tracking along the energy channels of arms and hands. Couldn't get heated up.

Woke this morning nauseous and scared stiff. Saw an ice-cold, glowing white, Saturn figure coming for me – the grim reaper with his sickle. Bad news. I had frozen the central meridians on my head by sitting in the icy wind without a hat. Half awake, I fantasized Father Time, the Ghost of Impermanence, or was he for real? Frantic, I fumbled through a clutch of mind-methods to counter my fear. Nothing worked, just as when a foot goes to sleep, you have to simply wait until circulation returns. But this was my head! Felt panic and had a big urge to give in, to simply curl up and let the cold gather me in.

Had to turn the urge to run for cover, to go anywhere to escape the diabolical wind that pushes all my affliction-buttons. The frozen head was a big scare, a show-stopper, not a joke. Dark, cold, alone, the resolve for Bodhi is a wish to wake every living beings from "the long sleep" of fear and pain.

If I had genuine spiritual skill or a Bodhisattva's courage, I could have turned this state; the brush with impermanence was vivid, a shock. But I dived for the blankets and cried for help instead. Ah, the wind. I'm going to have to face my hang-up and let go my attachment to comfort. I put my self first and hung on tight. That ain't how things are! The self is a wrong idea, and it creates all fear. Bodhisattvas erase all shadows of the self and feel no fear no matter where they are.

> "It is because these Bodhisattvas are free of the thought of self. They do not even cherish their own bodies, how much the less wealth and possessions. Therefore, they have no fear of not staying alive."

Ten Grounds Chapter
Avatamsaka Sutra

Heng Chau • December 4, 1978
Real compassion is often silent

"Happy Birthday To Who?"

The days and dates got scrambled and I missed my own birthday. The "big day" passed unnoticed and felt like any other day. The message: "Everything is made from the mind alone." If we think a particular day is special, then it becomes special. If we do not think about it, then the day returns to the level sameness of all dharmas. Things of themselves are still and empty; their nature is no-nature.

> All dharmas are uncreated;
> Their nature is no-nature.

Ten Transferences Chapter
Avatamsaka Sutra

In the primary meaning there is no self or what belongs to self, including birthdays. How many days from beginningless time past have I been born into this world and left it, only to return on another day, in another body, in another path, with another name, and another lifespan, and do it all over again? How many times in the future will I be born again and again? Birthday after birthday, funeral after funeral, turning on the wheel of the Six Paths without a moment's pause. Maybe today is my birthday from last life and tomorrow my birthday next life. Missing a birthday is nothing, but missing a day of cultivation is truly a loss.

"One turns and flows in birth and death and is unable to get out of this narrow dwelling of the skandhas (personality). The heap of suffering increases, and yet within it, there is no self, no one with a lifespan, no one with an upbringing or personal history, and no one who can grasp at numerous future births in the six paths.

"With no self and nothing that belongs to self, the past and future are the same: none of this exists at all. Empty and false, greedy longing are cut off and left behind. Whether these exist or do not exist, he knows it as it really is."

Ten Grounds Chapter, "Fifth Ground,"
Avatamsaka Sutra

* * *

"Solitary Places"

"Real Compassion is often silent."

Venerable Abbot Hua

"He vows that all living beings totally leave behind unbeneficial speech and take constant delight in solitary places, their minds without a second thought."

Ten Transferences Chapter
Avatamsaka Sutra

The "solitary place" is remembering how to be happy and comfortable alone. To be independent and self-reliant is the true and fundamental disposition of people. But where there's nothing going on we make trouble and have that second thought, "Oh, I feel lonely." With the second thought comes a third, fourth, and fifth, up to ten thousand. We forget our original face and leave the natural fullness of self, seeking to fill a trumped-up need that doesn't need to be filled. Moreover, this need can't be filled. Unbeneficial speech arises, emotions stir, feelings grow, excited, then hurt, and unbeneficial deeds follow. As the glamour wears off and waxes cold, love turns to hate and we end up feeling smothered and tied-down, far away from the delight of our solitary place.

"Monk" is from the Greek work *monachos*, *monos*, meaning "single, alone, solitary." We are all of us by nature "monks." Left-home people, monastics, are simply reclaiming their original home and natural heritage. In practice it means cleaving to the Middle Way: not attaching, not rejecting; not being sticky, yet not cold and inhuman. Part of returning the light to illumine within means not trampling on others' solitary place, so that even while together, we never lose the freedom to be alone. It is by grasping and attaching to people that we abandon them and lose ourselves. Therefore,

> He never discriminates or seeks among living beings.
> Nor does he false think about dharmas.
> Although he is not defiled by attachment
>   to the mundane world,
> At the same time, he does not abandon living beings.
>
> Ten Transferences Chapter
Avatamsaka Sutra

Ultimately, by taking constant delight in solitary places, we give the greatest benefit and contentment to others: the unattached, unbound, liberated mind. After a lecture in Alor Setar, Malaysia, the Abbot spoke informally and answered some of our questions. The topic of compassion and helping people came up.

"Master, what does real compassion mean? I don't feel it entails just being 'nice' to people, because that often is false," asked a nun.

The Master replied,

"Of course, compassion is not a mere external show of kindness, because that easily falls into the realm of artificiality. Compassion arises on its own as you understand more. As you grow up, it flows out from your self-nature because you are really able to see."

The Abbot gave the example of lecturing, saying that true eloquence cannot be learned or feigned, but can only arise when one is really sincere and spontaneously responding from the self-nature, without thought or self-calculation.

"People are born alone into this world, solitary," he continued. "When I was young and yet a student of the Way, I used to prefer to be by myself. I seldom talked and I looked really dumb. Many people looked down on me; even novices looked down on me, and ordered me around. I voluntarily took on the menial chores that nobody else wanted to do: washing vegetables, cooking, cleaning out the pit toilets. I gathered my essence and blended with the scenery."

The Master went on, "Even now at Gold Mountain and the City of Ten Thousand Buddhas, I am solitary. I enjoy most being in my little room, doing my own work. Most people who come to talk have nothing important to say. Why talk for the sake of talking? Why waste time on non-essentials?" he asked.

"When I help people I don't want it to be known that I am helping them. They need not thank me or get attached to any external aspects of Dharma. Real compassion is often silent."

Heng Sure • December 5, 1978
It has been years

"…Totally Without Reliance or Dwelling"

It's been years since I entered a bank, answered the phone, opened a bill, riffled a sports-page, totaled a tax return, sat on the aisle, talked to a store clerk, took an aspirin, uncapped a soft-drink, heard an advertisement, slept between sheets, shook a hand, or said "goodnight."

Before leaving the monastery base-camp, I never bowed beside roaring surf or covered hands and face with sap from sticky sea-daisies, or walked like a circus clown on rubber legs across a patch of springy ice-plant, or scaled a narrow chimney of shale above the road to find a private space for privy. Never before stood in wind strong enough to lean against, or hung laundry on a live-oak branch and looked up to meet a startled turkey buzzard eye-to-eye.

We don't live on a shoestring – our monk's shoes have no ties. Haven't touched an electric light for years, but every night, our eyes behold the radiance of wisdom; gradually learning to let go of hang-ups and fears. Happiest time of my life, dwelling nowhere, every moment of cultivation a step along the high road back home.

> In every country in all directions,
> They are totally without reliance or dwelling.
> Not seeking life itself or any of the host of dharmas;
> Nor do they falsely discriminate.

Ten Transferences Chapter
Avatamsaka Sutra

Heng Chau • December 5, 1978
A tribute to Great Strength Bodhisattva

Dream: The Master has his disciples do University "projects" of introducing the Buddha-dharma to all fields of study: math, sciences, literature, medicine, horticulture, architecture, and so forth. The results are mind-blowing. Brilliant mathematicians are working on a formula equation for "still quiescence," totally absorbed in dimensions they never dreamed of. Someone in plant-research/botany came up with a rich growth of never-before-seen or heard-of plants: funny green ones, wild creeping, hovering vines. Many were edible. The University people were really excited about plunging into new worlds that made what they had been studying seem like kinder-garten by comparison.

Waking up, I remembered a passage from the Avatamsaka where the Pure Youth, Comfortable Chief, one of Good Wealth's Advisors, describes his mastery of all manner of occupations and skills. He knows architecture, construction, chemistry, farming, and horticulture, business and trade, as well as physiognomy, medicine, psychiatry, prophecy, and divination, mathematics, and even alchemy. He says to Good Wealth,

> "Good Man, in the past at the Way Place of Dharma Prince Manjushri, I practiced and studied the dharmas of literature, numeration, mathematics, and self-making, and so forth. Thereupon, I enlightened to and entered the Dharma door of spiritual penetrations and wisdom of all clever arts and skills."
>
> Entering the Dharma Realm
> Avatamsaka Sutra

The ancients used the knowledge and skills obtained from worldly studies to gain transcendental wisdom. The mastery of "the Clever Arts and Skills" (also called the Five Sciences) served as a stepping stone to spiritual purity and world-transcending knowledge. They also were able to use these skills to benefit mankind and as expedient to lead people from worldly pursuits to the paths of ultimate wisdom. Comfortable Chief concludes,

> "I can cause living beings to study and practice these dharmas and to increase and grow in decisiveness until they are ultimately pure."

Perhaps the dream wasn't so far-fetched after all.

Note: The Five Sciences, or the Clever Arts and Skills are:

1. Science of Sounds – grammar, linguistics, philology.

2. Science of Arts and Crafts – mathematics, numeration, construction, alchemy, agriculture, trade and comer, divination.

3. Science of Medicine – curing diseases.

4. Science of Logic – study of the various realms and places.

5. Science of Philosophy – knowledge of cause and effect in the six paths of rebirth and the Three Vehicles.

"Great Strength"

Real strength is measured in self-control, not in controlling others. True power cannot be seen in big biceps, nor demonstrated with a show of brawn. Genuine power is invisible and expressed quietly in a gentle heart, and an unbreakable will for goodness. Only one who softens his mind and completely cuts off selfish desire can be called a strong person and a great hero.

> One who conquers others is strong,
> One who conquers himself is far stronger.
>
> Lao Tzu

Transforming ignorance into wisdom, smelting afflictions into Bodhi, is the *gung fu* of "gathering back." Cultivators gather back their natural endowment of enlightenment by reversing the habitual outward flow of the six sense faculties. These six organs, when allowed to run loose, scatter and drain away our precious treasures like Huns sacking a scared city. Gathering back requires great strength.

When the work of "subduing oneself and returning to principle" requires more strength and guts than I can muster, I find myself reciting the name of Great Strength Bodhisattva:

Namo Da Shr Jr Pusa, Namo Da Shr Jr Pusa.

When I recite his name help arrives along with the strength to gather back the six organs. It takes great strength and patience-power to do nothing, and by doing nothing, the light of wisdom returns itself. Part of a verse in praise of Great Strength Bodhisattva reads,

> Gather back the six organs,
> This is wonderful beyond words!
> I vow to make it known throughout the land.
> Namo the Western Land of Ultimate Bliss,
> Body of boundless, flickering light,
> Great Strength Bodhisattva

We wrote a ballad today in praise of Great Strength Bodhisattva:

"The Ballad of Super Strong"

Come gather 'round friends
And I'll sing you a song,
About a Bodhisattva,
His name is Super Strong.

With a burst of blazing light,
He opened eyes asleep and blind,
'Cause Super Strong's *gung fu*
Was the power of his mind.

Now Super Strong was awesome,
But his heart was solid kind,
"All suffering and disasters
I'll end for all mankind."

CHORUS:
Super Strong's inside you,
Cultivate with all your might,
Pure thoughts continue;
Don't fight, return the light.
Pure thoughts continue,
Don't fight, return the light.

* * *

So he gathered in his stealin' eyes,
His ears and nose and tongue.
Tamed his mind and wild body,
And when all the work was done,

A blinding blaze of light,
Shot forth from toe to crown;
'Cause he plugged into the Source,
Tried his best and laid it down.

CHORUS:
"The six organs gather back
Recite the Buddha's name,"
Throughout the Dharma Realm
Ya' can hear Great Strength proclaim.

* * *

Now dragons curl their tails,
And spirits fold their hands.
Tigers crouch in corners,
And ghosts obey commands.

CHORUS:
Guan Yin and Amitabha
With Super Strong join hands;
Riding vows made long ago,
They roam the Western Land.

* * *

Ain't no better thing to do
Than savin' all mankind.
And to the Buddha City
Bowing with a single mind.
The world is ripe and waitin',
Can't you see that now's the time?
To the Buddha City,
Bowing with a single mind.

CHORUS:
The world is ripe and waitin'
Can't you see that now's the time,
To the Buddha City,
Bowing with a single mind.
Ya, to the Buddha City,
Bowing with a single mind.

* * *

"At all times we are reciting our sutra. Some of us recite fluently, others not so well. If we can be familiar with our sutra we need not be dragged all over the universe by our karma. If we are unfamiliar with our sutra, it recites us instead, and drags us all over. But bit by bit we can become fluent and then we have some leverage on our destiny."

Venerable Abbot Hua, 1978
Gold Wheel Temple, L.A.

Admonition to myself: Take apart and get to know your Sutra, the core ideas, views, and thoughts that flow through your mind in an unbroken stream. Carefully watch over your three karmas of body, mouth, and mind. Observe how everything that happens to you is a rebound of what you created, a reflection of your mind's Sutra.

In over forty-nine years of speaking Dharma, the Buddha never laid down a single Dharma, save to "learn to recite your own sutra;" that is to say, "return the light and illumine within, light up your mind and see the Nature." After bowing long in repentance and reform, sometimes I can see it is all there, in the Buddha's profound teaching, states in such simple words: "All beings have the Buddha-nature; all can become Buddhas." The trick is to not interfere and to not smother the pure nature with my greed, anger, stupidity, pride, and doubt. Truly,

"What is spoken is false, what is practiced is true."

The Sixth Patriarch Sutra

Heavy winds and winter storms continue to pound the coast. Nights are cold. Our cotton Bhikshu robes and blankets keep out the hill and protect our bodies from the wind. The Avatamsaka fills our hearts with a warm light and keeps our souls from blowing away.

In the beginning, the pilgrimage was mostly outside: the streets and people, the weather, long miles, and aching muscles. But the bowing and Sutra change us like the inexorable waves of the mighty ocean wear down and soften the hardest boulder. The bowing moves us deeper into our own minds and the Avatamsaka opens up and beckons us into measureless worlds without limit. And yet the deeper we travel within, the more inside and outside merge. Sometimes everything starts to interlace and fuse into one size, one number, one place, and one time. The urge to grab for the old and familiar is offset by the joy of discovery and the freedom of letting go. As the poem says,

"Cultivation! How could there be anything more esoteric or wonderful!?"

Venerable Abbot Hua

* * * * * * * * *
January 1979

Heng Chau • January 2, 1979
The "Fly" invades planet Earth

Dear Shr Fu,

I had a dream last month that really moved me to work harder:

Dream: It came silently gliding in from outer space, passing galaxies and covering incredible distances in seconds. It was huge, black and a totally evil thing. Attracted by a foul, amber smog, it was honing in on our galaxy. The smog was a color, a smell, a texture and vibes of a bad energy that permeated our whole universe. This "fly" was drawn to it like a bee to honey.

Everyone thinks the smog is beautiful – like looking at a colorful sunset through layers of air pollution. No one notices the fly as it quietly zeros in on our galaxy, then our solar system, and finally Earth itself. The Earth is center of the bad *ch'i* the fly is attracted to. The fly is diamond-hard concentrated evil and destruction. There is no goodness whatsoever to it.

It banked around the moon. You could see the footprints of the astronauts on its surface. The astronauts were jumping and playing around like kids digging in a sand-box. They never noticed the fly. It could change shape from the size of the Milky Way down to an atom particle faster than a thought.

At the top of a tiered flight of stairs, in an awesome, idyllic place, lived an absent-minded professor-type. I asked who he was, "Oh that's God," someone said. "God the Father." It blew my mind! "I'm going back to work!" I thought, "to fight the fly." The force of the fly was way beyond God's power of influence. He was having a party, and, like the carefree child, waiting for the next surprise delight. He knew only bliss.

In a weird, *yin* mortuary-temple, devotees dressed in long, white Greco-Roman robes were engaged in bizarre rites about death and the dead. It was like a deviant Forest Lawn. They were pouring oils and wines over a corpse, laughing and merrymaking. The fly was there, unemotional and very at home.

A radio station in a big city: it looks on the up-and-up out front, but inside it's a nerve center for the fly. It may have even beamed the fly in with its broadcasts.

An urbane, young, unmarried "people's politician" is at the radio station. It's his campaign headquarters. His aides excitedly tell him there's a major revolution going on in the High Schools and Junior Highs. The station is broadcasting the take-overs of the schools and fomenting the violence: "Orange Jr. High has been occupied by… Glendale High School has been taken over by… The east wing of…" The politician is cool and calculating. He is going to ride the revolution to political power. There is a bloodbath – children are killing their parents and teachers.

People were in heavy trances, as if under a spell. Their hearts and minds were numb and beyond the reach of reasoning or pity.

On an airport runway all ready to go like a 707 fighter jet plane with an ominous rocket/missile mounted on its nose. The rocket could not be stopped. It could penetrate anything and be shot anywhere. The missile was like a silver metal sliver and it could kill a single person by entering the eye, or wipe out an entire country. There were lots of them.

The Sangha was working day and night in groups and teams. They were not under the spell and could see the deviant energy of the fly in all its manifestations. We travelled everywhere fighting it and planting good seeds, neutralizing noxious vapors. Our method was the Great Compassion and other mantras. Wherever the Great Compassion Mantra was recited a circle of pure, bright light was produced. The light was sunny and correct, like the colors on the coast after a rainstorm when the sun comes out. The color of the fly-

smog was the dense, choking amber of an old photograph, a stuffy attic without windows.

"I should be a light for all living beings, and cause them to attain the light of wisdom which eradicates the gloom of stupidity. I should be a torch for all living beings which breaks through the gloom of ignorance. I should be a lamp for all living beings and cause them to dwell in the place of ultimate purity."

Avatamsaka Sutra

The Sangha was pure light travelling to all places, afraid of nothing. We told people just to sincerely recite the Mantra and "light up their minds, see the nature." The Mantra helped all invisibly. Lots of people had responses to the Great Compassion Mantra. "Lighting up your heart" – these words registered deep inside and cut through the smog. Wherever it was recited, a clear and wholesome goodness broke through the gloom. All who saw it returned to the good.

We moved around on foot, on bikes and scooters, telling our friends and all with whom we had conditions and affinities. But the fly was huge and our efforts seemed like trying to stop a typhoon with an eyelash. And yet the power of the Mantra was indestructible and unsurpassed.

An electrician teamed-up with us and was able to cross some wires in a panel in the bowels of the radio station. The station looked like an ordinary public service company, but with the electrician's skill we were able to see that inside were the fly, the deviant death rites, the politician and a constant wave of broadcasted evil.

Everyone knew about the fly. But they saw it as auspicious. They were blind to its true nature because they were immersed in the smog. People said, "Oh, groovy, far out – just like science fiction!" They were merging their minds with it like in the mortuary cult. Even though the fly was eating them up and sucking up their lives, they were in a trance and getting off on it. No one could tell right from wrong, true from deviant – they didn't have "true eyes" anymore. The collective blindness was chilling and horrible.

It was all tied together: the fly, the jet-rocket, the radio station, the revolution in the schools, the strange religions and the slick politician. The fly was going into underground missile silos to spawn its eggs. The radio station and mortuary were its nest. Much of what went on was behind the scene. It took the mysterious electrician to penetrate the radio station.

God was like the card-playing fire chief who doesn't notice he's about to be burned by a forest fire. Right below his happy heaven were all these destructive missiles in silos, ready to be shot off. The missile silos looked like organ pipes or art sculpture and no one could see the fly go in and lay its eggs.

The electrician let us listen to the radio announcer say in a polished, sonorous voice, "And remember friends… kill, kill, kill…" There was a fade-in to a popular folk singer masking the evil message with a simple song, "This land is your land…" It made it palatable.

There were lots of people engaged in a colorful ceremony hanging themselves. It was a religious group. They were killing themselves in order to obtain some kind of spiritual state and salvation. Death and ignorance were feeding each other. They were in a trance, too, and had no light of wisdom.

When I awoke, my resolve was deepened. Heavy demonic forces and darkness created from bad karma could only be stopped by cultivation. What really counts is the Forty-Two Hands and Eyes, the Great Compassion Mantra and the Shurangama Mantra. And most of all, a *pure heart* – a vast, unselfish, kind and pure heart. That's where the light was coming from in the dream, pure, peaceful, happy people reciting mantras and transferring the benefit to all living beings. The politician had color but no light. It was the color of good food and cosmetics, not the light of wisdom and compassion. The people of goodness in the dream were like little suns of kindness, compassion, joy and giving. Even though our efforts seemed small in the face of big darkness, they were pure and done with big hearts for everyone.

"I should be like the sun which shines universally on everything without seeking repayment for its kindness. No matter what kind of evil comes from living beings, I can handle it. I would never give up my vows on account of it...

"Rather, I vigorously cultivate the transference of good roots to universally cause living beings to obtain peace and happiness.

"Even though my good roots may be few, I gather in all living beings and using a mind of great happiness, I transfer it on a vast scale.

"If there were good roots and I did not desire to benefit living beings, this could not be called transference."

Avatamsaka Sutra

Unselfishness and great compassion is where it's at.

Peace in the Way,
Disciple Guo Ting (Heng Chau)
bows in respect

Heng Sure • January 3, 1979
Kerzatz! Pain to the extreme!

Venerable Master,

"He vows that all beings get pure Ch'an gates."

Avatamsaka Sutra

Patient Ch'an meditators know that when pain in the knees and ankles, legs and back occur after long hours of sitting, one reaches a point when the pain suddenly disappears. It's as if a gate opens and one passes through to another world, free of affliction. It's a wonderful experience.

On the way through the gate, however, it takes determination and patience not to be moved by the discomfort.

"What others cannot endure, you must endure. While sitting in Ch'an everyone must go through the experience of leg pain. We all must pass through the stage of taking what others cannot take. And when we reach the point of bearing the pain that others cannot bear, then we can get good news. This is called 'getting through the gate that is difficult to enter,' and 'breaking through the difficult barrier.'"

Master Hua, Ch'an instruction
December 1977

In our station wagon I sit in the well where the back seat folds down. Heng Chau has to crawl over my knees to reach his seat in the back. Our meditation schedules are different and one evening he was returning from standing meditation just as I was reaching the point of extreme pain in the knees during Ch'an. I was really sweating. My body hurt a lot, but I was determined to take it. The happiness on the other side of the gate is quite fine.

"Now we are in the Ch'an Hall and why don't we have any samadhi power? You hurt a little and can't take it... even to the point that in being unable to take it, you want to cry... you haven't broken through the barrier of pain. Now, we want to break through it. We break through these barriers and we can be at ease with the pain..."

Listen and Think

I was at the point of extreme pain and because of my normal impatience I was debating whether or not I could make it through the gate. The pain had gone on for what seemed like aeons. In fact, it was more like half an hour, but I was ready to cry and moan. Had a fly landed on my leg, it would have been too much to take. Every cell was straining to hold on to full lotus.

"...pain to the extreme, to the point that we forget there is ourselves and others."

Listen and Think

Heng Chau has a trick of closing the car door with his foot as he climbs on over my seat. He hooks his toes onto the door handle and pulls with his leg. The door swings shut without his having to turn around on the narrow door jamb. It's a nifty move, only this time it didn't work. Heng Chau slipped on the ledge and landed with all his weight right smack on my long-suffering knee.

Kerzatz! Pain to the extreme! Electric blue and white pain! So much pain that there wasn't any pain any more.

> "How can there be pain? There is no pain. No matter what it is you do, you should do it to the ultimate point. When you've cultivated to the extreme, your light is penetrating."
>
> Listen and Think

If I have ever emitted light, this was surely the time. I must have blazed like a torch for a few seconds. Tears ran down – tears of laughter. My nose watered and I could only laugh. It was such a ridiculous scene and the pain was just huge. Heng Chau apologized, he knows this point of pain in meditation, and he felt compassion for my misery. His comment, "Did I put you through the gate?" was right on. He had. As my eyes dried I realized that I was still in full lotus and I was on the other side of the difficult barrier. The pain was gone and my mind was quiet and still.

There was no Heng Sure and no Heng Chau. No Plymouth and no Ch'an meditation. It was really a tranquil state. Cultivating the Forty-two Hands and Eyes in this place of stillness was a brand new experience.

I don't recommend that Ch'an cultivators rely on externals to pass through Ch'an barriers, but sometimes unexpected expedients appear to take us across when our determination to endure the pain is solid and firm.

Disciple Guo Chen (Heng Sure)
bows in respect

Heng Chau • January 3, 1979
Ants were biting and crawling all over my legs

Dear Shr Fu,

It's truly as you say, "The straight mind is the Bodhimanda." I remember when I took precepts, it was said that each precept brings with it five Dharma-protecting Spirits. As long as one holds the precepts, these spirits protect one. But if one breaks a precept, they retreat, leaving one wide open to attack from the retinue of demons. Why do things go wrong with our lives? Why do we meet with disasters and bad luck? It's just because of not following the rules, not keeping the precepts. When the mind is straight, one's Bodhimanda is secure and lucky. When the mind is crooked, the Bodhimanda meets hard times. The Bodhimanda is just our own bodies and minds.

Out here, bowing, every time we break a rule or false think we get trouble. In the Avatamsaka Sutra it says:

"As one thinks, so one receives in return."

This week, we really put our minds to working hard and keeping the rules. It was very peaceful and natural. The car, supplies, weather, our health – all effortlessly worked out just right and went well. Then I attached to a pleasant state in meditation and felt, "Hey, I've got something here." Within minutes, cars were honking and people were yelling at us. Strange people appeared, pale-looking and hungry for our light, wanting "to talk and rap." You see, after I got my state I got sloppy. I figured, "You don't have to start on time; relax, don't force it." So I got lazy and hung around the car making tea. Then I thought, "Well, I'm still hungry and that half an apple should be eaten." So I ate it, even though we have ended the meal. I didn't protect the Bodhimanda but left it open to strange energies and hassles with my false thoughts and broken rules. .

I realized that all the disasters in the world begin in this way. There is no boundary or fence for our thoughts. They are free to purify or pollute to the ends of empty space. If I kept the rules and purified my thoughts, it could have benefitted a lot of living beings and improved the world. The Bodhimanda begins with a single thought and our own persons, but it has no end. The self and the Dharma Realm are not two.

When we were in Hong Kong, the delegation went to visit Western Bliss Gardens, a Bodhimanda the Master built years ago on the steep hills of that city. It is a very pure place. Even though Western Bliss Gardens is surrounded by urban noise, smog and pollution, as soon as you enter the gate, it's as quiet as mountain wilderness. The air is clean and the water that flows out of a rock is the purest I ever drank.

There's a Bodhi tree growing in a corner and I got the notion to pick a leaf from it to bring back to the U.S and carry with us on our pilgrimage. Clearly this was just greed and climbing on conditions. While everyone was inside, I ran over to pick a leaf. But every time I reached for one, I couldn't touch it. It was as if I was being restrained. Not only that, but every time I found a perfect leaf – just the right shape and size, etc. – when I reached for it, the perfect leaf suddenly revealed a flaw or didn't look like the one I wanted. This went on for about five minutes. Just as I finally found the leaf I wanted, when I touched it, I felt all sorts of itching and stinging on my legs. My socks were full of ants! They were biting and crawling all over my legs. I ran out from under the tree and started jumping up and down, shaking off the ants and scratching the bites. Then the Master came out and someone said, "Come on, time to leave." I never got the leaf, but I got a good lesson: greed and self-seeking bring disasters; and, "everything is made from the mind alone." The Bodhimanda is created by pure thoughts. It's not outside.

In the midst of a Hong Kong slum is a peaceful and well-protected Way-place. In the midst of the pure and peaceful California coast and countryside we can encounter hassles, weird people and feel insecure. Why? Thoughts. A pure mind can turn any place into a pure place. A defiled mind can transform even the purest place into mud. If I want a peaceful and well-protected Bodhimanda, I should clean up my own mind and not try to steal it by picking other people's Bodhi trees.

> Defilement and purity,
> In measureless kshetra-seeds
> Come about from living beings' thoughts;
> They are held up by the strength of Bodhisattvas.
>
> Avatamsaka Sutra

Peace in the Way,
Disciple Guo Ting (Heng Chau)
bows in respect

Heng Chau • January 24, 1979
Wait 'til you get to Devil's Slide

Dear Shr Fu,

Here's a rundown of the last two days' bowing to the City of Ten Thousand Buddhas:

Sunday, January 22: Quiet morning. Horseback riders trot by, "Hey, what you're doing is great. I'd do it myself if I had the time." And off they gallop. A young family in an old car stops. "We're going back to the East Coast, but we really feel like we have to see the Ten Thousand Buddhas place before we go."

"The City of Ten Thousand Buddhas," I say.

"Yes. There's something about it… we would not feel ready to travel back East until we have visited it. We are looking for a pure and holy place to christen our new baby and the City of Ten Thousand Buddhas feels right." The mother proudly holds up the little baby. "I chant Om Mani Padme Hum. I learned it from a Tibetan Buddhist monk in New Jersey. He was a good person, but there wasn't any heart there, you know? I mean, it was all very intel-lectual. We are looking for a method, a Path to really practice and walk. We saw a picture of the City of Ten Thousand Buddhas. It feels clean and has lots of light."

A man in the back seat asks, "What kind of Buddhism do you follow?"

"Buddhism is just the best in the hearts of all living beings. It has no country or sect. It belongs to everyone. Buddhism is the teaching of all beings. Nothing is excluded, we don't discriminate."

Big smiles and nods of agreement. "What system do you practice?"

"World Buddhism. All traditions, all schools are practiced and taught. Whatever suits you is available – Ch'an, Vinaya, Secret School, Pure Land, or Teaching – and someone to teach the method. All paths for all beings." More smiles.

"Got a map?" "Is it near Mt. Shasta?" "Far out, that's great."

After they left, two young Mormon missionaries in spotless vested suits walk up. "This is Elder _____ and I am Elder _____. We were wondering what you're doing."

"We're Buddhist monks on a bowing pilgrimage."

"Oh, Buddhists. We thought so. For what purpose?"

"To get rid of our faults and help the world." I am half expecting a sermon and conversion pitch, but they simply say:

"That's wonderful! We're behind you 100%. Good luck!" and they leave. Good vibrations there.

Tollgate.

As we bowed up to the last intersection out of town, a strange man appeared. He moved slowly, totally in control. His face was hidden from view behind a full beard and the shade of the tall black hat he wore. He circled us and then positioned himself in a field about 75 yards ahead and watched us. From a large shopping bag he pulled bottles of whiskey and beer and downed one after another like they were water. The vibes he put out were black and cold. As soon as I saw him, I found myself doing a couple of the Forty-two Hands.

After he settled in, strange things began to happen. Fire trucks and police cars went roaring through the intersection and then weird people started showing up. A car skidded to a stop inches from Heng Sure's head and then a woman offered him a ride. A man kept hollering from behind the black-hatted man, "What religion are you?" and laughing strangely. People in bizarre clothes and long scraggly hair walked by mumbling. The man in the black hat calmly watched over it all, nodding his head and laughing. Then he rang some bells that hung from his neck.

Immediately, five or six yelling and cursing men appeared on the embankment across the road from us. They were angry and violent. "This is devil's land here," said one. "May you be cursed!" cried another. "Wait 'til you get to Devil's Slide," threatened one with a menacing laugh. (Devil's Slide is a steep and narrow stretch of sheer cliffs and mountains about seven miles north. We've had many warnings about it.) They tossed some rocks but they missed us. The man in the black hat downed another bottle in one long swallow. Then he rang his bells and waved to the men. They climbed back over the embankment and disappeared, cursing and howling.

The black-hatted man approached to check us out up close. He laughs under his breath, "Heh, Heh, Buddhists, Krishnas, Buddhists, heh, heh…" I catch a glimpse of his face. It sends a shiver through me. I couldn't describe it except to say that it was full of delight for evil and harm, flushing red and full. He wanders over across the intersection and stands next to our car. He just stares and drinks. Without moving an inch, you can feel him directing the whole negative show with his presence. He gestures and the men and weird people return and start coming toward us.

This could be tight. Heng Sure and I have discovered that no matter what happens, we can come through it just fine if we don't let our spirits sag. If we don't let fear or anger or bad vibrations come into our hearts, we can slide through the tightest spots like greased fish. We are learning to counter-punch with kindness, compassion, joy, and giving instead of our fists, words, and false thoughts. "Everything is made from the mind alone... as one thinks, so one receives in return" (Avatamsaka Sutra). It's so true. Our survival has come down to not allowing an inch of doubt or *yin* energy to enter and pollute our minds. Put out light and the sun shines; put out darkness and it rains. The heavier it comes down, the brighter you've got to rise up and shine.

So here they were, all these hostile, strange people gathering to test our temper and resolve and maybe worse. What to do? Just the day before, we read from the Avatamsaka, and the verse came into my mind as we bowed into this tense "tollgate,"

> It's just like the sun
> Which appears in the world
> But does not hide or fail to appear
> Because there are blind people who fail to see it.
>
> When the Bodhisattva takes on
>   all this grievous suffering,
> His vigor increases.
> He does not cast it off,
> He does not hide from it.
>
> He is not scared or startled.
> He does not retreat,
> He is not frightened.
> He has no fatigue.
>
> I do not seek liberation for my own body,
> But only to save all living beings.
> So that they all attain the mind of All-Wisdom, and
> Cross over the flow of birth and death, and
> Gain liberation from all their suffering.

As I recited these lines in my mind, Heng Sure and I were engulfed in a sea of children. A school bus had pulled up across the road and about forty happy, pure-faced little Dharma protectors ran over. They completely surrounded us – some sitting, some on bikes, some standing. They made offerings from their lunch pails and piggy-banks. The strange men were confused and thwarted. They couldn't get near us. A couple of men came up and tried to pester Heng Sure, but the kids' innocence and good energy mellowed them right out. The evil men got very polite and quiet in a hurry.

"Are there really 10,000 Buddhas up there?" "Is it hard bowing all day?" "It's neat helping the world, huh?" "Do you take baths?" asked a little one. His sister kicked him gently and scolded him for getting too personal. "Of course, they take baths," she said quietly. "But how?" he persisted, "I want to get the inside scoop."

"What if bad people throw rocks?" asked a child.

"We only see good things," I answered.

"What if people come by and call you weirdos?" wondered another.

"We only hear good things," I said.

"What do you say when you pray? Does he (Heng Sure) talk to pray?"

"Real softly, huh? Shhh! Listen, maybe we can hear him." They all stand quietly there on busy Highway 1 listening to the sounds of "Hua Yen Hai Huei Fwo Pu Sa," as Heng Sure comes up from a bow.

The angry, dark men one by one drift away, muttering. The first to come and the last to go is the dark figure in the tall black hat. He is waiting on the other side of the intersection. But as we cross, the kids ride/escort us on their bikes and he slowly turns and leaves.

On the other side of the intersection is a little stretch of open country. The intersection marks the geographical end of Half Moon Bay. Scores of enthusiastic supporters load us up with offerings and kind words. They are happy and full of light. The kids slowly head for home.

"It's fascinating," says an older woman making an offering. "A wonderful idea. I wonder where all those kids came from back there all of a sudden… Did you see them?"

"Yeah. We saw them. We certainly did!" I said.

The sign says "25 miles to San Francisco." Ahead is Devil's Slide. Our map is the Avatamsaka. Everybody's a teacher. "Everything's okay. No problem."

Peace in the Way,
Disciple Guo Ting (Heng Chau)
bows in respect

Throughout the pilgrimage, devotees made offerin

ood and supplies. They also joined the bowing.

Gold Wheel Temple, where the monks started their journ

GOLD WHEEL TEMPLE

...y have returned here for instructions from the Master.

Throughout the bowing pilgrimage, the Master has
patiently and compassionately guided and
protected the bowing monks.

Buddhist Text Translation Society Publication

Buddhist Text Translation Society
International Translation Institute

http://www.bttsonline.org

1777 Murchison Drive,
Burlingame, California 94010-4504 USA
Phone: (650) 692-5912 Fax: (650) 692-5056

When Buddhism first came to China from India, one of the most important tasks required for its establishment was the translation of the Buddhist scriptures from Sanskrit into Chinese. This work involved a great many people, such as the renowned monk National Master Kumarajiva (fifth century), who led an assembly of over 800 people to work on the translation of the Tripitaka (Buddhist canon) for over a decade. Because of the work of individuals such as these, nearly the entire Buddhist Tripitaka of over a thousand texts exists to the present day in Chinese.

Now the banner of the Buddha's teachings is being firmly planted in Western soil, and the same translation work is being done from Chinese into English. Since 1970, the Buddhist Text Translation Society (BTTS) has been making a paramount contribution toward this goal. Aware that the Buddhist Tripitaka is a work of such magnitude that its translation could never be entrusted to a single person, the BTTS, emulating the translation assemblies of ancient times, does not publish a work until it has passed through four committees for primary translation, revision, editing, and certification. The leaders of these committees are Bhikshus (monks) and Bhikshunis (nuns) who have devoted their lives to the study and practice of the Buddha's teachings. For this reason, all of the works of the BTTS put an emphasis on what the principles of the Buddha's teachings mean in terms of actual practice and not simply hypothetical conjecture.

The translations of canonical works by the Buddhist Text Translation Society are accompanied by extensive commentaries by the Venerable Tripitaka Master Hsuan Hua.

BTTS Publications

Buddhist Sutras. Amitabha Sutra, Dharma Flower (Lotus) Sutra, Flower Adornment (Avatamsaka) Sutra, Heart Sutra & Verses without a Stand, Shurangama Sutra, Sixth Patriarch Sutra, Sutra in Forty-two Sections, Sutra of the Past Vows of Earth Store Bodhisattva, Vajra Prajna Paramita (Diamond) Sutra.

Commentarial Literature. Buddha Root Farm, City of 10 000 Buddhas Recitation Handbook, Filiality: The Human Source, Herein Lies the Treasure-trove, Listen to Yourself Think Everything Over, Shastra on the Door to Understanding the Hundred Dharmas, Song of Enlightenment, The Ten Dharma Realms Are Not Beyond a Single Thought, Venerable Master Hua's Talks on Dharma, Venerable Master Hua's Talks on Dharma during the 1993 Trip to Taiwan, Water Mirror Reflecting Heaven.

Biographical. In Memory of the Venerable Master Hsuan Hua, Pictorial Biography of the Venerable Master Hsü Yün, Records of High Sanghans, Records of the Life of the Venerable Master Hsüan Hua, Three Steps One Bow, World Peace Gathering, News from True Cultivators, Open Your Eyes Take a Look at the World, With One Heart Bowing to the City of 10 000 Buddhas.

Children's Books. Cherishing Life, Human Roots: Buddhist Stories for Young Readers, Spider Web, Giant Turtle, Patriarch Bodhidharma.

Musics, Novels and Brochures. Songs for Awakening, Awakening, The Three Cart Patriarch, City of 10 000 Buddhas Color Brochure, Celebrisi's Journey, Lots of Time Left.

The Buddhist Monthly–Vajra Bodhi Sea is a monthly journal of orthodox Buddhism which has been published by the Dharma Realm Buddhist Association, formerly known as the Sino-American Buddhist Association, since 1970. Each issue contains the most recent translations of the Buddhist canon by the Buddhist Text Translation Society. Also included in each issue are a biography of a great Patriarch of Buddhism from the ancient past, sketches of the lives of contemporary monastics and lay-followers around the world, articles on practice, and other material. The journal is bilingual, Chinese and English.

Please visit our web-site at **www.bttsonline.org** for the latest publications and for ordering information.

Dharma Realm Buddhist Association Branches

The City of Ten Thousand Buddhas
4951 Bodhi Way, Ukiah, CA 95482 USA
Tel: (707) 462-0939   Fax: (707) 462-0949
Website: **http://www.drba.org** Email: **cttb@drba.org**

Buddhist Text Translation Society Online Catalog
Website: **http://www.bttsonline.org**

Institute for World Religions (Berkeley Buddhist Monastery)
2304 McKinley Avenue, Berkeley, CA 94703 USA
Tel: (510) 848-3440 Fax: (510) 548-4551 Email: paramita@drba.org

Dharma Realm Buddhist Books Distribution Society
11th Floor, 85 Chung-hsiao E. Road, Sec. 6, Taipei, Taiwan R.O.C.
Tel: (02) 2786-3022 Fax: (02) 2786-2674 Email: drbbds@ms1.seeder.net

The City of the Dharma Realm
1029 West Capitol Avenue, West Sacramento, CA 95691 USA
Tel: (916) 374-8268 Fax: (916) 374-8234 Email: cdrclasses@yahoo.com

Gold Mountain Monastery
800 Sacramento Street, San Francisco, CA 94108 USA
Tel: (415) 421-6117 Fax: (415) 788-6001

Gold Wheel Monastery
235 North Avenue 58, Los Angeles, CA 90042 USA
Tel: (323) 258-6668 Fax: (323) 258-3619

Gold Buddha Monastery
248 East 11th Avenue, Vancouver, B.C. V5T 2C3 Canada
Tel: (604) 709-0248 Fax: (604) 684-3754 Email: drab@gbm-online.com
Website: http://www.drba/gbm-online.com

Gold Summit Monastery
233 1st Avenue, West Seattle, WA 98119 USA
Tel: (206) 284-6690 Fax: (206) 284-6918
Website: http://www.goldsummitmonastery.org

Gold Sage Monastery
11455 Clayton Road, San Jose, CA 95127-5099 USA
Tel: (408) 923-7243 Fax: (408) 923-1064

The International Translation Institute
1777 Murchison Drive, Burlingame, CA 94010-4504 USA
Tel: (650) 692-5912 Fax: (650) 692-5056

Long Beach Monastery
3361 East Ocean Boulevard, Long Beach, CA 90803 USA
Tel: (562) 438-8902

Blessings, Prosperity, & Longevity Monastery
4140 Long Beach Boulevard, Long Beach, CA 90807 USA
Tel: (562) 595-4966

Avatamsaka Vihara
9601 Seven Locks Road, Bethesda, MD 20817-9997, USA
Tel/Fax: (301) 469-8300 Email: hwa_yean88@msn.com

Avatamsaka Monastery
1009 4th Avenue, S.W. Calgary, AB T2P OK8 Canada
Tel: (403) 234-0644 Fax: (403) 263-0537
Website: http://www.avatamsaka.ca

Dharma Realm Guanyin Sagely Monastery
161, Jalan Ampang, 50450 Kuala Lumpur, West Malaysia
Tel: (03) 2164-8055 Fax: (03) 2163-7118

Prajna Guanyin Sagely Monastery (formerly Tze Yun Tung)
Batu 5½, Jalan Sungai Besi, Salak Selatan, 57100 Kuala Lumpur, Malaysia
Tel: (03) 7982-6560 Fax: (03) 7980-1272

Lotus Vihara
136, Jalan Sekolah, 45600 Batang Berjuntai, Selangor Darul Ehsan, Malaysia
Tel: (03) 3271-9439

Source of Dharma Realm – Lot S130, 2nd Floor, Green Zone, Sungai Wang
Plaza, Jalan Bukit Bintang, 55100 Kuala Lumpur, Malaysia
Tel: (03) 2164-8055

Buddhist Lecture Hall – 31 Wong Nei Chong Road, Top Floor, Happy
Valley, Hong Kong, China
Tel: (02) 2572-7644 Fax: (2) 2572-2850

Dharma Realm Sagely Monastery – 20, Tong-hsi Shan-chuang, Hsing-lung
Village, Liu-kuei Kaohsiung County, Taiwan, R.O.C.
Tel: (07) 689-3717 Fax: (07) 689-3870

Amitabha Monastery – 7, Su-chien-hui, Chih-nan Village, Shou-feng,
Hualien County, Taiwan, R.O.C.
Tel: (07) 865-1956 Fax: (07) 865-3426

Gold Coast Dharma Realm
106 Bonogin Road, Mudgeeraba, Queensland 4213 Australia
Tel/fax: (07) 61-755-228-788 (07) 61-755-227-822

The Dharma Realm Buddhist Association

Mission

The Dharma Realm Buddhist Association (formerly the Sino-American Buddhist Association) was founded by the Venerable Master Hsuan Hua in the United States of America in 1959. Taking the Dharma Realm as its scope, the Association aims to disseminate the genuine teachings of the Buddha throughout the world. The Association is dedicated to translating the Buddhist canon, propagating the Orthodox Dharma, promoting ethical education, and bringing benefit and happiness to all beings. Its hope is that individuals, families, the society, the nation, and the entire world will, under the transforming influence of the Buddhadharma, gradually reach the state of ultimate truth and goodness.

The Founder

The Venerable Master, whose names were An Tse and To Lun, received the Dharma name Hsuan Hua and the transmission of Dharma from Venerable Master Hsu Yun in the lineage of the Wei Yang Sect. He was born in Manchuria, China, at the beginning of the century. At nineteen, he entered the monastic order and dwelt in a hut by his mother's grave to practice filial piety. He meditated, studied the teachings, ate only one meal a day, and slept sitting up. In 1948 he went to Hong Kong, where he established the Buddhist Lecture Hall and other Way-places. In 1962 he brought the Proper Dharma to the West, lecturing on several dozen Mahayana Sutras in the United States. Over the years, the Master established more than twenty monasteries of Proper Dharma under the auspices of the Dharma Realm Buddhist Association and the City of Ten Thousand Buddhas. He also founded centers for the translation of the Buddhist canon and for education to spread the influence of the Dharma in the East and West. The Master manifested the stillness in the United States in 1995. Through his lifelong, selfless dedication to teaching living beings with wisdom and compassion, he influenced countless people to change their faults and to walk upon the pure, bright path to enlightenment.

Dharma Propagation, Buddhist Text Translation, and Education

The Venerable Master Hua's three great vows after leaving the home-life were (1) to propagate the Dharma, (2) to translate the Buddhist Canon, and (3) to promote education. In order to make these vows a reality, the Venerable Master based himself on the Three Principles and the Six Guidelines. Courageously facing every hardship, he founded monasteries, schools, and centers in the West, drawing in living beings and teaching them on a vast scale. Over the years, he founded the following institutions:

The City of Ten Thousand Buddhas and Its Branches

In propagating the Proper Dharma, the Venerable Master not only trained people but also founded Way-places where the Dharma wheel could turn and living beings could be saved. He wanted to provide cultivators with pure places to practice in accord with the Buddha's regulations. Over the years, he founded many Way-places of Proper Dharma. In the United States and Canada, these include the City of Ten Thousand Buddhas; Gold Mountain Monastery; Gold Sage Monastery; Gold Wheel Monastery; Gold Summit Monastery; Gold Buddha Monastery; Avatamsaka Monastery; Long Beach Monastery; the City of the Dharma Realm; Berkeley Buddhist Monastery; Avatamsaka Hermitage; and Blessings, Prosperity, and Longevity Monastery. In Taiwan, there are the Dharma Realm Buddhist Books Distribution Association, Dharma Realm Monastery, and Amitabha Monastery. In Malaysia, there are the Prajna Guanyin Sagely Monastery (formerly Tze Yun Tung Temple), Deng Bi An Monastery, and Lotus Vihara. In Hong Kong, there are the Buddhist Lecture Hall and Cixing Monastery.

Purchased in 1974, the City of Ten Thousand Buddhas is the hub of the Dharma Realm Buddhist Association. The City is located in Talmage, Mendocino County, California, 110 miles north of San Francisco. Eighty of the 488 acres of land are in active use. The remaining acreage consists of meadows, orchards, and woods. With over seventy large buildings containing over 2,000 rooms, blessed with serenity and fresh, clean air, it is the first large Buddhist monastic community in the United States. It is also an international center for the Proper Dharma.

Although the Venerable Master Hua was the Ninth Patriarch in the Wei Yang Sect of the Chan School, the monasteries he founded emphasize all of the five main practices of Mahayana Buddhism (Chan meditation, Pure Land, esoteric, Vinaya (moral discipline), and doctrinal studies). This accords with the Buddha's words: "The Dharma is level and equal, with no high or low." At the City of Ten Thousand Buddhas, the rules of purity are rigorously observed. Residents of the City strive to regulate their own conduct and to cultivate with vigor. Taking refuge in the Proper Dharma, they lead pure and selfless lives, and attain peace in body and mind. The Sutras are expounded and the Dharma wheel is turned daily. Residents dedicate themselves wholeheartedly to making Buddhism flourish. Monks and nuns in all the monasteries take one meal a day, always wear their precept sash, and follow the Three Principles:

> *Freezing, we do not scheme.*
> *Starving, we do not beg.*
> *Dying of poverty, we ask for nothing.*
> *According with conditions, we do not change.*
> *Not changing, we accord with conditions.*
> *We adhere firmly to our three great principles.*
> *We renounce our lives to do the Buddha's work.*
> *We take the responsibility to mold our own destinies.*
> *We rectify our lives to fulfill the Sanghan's role.*
> *Encountering specific matters,*
>   *we understand the principles.*
> *Understanding the principles,*
>   *we apply them in specific matters.*
> *We carry on the single pulse of*
>   *the Patriarchs' mind-transmission.*

The monasteries also follow the Six Guidelines: not contending, not being greedy, not seeking, not being selfish, not pursuing personal advantage, and not lying.

International Translation Institute

The Venerable Master vowed to translate the Buddhist Canon (Tripitaka) into Western languages so that it would be widely accessible throughout the world. In 1973, he founded the International Translation Institute on Washington Street in San Francisco for the purpose of translating Buddhist scriptures into English and other languages. In 1977, the Institute was merged into Dharma Realm Buddhist University as the Institute for the Translation of Buddhist Texts. In 1991, the Venerable Master purchased a large building in Burlingame (south of San Francisco) and established the International Translation Institute there for the purpose of translating and publishing Buddhist texts. To date, in addition to publishing over one hundred volumes of Buddhist texts in Chinese, the Association has published more than one hundred volumes of English, French, Spanish, Vietnamese, and Japanese translations of Buddhist texts, as well as bilingual (Chinese and English) editions. Audio and video tapes also continue to be produced. The monthly journal Vajra Bodhi Sea, which has been in circulation for nearly thirty years, has been published in bilingual (Chinese and English) format in recent years.

In the past, the difficult and vast mission of translating the Buddhist canon in China was sponsored and supported by the emperors and kings themselves. In our time, the Venerable Master encouraged his disciples to cooperatively shoulder this heavy responsibility, producing books and audio tapes and using the medium of language to turn the wheel of Proper Dharma and do the great work of the Buddha. All those who aspire to devote themselves to this work of sages should uphold the Eight Guidelines of the International Translation Institute:

1. One must free oneself from the motives of personal fame and profit.
2. One must cultivate a respectful and sincere attitude free from arrogance and conceit.
3. One must refrain from aggrandizing one's work and denigrating that of others.
4. One must not establish oneself as the standard of correctness and suppress the work of others with one's fault-finding.
5. One must take the Buddha-mind as one's own mind.
6. One must use the wisdom of Dharma-Selecting Vision to determine true principles.
7. One must request Virtuous Elders of the ten directions to certify one's translations.
8. One must endeavor to propagate the teachings by printing Sutras, Shastra texts, and Vinaya texts when the translations are certified as being correct.

These are the Venerable Master's vows, and participants in the work of translation should strive to realize them.

Instilling Goodness Elementary School, Developing Virtue Secondary School, Dharma Realm Buddhist University

"Education is the best national defense." The Venerable Master Hua saw clearly that in order to save the world, it is essential to promote good education. If we want to save the world, we have to bring about a complete change in people's minds and guide them to cast out unwholesomeness and to pursue goodness. To this end the Master founded Instilling Goodness Elementary School in 1974, and Developing Virtue Secondary School and Dharma Realm Buddhist University in 1976.

In an education embodying the spirit of Buddhism, the elementary school teaches students to be filial to parents, the secondary school teaches students to be good citizens, and the university teaches such virtues as humaneness and righteousness. Instilling Goodness Elementary School and Developing Virtue Secondary School combine the best of contemporary and traditional methods and of Western and Eastern cultures. They emphasize moral virtue and spiritual development, and aim to guide students to become good and capable citizens who will benefit humankind. The schools offer a bilingual (Chinese/English) program where boys and girls study separately. In addition to standard academic courses, the curriculum includes ethics, meditation, Buddhist studies, and so on, giving students a foundation in virtue and guiding them to understand themselves and explore the truths of the universe. Branches of the schools (Sunday schools) have been established at branch monasteries with the aim of propagating filial piety and ethical education.

Dharma Realm Buddhist University, whose curriculum focuses on the Proper Dharma, does not merely transmit academic knowledge. It emphasizes a foundation in virtue, which expands into the study of how to help all living beings discover their inherent nature. Thus, Dharma Realm Buddhist University advocates a spirit of shared inquiry and free exchange of ideas, encouraging students to study various canonical texts and use different experiences and learning styles to tap their inherent wisdom and fathom the meanings of those texts. Students are encouraged to practice the principles they have understood and apply the Buddhadharma in their lives, thereby nurturing their wisdom and virtue. The University aims to produce outstanding individuals of high moral character who will be able to bring benefit to all sentient beings.

Sangha and Laity Training Programs

In the Dharma-ending Age, in both Eastern and Western societies there are very few monasteries that actually practice the Buddha's regulations and strictly uphold the precepts. Teachers with genuine wisdom and understanding, capable of guiding those who aspire to pursue careers in Buddhism, are very rare. The Venerable Master founded the Sangha and Laity Training Programs in 1982 with the goals of raising the caliber of the Sangha, perpetuating the Proper Dharma, providing professional training for Buddhists around the world on both practical and theoretical levels, and transmitting the wisdom of the Buddha.

The Sangha Training Program gives monastics a solid foundation in Buddhist studies and practice, training them in the practical affairs of Buddhism and Sangha management. After graduation, students will be able to assume various responsibilities related to Buddhism in monasteries, institutions, and other settings. The program emphasizes a thorough knowledge of Buddhism, understanding of the scriptures, earnest cultivation, strict observance of precepts, and the development of a virtuous character, so that students will be able to propagate the Proper Dharma and perpetuate the Buddha's wisdom. The Laity Training Program offers courses to help laypeople develop correct views, study and practice the teachings, and understand monastic regulations and ceremonies, so that they will be able to contribute their abilities in Buddhist organizations.

Let Us Go Forward Together

In this Dharma-ending Age when the world is becoming increasingly dangerous and evil, the Dharma Realm Buddhist Association, in consonance with its guiding principles, opens the doors of its monasteries and centers to those of all religions and nationalities. Anyone who is devoted to humaneness, righteousness, virtue, and the pursuit of truth, and who wishes to understand him or herself and help humankind, is welcome to come study and practice with us. May we together bring benefit and happiness to all living beings.

Verse of Transference

May the merit and virtue accrued from this work,
Adorn the Buddhas' Pure Lands,
Repaying four kinds of kindness above,
And aiding those suffering in the paths below.

May those who see and hear of this,
All bring forth the resolve for Bodhi,
And when this retribution body is over,
Be born together in the Land of Ultimate Bliss.

Dharma Protector Wei Tuo Bodhisattva